THE PEACEMAKER
AND THE KEY OF LIFE

By William Henry

Earthpulse Press, Inc.
P. O. Box 201393
Anchorage, AK 99520

Printed in the United States of America

ISBN – 0-9648812-9-2

Cover Image: Seal of the Peacemaker. (From: Harold Bayley, *Lost language of Symbolism*, Citadel Press)

Earthpulse Press
P. O. Box 201393
Anchorage, Alaska 99520

First Printing

Printed in the United States of America
Anchorage, Alaska

To the Peacemakers past, present and future

And to the heron whose presence imbued my life with inspiration. As Mahatma Gandhi once said, "With every true friendship we build more firmly the foundations on which the peace of the whole world rests." Thanks, my friend, for loving me enough to let me use your wings.

Acknolwedgments

I am deeply grateful to the original scholarship of Zecharia Sitchin, Peter Lemesurier, Graham Hancock, Gregory Shaaf, G. Cope Schellhorn and others without whose bravery and insight this work would not have been possible.

Every effort has been made to acknowledge the ownership of the illustrations, quotations and insights which made this such a wonderful project to be a part of. Should any error or omission of acknowledgment have been made I offer my humblest apology and will make the necessary correction in future editions.

In Appreciation

I especially wish to express my gratitude to Ernie Stokes for proofreading, and to Dan Hayes for his drawing of Tula.

Thanks to all the wonderful people who have contributed richly to my life and learning, and whose belief in me brought forth this book: My parents Bee and Bob Schmidt, Diane Schmidt, Kim and Donny Hinkle.

TABLE OF CONTENTS

The Way of the Tree of Peace

The Way of the Tree of Peace
which is the perfect secret
that God has guarded
from the curious and profane
remains a penetrable mystery
to him who is not ashamed
to wear his wings,
to him who understands
the diligence of each day.
To him who is content to place his hand
in loving trust that destiny is ours,
to him who is willing to forsake
a past that has not produced
the blossoming beauty he craves.
To him whose heart reaches up as a cup
to the highest and sweetest,
the noblest and best Lord of All
in the desire to have imparted to himself
and every part of life
the best of gifts.
He speaks in summoned, loving tones
of inward communion,
"O Father, not my will but Thine be done!"
To him there is conveyed the highest crown,
the word "Dominion."
He is the Son, the Alchemist.
The Beloved One
He can divide the loaves and fishes
walk upon the waves,
fulfill his own and others wishes,
and be the greatest benefactor.
In him the Immortal Spirit prevails,
The Ultimate Tula is seen.

Saint Germaine

INTRODUCTION

"Blessed are the Peacemakers;
God shall call them His sons."
– Matthew 5:9

APPOINTMENT WITH DESTINY

The premise of this book is at once simple and startling: the Earth Teacher (the Planetary Christ, Messiah or head of the spiritual hierarchy) has a fore-runner called the Peacemaker.

Whether ancient or modern, pagan or Jewish, Christian, Hindu, Mayan, Egyptian or Muslim, history's prophets tell us to expect the return of the Peacemaker between 1996 and 1999, bringing with him a time of unprec-edented spiritual awakening.

The Peacemaker and the Key of Life is the first book to disclose this ancient sacred figure and the far-reaching influence he has had in the upliftment of humankind from Eden to angel. Out of this extraordinary search the Peacemaker will return with an outpouring of long buried esoteric se-crets including those of a mystical place called Tula – knowledge of the existence of which surpasses even the reality of extraterrestrial life in its potential effect on mass human consciousness.

WHO IS THE PEACEMAKER?

The great holy books of the Christians and Jews are probably the best known accounts of the Peacemaker (yet many more will be examined in-cluding the traditions of the Iroquois, Hopi, Egyptian and Maya). According to Jewish tradition the Day of the Lord, the coming of the Messiah for Jews, the Christian Second Coming, is preceded by seven signs beginning with the reappearance of Elijah (Mal. 4:5; Revelation 11:3-6).

Elijah (850 B.C.) was seen as one who would in the end bring peace to the world and as one who would be precursor or forerunner of the Messiah. Therefore, he is called the Peacemaker.

The Peacemaker, which is an office subordinate to the Christ akin to an ambassador representing a President in an alien land, represents an ancient interface between mankind on earth and a tribe of beings who are believed to live in the inner realms, and in whose company we live between death and rebirth.

The Peacemakers have accompanied the Christ on His evolutionary mission through long centuries of preparation for the awakening that is presently occurring on earth. Remembered in the Old Testament as the "Sons of God," exalted in the New Testament as the Order of Melchi-zedek, of which Jesus himself was "a priest for ever after the order of Melchizedek" (Hebrews 5:5-6), the Peacemakers have touched and been touched by every earth civilization from Africa to Australia to the Americas and Asia.

An examination of a partial listing of the names by which the tribe or family the Peacemaker represents have been known as down through the centuries is instructive in itself: the Spirits of the Stars, the Elder Race, Els (or Shining Ones), the Solar Clan, the Bird Tribe, the Guardians, the Sons of the Morning, the Watchers, the Brotherhood of the Snake, the Great White Brotherhood, the Grail Kings, Lords of the Flame, Space Brothers, Consciousness Agents, the Keyholders and the Arthurs.

As representatives of the Creator, these beings watch over humanity, make plans for humanity and because they are designed to blend with humans they occasionally incarnate as humans, possess humans or are intuited by humans to directly intervene in human affairs. The more familiar term for what these beings, including the Peacemakers, are is angels, time spirits or non-corporeal spirit beings. Here since the beginning, staying till the end of time, the Peacemaker and his tribe are the spiritual guardians of the earth.

THE TREE OF PEACE

Until the discovery of the ancient Dead Sea Scrolls of the Essenes in 1947, little was known in the Christian world about the role of the Peacemaker. With the discovery of the Scrolls this profound and ageless figure who once permeated the religions of Egypt, India, Persia, Greece, China, Tibet, America and Palestine came to light.

The Scrolls reveal that the Essenes – the mystical Jewish sect out of which Jesus preached – synthesized ancient (possibly antediluvian) teachings which they called the *Gospel of Peace* or *Tree of Peace* and which were centered upon harmonizing or balancing the forces of heaven and earth.

Furthermore, the Essenes viewed the earth as a training ground for souls. Their goal was to create a Kingdom of God on earth, which meant "Thy will be done on earth, as it is in heaven." Unfortunately, there is opposition to this goal. Earth, say the Essenes, is a battlefield between the Children of Light and the Children of Darkness. The battles have to be fought and the victory won here before the Kingdom could be established and we could be transferred elsewhere.

NOT ONE, BUT TWO MESSIAHS

The Scrolls document the Essenes as anticipating the coming of not one but *two* Messiahs ('anointed ones') working together. The first would be a priest who would create peace and redeem his followers through suffering. He is called the Peacemaker and is the leader of the Children of Light. The second anointed one would be a king who would be wise and kind. Scholars believe John the Baptist fulfilled the role of the Peacemaker and Jesus the king of love. We, however, will bring information to light which may question this dogma.

Many are familiar with John the Baptist and the role he is believed to have played in the mission of Jesus. John was the forerunner of the Christ. (For the moment we will accept this description of John. Bear in mind, however, that a revelation of possibly enormous consequence awaits all who seek the mysteries of the Peacemaker.) He was considered by wise men to be the earthly ambassador of the heavenly Savior. As we know, John was the son of Mary's cousin Elizabeth. His role as the advance man of Jesus began while they were still in their mother's wombs. Later, John baptized Jesus, a mystical act which many believe introduced the Christ energy into the body of Jesus.

Jesus stated clearly that John the Baptist was the reincarnated Elijah, the Peacemaker (Matt. 11:17:15 and 17:10-13). This testimony, and the fact that he is expected to return in our time, almost certainly implies the Peacemaker is a figure who is reincarnating over time to perform a specific function.

No one, until now, has ever asked the question of who the Peacemaker has been in what may be many past lives or reappearances. These lives, as recorded in scriptures and texts from around the world, present an amazing and fascinating saga. It is the story of a man who was taught heavenly secrets in order to be an interceder for humanity. He is the leader of the Children of Light who are fighting to lead us home. He is the link, the seal, binding past, present and future of the Divine Plan for the spiritual upliftment of humanity.

The Peacemaker's story began before the Flood, continued in Egypt, Central America, and, astonishingly, may find its climax in America. We shall examine the evidence of a few of the Peacemaker's lifetimes. Space permits us to look at only those appearances which have the most direct relevance to our lives. As we will see, events which occurred in antiquity will soon reverberate through the lives of this age's faithful.

THE KEY OF LIFE

As we begin to connect the lifetimes of the Peacemaker we will notice a thread running through each of these lives. The souls who incarnate as or represent the Peacemaker appear at times to be following a path in which they repeat many of the same experiences or duties. This path was illuminated by Father John Rossner, Phd. when, in his work *The Primordial Tradition and the Cosmic Christ*, he describes the Peacemaker's path as that of the salvation hero.

The function of salvation heroes and their myths wherever they occur in the world's religious/mystery traditions (whether in India, Persia, Asia, Egypt, Greece or America) is to set forth, to enact, and to explain the archetypal cosmic drama by which 'fallen man' regains his divinity. Salvation heroes have generally performed the great function of providing a blueprint or archetypical symbol of the 'way', or 'path' for humanity to achieve Christ consciousness and immortality.

The immediate mission of the Peacemaker, often referred to as the Messianic or Divine Plan, is the spiritual upliftment and physical evolution of humanity in preparation for more fully receiving Christ consciousness.

Like Sir Galahad's quest for the Holy Grail, the Peacemaker's soul awakening begins with the search for the Key of Life, which, like the Grail, is at once a physical technology and a spiritual process. The Key of Life represents a teaching which leads to the perfection of the human soul and can be learned by all seekers. This ancient artifact is the Messiah's 'rod of power', immortalized as the holy relic once used by Moses to part the Red Sea and by Jesus to perform many of his miracles.

Discussing the Peacemaker without mentioning the Key of Life is akin to a music archaeologist in 3,500 A.D. telling Eddie Van Halen's story without mentioning a thing about his relationship to the guitar, which in that far-off time may be long forgotten, and therefore unimaginable, just as the Key of Life may be unimaginable to sophisticated moderns like us. As U2 guitar player Edge once observed, with the emergence of electric guitars things are looking pretty tough for the acoustical guitar these days. Perhaps in the distant past the Key of Life also faced extinction and was replaced by the next new idea. We shall investigate its convoluted history and profound secrets in the following pages.

Among the secrets of the Key of Life is the secret of overcoming matter, the key to immortality. The Bible terms these secrets the miracles of resurrection and ascension. Learning them will enable us to become immortal inhabitants of the indescribably beautiful worlds that are built on the higher planes of existence.

The Essenes, forerunners of Christianity, called the Peacemakers 'Those of the Way', because their purpose is to lead us to the means to resurrect and ascend to these higher planes. Jesus Christ, as a member of their order, modeled the means for us to elevate ourselves to these planes. Tragically, much of Jesus' direct instruction for this process of resurrection and ascension has been lost or scattered like so many pieces of a puzzle and now remains hidden in mystery traditions the world over from the Egyptians to the Mayans to the indigenous peoples of the Americas and Australia.

For centuries the Peacemakers have been preparing the way, planting the seeds for the return of the Earth Teacher, the Christ, in different societies, places and times with knowledge that some day humanity would unite in a spirit of love, cooperation and harmony. In that day the pieces of the puzzle, the Key of Life, will be put together and the secrets of individual and planetary ascension, finally apprehended.

That day, a highly planned event, has been known for thousands of years in every culture and civilization by numerous names: the New Age, the Second Coming, the Fourth Dimension, the Tribulation, the Rapture, the Axis Shift, the Golden Age, the Age of Aquarius, the Sixth World, Armageddon, the Photon Belt, the Age of Light, and the Christing of earth.

Prophecies and calendars from every culture the Peacemakers had contact with universally point to the years 1999 to 2012 as times of startling changes for humanity, perhaps even catastrophic earth changes, a necessary cleansing, that will precede the birth of a new world and a new mind.

TULA: THE LOST KINGDOM OF GOD

At the apex of the Key of Life mystery is a secret so extraordinary that merely acknowledging its existence seems to trigger deeply embedded soul memories in our collective imagination. The Key of Life is a secret teaching which enables the Children of Light to enter the Promised Land which is biblical code for the ultimate human experience. It is called Tula (Sanskrit for 'balance') in the ancient texts.

Although you may have never heard of Tula, it is almost certain you have heard of one of the many colorful legends which are derived from it. Zion, the New Jerusalem, Camelot, Avalon, even Oz (Hebrew for 'strength is within') – all are attempts at recreating Tula and finding something of value within us that will enable our metamorphosis from human to angel.

The recent evolutionary jumps humanity has accomplished have served the purpose of awakening us to the reality that our world is connected to a higher dimension. Tens of millions of ordinary people have had soul-awakening experiences with angels, spirits, extraterrestrials and all other manner of beings who populate our universe. Now, the time has come to relearn the wisdom of the ancients: humans and all other beings in our galaxy all emanate from and share a common home. This home is at the center of our Milky Way galaxy and is called Tula.

Tula is sacred to a number of religious traditions. Her lore dominated the thinking of the ancients who believed the soul's mission on earth was to learn how to become a human being and then learn to return to Tula. It is awareness of the original concepts of Tula, including those of Jesus, that we are now being asked to absorb. Furthermore, we are being asked to learn the teachings which will place us in attunement and resonance with Tula in preparation for our return home.

The classic conception of heaven is derived from earlier recollections of Tula. In these pages we shall consider the questions: what did the ancients really mean when they talked about heaven? And, what did they mean when they talked about learning to return there? One point is clear. Whenever Tula (heaven) is mentioned its meaning is dualistic: one Tula is on earth, another Tula is 'out there'. At specific times in history earthly counterparts, also called Tulas, are constructed. These temples house the teachings which will enable our return to Tula.

TULA: THE PLACE OF PEACE

Tula is a place and a process of becoming. In Tula our thoughts, desires or fears will become instantly 'real'. What is in our hearts cannot remain hidden. What is felt in the heart is what is seen in the world. Only love can flow through our hearts in Tula.

This relationship between heart and mind is signified by the term *synchronicity* which is used to define meaningful coincidences. Have you ever been thinking of a long lost friend right when that person called you on the phone? That's synchronicity.

Spiritually, synchronicities open us to a new dimension of experience, Tula. Jesus called this dimension the kingdom of God. What outwardly appears to be coincidence is actually inwardly the result of the breaking down of the buffer or lag time between thought and result. Desire, thought and action/result – all three happen at the *same time* in an instant of synchronicity. When Jesus performed many of his healings and miracles he first took his subjects to the kingdom of God, a trance state, where instant manifestation is possible. As Jesus demonstrated, these experiences leave one with a feeling of spiritual solidarity with others and offer tremendous energies for healing ourselves and our world.

Mahatma Ghandi once prophetically observed that there never would be peace on earth unless there was first peace among the religions. Synchronicities are the highest, deepest, closest, most universal, every day sacred bond with God that we have. They are the secret, sacred bridge that can unite the people of earth and create peace among the religions. The ability of every individual to experience synchronicity is the golden link in the chain of peace and harmony. Think peace in our hearts and we will create peace in the world. Peace and harmony between people is the kingdom of God.

The timing of the reappearance of the 'vital magic' of these Tula energies and legends in our time of planetary ascension is not a coincidence. In our time the Children of Light will gather at Tula and from there the Messiah will rule (Psalm 132:13-14).

THE CURRENT ERA PEACEMAKER

This book becomes two books in one, a history of the Peacemaker, the Key of Life and Tula and an investigation into the mission and identity of the Peacemaker. In this way we will cut to the core of the most mysterious prophecy ever known – the Second Coming of a Christ, Messiah or Earth Teacher who will usher in a Millennium of Peace and the creation of the Kingdom of Tula on earth.

Scriptures tell us the time schedule of the arrival of the Teacher is a mystery. Few students of the Bible, however, fail to see that events in the world today are signs leading up to and presaging this return. In particular, the shifting of the earth's spiritual vibration, the movement toward awareness of the earth as one world connected to many, and the extraordinary spiritual revolution that will make this possible. Petty earthly politics and racial prejudices simply evaporate once we reconnect ourselves with the universe, the 'Garden' of billions of galaxies of which we are a member.

Remembrance of Tula serves this greater purpose. Many are familiar with the idea of Christ consciousness, the conception of the Second Coming as a spirit rather than as an individual. This consciousness will introduce an era of peace. A consciousness cannot just 'sit there' like a cloud. It must unfold so that its contents can be absorbed. Indeed, it is meant to flow through us.

Eastern teachers predict that only one-tenth of one percent of the human race is needed to create powerful enough chaotic vibrations in the 'thoughtsphere' of earth to cause the entire planet to reorganize into a peaceful 'thoughtsphere'. Presently, slightly more than six billion people inhabit the garden of earth. All it takes is 6,000,000 people to change their thinking to create a 'thoughtsphere' of peace. All it takes is one of these humans to 'flower' or blossom and the entire earth will bloom!

Ancient Judaic prophecy reveals that, perhaps in the manner just described, the Peacemaker will fulfill the yearning of our day. He will create a Divinely inspired world peace and harmony. As we shall see, the means to create this peace have been preserved in various cultures and traditions.

The Peacemaker's mission is also to bring Moses back to life, level the mountains of the Holy Land, recover the Ark of the Covenant and construct the new temple. This temple is known in Judaism as *Zion* and in Christianity as the *New Jerusalem*. Both of these temples are derived from legends of Tula.

Finally, the Peacemaker will introduce the Earth Teacher. The Peacemaker will then be murdered in the streets of Israel. The Children of Darkness will believe they have conquered the earth. Then, the Messiah will resurrect the Peacemaker in front of the entire world. The Millennium of Peace will begin.

Astonishingly, the person who may have had the most to say about the Peacemaker's mission is Nostradamus (1503-1566). Considered by many to be the greatest European prophet, many of his prophecies, first made public in the 1500's, have come true. What most catches our attention is the amazing detail of his revelations concerning the Peacemaker and his mission. Nostradamus even named the name of the returning Peacemaker.

WHAT IF THE PEACEMAKER WAS ONE OF US?

Throughout this book we will be exploring Tula, the Peacemaker's mission and all that it portends in our world. Who will be involved in creating this divinely inspired world peace? What is the role of each soul on earth during these extraordinary times? What if the Peacemaker really was one of us? These are the questions upon which human destiny in our new Millennium hinges.

The Earth Teacher has been widely prophesied to return for the Millennium, the dawn of the Age of Aquarius. Many believe this began in 1962 when, astrologically, earth entered Aquarius. This has led students of prophecy to speculate the Teacher or his prophet, the Peacemaker, were born in 1962. In those innocent days President and Mrs. Kennedy were ruling over Camelot and inspiring the inhabitants of earth like none before or since, setting the stage for a new Grail quest. Could there possibly be a better time for a modern 'Christ' Galahad, the pure knight of Camelot's Round Table who was the last to see the Holy Grail, to return to recover the Holy Grail and with it the secret force of Christ consciousness?

Today, this 'force' is stirring deep within every cell of our bodies and in the psyche of the human family in every nation, culture and religious tradition. Some describe this feeling as a 'speeding up'. These changes are already beginning to have a profound effect on human consciousness and physiology. Have you noticed an increase in friends and family seeking to raise their level of consciousness? That's just one facet of this. Another major development is changing weather patterns and increased seismic activity. Mass migrations of people are occurring. Economic, political and social systems are realigning. New biological forms, both man-made and natural, are emerging. We are changing the biochemistry of the planet, altering the geological structure. Population is growing exponentially. A world-wide communications web provides instant communications capabilities everywhere. Extraterrestrial encounters are occurring with increasing frequency and intensity. Miracles are the subject of television shows. The Dalai Lama is partying with movie stars in L.A. Crop circles are appearing on a large-scale planetary basis.

This sequence of events appears to be setting the stage for *something*. Could it be that all of the changes we are experiencing are birth pains, part of a sequence of events preparing earth for the birth of something wonderful, an indescribably awesome state of existence, a Golden Age sparked by a Christ visitation?

That the Christ visitation would involve a sequence of events, a preparation of individual, societal and planetary proportions, should be obvious. Would the Earth Teacher just appear out of thin air? Think of the logistics involved when a head of state travels from his home country to a foreign land. There are travel arrangements, security precautions, itineraries, meetings, etc. Doesn't it make sense that during a Messianic visitation similar logistics and criteria would also be involved?

In addition to creating the proper planetary environment other criteria, apart from prophecy, would have to be fulfilled. This book will show that one such criteria would be the arrival of the Christ's forerunner, the Peacemaker.

JULY, 1999

While the exact time of arrival of the Christ may be unknowable, the inception and activities of the Peacemaker can be known and documented. Judaic prophecy holds the Peacemaker will return either three days or three years before the Advent of the Earth Teacher. Correspondingly, Nostradamus has the Peacemaker arriving in July, 1999 and the Earth Teacher three years later in June, 2002.

According to Jesus' own prophecy in Matthew 24:32-34, the generation that saw Israel become a nation will live to see the return of Christ. When Israel was recognized as an independent state on May 14, 1948 and her exiles returned home, it was a signal to many that 'the age of redemption' had begun.

Consider, for example, the following events surrounding the Peacemaker and the role they might be playing for the events prophesied in the Bible and other sacred texts of the world:

In 1990 President George Bush signed a resolution stating that the ideas for the United States Constitution were derived from the Great Tree of Peace. This set of universal principles based on brotherly love was set forth a thousand years ago by an Iroquois Indian named *Deganawidah,* who was called the Peacemaker. This would make the Peacemaker the true founding father of America.

In 1991, according to Sun Bear, the Chippewa Indian teacher, a thousand year old prophecy given by Deganawidah was fulfilled when America tangled with Saddam Hussein in the Gulf War. In this ancient prophecy, the Black Serpent (Hussein), would be defeated by the "great light of Deganawidah" (America) which would appear to frighten him away. In this prophecy the Black Serpent dies to make way for the return of the Peacemaker.

In 1992, a Hopi Indian spiritual leader, Thomas Banyacya, stood before the United Nations General Assembly to release centuries-old Hopi prophecies concerning the collapse of our modern world. These traditions center on the return of the 'true white brother' who would lead a Great Purification and restore balance and harmony to the earth.

In 1994, Miracle, the white buffalo calf was born. Her birth has been heralded by Native American tribes as a sacred event. She signals a new era of reconciliation among the races and a new respect for the earth. She also announces the return of the Peacemaker which many believe occurred in 1996.

In January, 1996 filmmaker Steven Spielberg announced production of *The Peacemaker*, the first feature film for his new powerhouse film company. In this oddly misnamed movie, Spielberg performs an amazing wholesale rewrite of religious history by portraying the Peacemaker not as a holy figure, but as an action hero seeking out black market nuclear materials. This is like making a movie that portrays the Buddha as a machinegun-toting redneck. It is not merely coincidental that the influential filmmaker would choose this unusual title at this peculiar time in history. Spielberg now has his sights set on redefining Moses. *The Prince of Egypt*, an animated film, purports to tell the story of Moses. To insure the movie's financial success, Spielberg has hired Christian Coalition leader Ralph Reed as a consultant.

In 1996, the United Nations entered into a Peacekeeping mission centered in *Tuzla*, Bosnia. Tuzla, as we can see, is one letter away from Tula. In the world of prophecy this is close enough. Remember, when Nostradamus prophesied the rise of Hitler he called him by the name "Hister." When the man arrived the world knew he was the figure of prophecy.

Also in 1996, the Centennial Olympic Games were held in Atlanta, Georgia. Is it just a coincidence that the letters T-L-A in the word Atlanta signify Tula? The ancients believed the world would come together at the City of Peace, Tula, to build a new and better civilization. Did the Atlanta Olympic Games inaugurate the creation of this city?

The archetypal story of the return of the Christ is that of a hero who rides in on or is preceded by a white horse, is exalted by the goddess and resurrects the sun god. The Peacemaker is the white horse, a symbol for a man.

Recently the world was hypnotized by the opposing or anti-Christ story when it was fulfilled beat for beat in the O.J. Simpson drama. Millions of people witnessed this coward riding out of town curled up in the back of his *white bronco* after being accused of *murdering the goddess* (the fair-haired Nicole often photographed with a large cross around her neck) and *murdering the sun god* (a handsome young man named Gold-man).

In physics every action has an equal and opposite reaction. By this rendering, potentially one shoe of the Christ story has dropped. We can now expect to see signs for the positive fulfillment of the Christ story to unfold.

As we can see, the world has already begun to discover Tula and its prophet. Today, it is of vital importance to realize that the experience of Tula on earth is the goal for which we must strive. The first Tula was a time when humankind interacted with the 'gods'. Our Tula, the ancient prophets believed, will be a time when the etheric or invisible worlds 'above' the earth become visible to humanity and we see Christ never left us, we merely needed to sip from the Holy Grail and develop our eyes or 'Christ consciousness' to see him anew. This process has been called the 'Christing of earth' or 'enchristing', a time when Christhood will be available to all.

In seeing Christ and our present Tula this way we will see the truth of who we are, as Jesus said when he quoted the 82nd Psalm: "Is it not written in your law: 'I said, you are Gods'" (John 10:34).

When I began my quest for the Peacemaker, the Key of Life and Tula my starting point was a round room deep within my imagination. On the floor of this room lay scattered pieces of a puzzle. I picked up piece after piece, putting them on the wall. Soon, a story unfolded. I didn't know all the names of the people and places in this story. Sometimes, I couldn't correctly pronounce them either. Still, a timeless message emerged from simply looking at the pictures and absorbing their subconscious messages.

As the key to my round room turns and the door opens, the Peacemaker is resting silently in one of these pictures in the suspended animation of history. Dare we rouse him?

CHAPTER ONE

THOTH/ENOCH:
PROPHET AND PEACEMAKER

"I am Thoth,
the skilled scribe whose hands are pure,
a possessor of purity,
who drives away evil,
who writes what is true,
who detests falsehood,
whose pen defends the Lord of All;
Master of Laws who interprets the writings,
whose words established the Two Lands."
— The Egyptian Book of the Dead

Long ago, a man named Enoch was unexpectedly roused from his sleep by a light so bright it frightened him. Suddenly, from out of the light appeared two men, very tall, such as he had never seen before. Their faces shone like the sun, and their eyes were like burning lamps. They stood at the edge of his bed and identified themselves as dignitaries from the other side, "messengers of God" to be exact.

Asleep in another room was Enoch's wife and partner, Seshet. Enoch worries over her. The messengers of God tell him to wake up his family and servants, tell them good-bye and ask them not to look for him for a while, "till the Lord brings him back to them."

Next, the men place Enoch in a moving "cloud." Before he knows it he is in a "sea greater than the earthly sea," and is looking upon the whole earth.

Sailing the deep sea of space, Enoch and his messengers travel for thirty days through the six heavens to the seventh heaven. There, for over thirty days, Enoch is trained by the Lord and sent back to earth with a secret teaching.

Theologians and Biblical scholars are uncertain why, of all people, Enoch was chosen to go to heaven. The simple answer, and therefore the consensus, is it had something to do with one of the several meanings of his name, "righteous one."

There is a more enlightening explanation.

The editors of the Bible had a tendency to diminish the key men in the Old Testament, not wanting to exalt a particular man for fear of creating a cult of personality. So, they portrayed them as simple-minded shepherds, carpenters and cobblers. The truth is, Enoch, like most of the other teachers in the Bible, including Abraham and Moses, was no ordinary man.

The picture that emerges of Enoch: a 'sleeping' man who leaves his body, passes through a series of heavens and communicates with a variety of spirits who give him a teaching that benefits his society, is the picture of a *shaman* as described in Mircea Eliade's *Encyclopedia of Religion*.

Eliade defines the shaman in terms of his or her power to release his soul from his body in order to communicate directly with divine powers. By working with unseen forces in another reality or dimension, the shaman provides a link with the spiritual world and from the knowledge gained there protects his fellow man from darkness and leads them toward the light.

ENOCH/THOTH

The picture of Enoch enlarges considerably when we realize he was called *Thoth* or *Tehuti* by the Egyptians and is one of their most popular 'gods'. Thoth, in turn, was called *Hermes* by the Greeks.

To the ancient Greeks, Hermes was a psychopomp, or 'guide of souls' to the realm of eternal life. The tool of his trade is called the *caduceus* – the Greek form of the Key of Life. The caduceus is a rod with two intertwining serpents often topped by a dove signifying the unity of the Holy Spirit.

1. Hermes/Thoth releasing souls from the underworld.

Often the shamans needed a little help to communicate with the other dimension. Sex and alcohol often served to facilitate this, as did music and drugs. Typically shamans learned their craft as highly trained initiates of ancient occult priesthoods, doubling as custodians of the secret wisdom, the Key of Life.

It is significant to note that the shamans of yore were not far-out mystics or flakes. All of them had advanced training in one of the arts such as medicine, astronomy, engineering, music, etc. It was their job to channel the mystic insights gained in their shamanic practice into practical application in the 'real world' (which, they knew, was actually the 'weird world'; the true 'real world' being that which resides in the higher dimensions).

Enoch's day job was scribe. Scribes acted as bridges between worlds, filters of secret or protected wisdom. They then preserved and disseminated this knowledge, becoming librarians of sacred wisdom. Thoth was described by the Egyptians as "lord of the divine words." He is shown in this aspect here, with what looks strangely like a modern notebook computer in his hand. He is also known as the patron of learning, magic, truth, books and libraries, keeper of the Akashic records, and Time Lord.

2. Thoth with a notebook computer?

Because of his wisdom the Egyptians said Thoth was a 'god'. This is an exaggeration. His Hebrew name *Enosh* or *Enoch*; a Hebrew term meaning 'human, mortal', shows this. Additional confirmation comes from the Sumerians who preserve the record of Thoth's conception and lineage.

According to Sumerian scholar Zecharia Sitchin (*Divine Encounters*), the Sumerians called Thoth *Ningishzidda*, which means 'Lord of the Artifact (Key) of Life'. The Sumerians hint Thoth is the offspring of their god *Enki* ('Lord Earth'), whom Sitchin upholds as an extraterrestrial bio-engineer, and a mortal woman, *Inanna/Ishtar*.

During a night of wild drink and sex, Inanna, a cunning and ruthless beauty, seduced Enki and made off with the ME-tablets, the divine formulas which were the basis of high civilization (we will discuss these further in a later chapter). In addition, she acquired the Exalted Scepter and Staff or Key of Life. That night Inanna also conceived a son, Thoth.

3. An unusual wall sculpture of Inanna at her temple in Ashur shows the goddess with a tight-fitting decorated helmet and very distinct goggles that are part of the helmet. (Copyright Z. Sitchin, *The Twelfth Planet*)

Raised by priestesses in Inanna's temple, the half-human, half-divine Thoth appears to have been privileged to learn the secrets of the universe, including those of the Key of Life. Not just any priest in Inanna's temple was given this honor. The Sumerians record Thoth's brother, Ra/Marduk (later transformed by the Christians into the Archangel Micha-El), as being jealous of Thoth. It was the humble Thoth who was chosen over Ra to learn the principles of the Key of Life, which included the ability to infuse lifeless matter with the life force.

While mastering the Key of Life is certainly on the Peacemaker's 'to do' list, he is often obsessed by another matter altogether: the search for his beloved. He is virtually incomplete without her. She anoints him, she protects him, she blesses him. In Greek, their union is called the *hiero gamos* or 'Sacred Marriage'. Through their union he becomes known as the "anointed one" – in Hebrew, a 'Messiah', in Greek, a 'Christ'.

4. Seshet. (Copyright Z.Sitchin, *When Time Began*)

It is entirely possible that while at Inanna's temple Thoth met his beloved Seshet. In temple paintings she is shown dressed in a leopard skin, the attire of those who escort souls to the light of higher dimensions. She is also shown with an emblem upon her head in the form of a seven-pointed star, the symbol of a special wisdom tradition connected with a star cluster known as the Pleiades.

Like Thoth, Seshet was a psychopomp and kept sacred wisdom. She was called 'Mistress of the Hall of Books' and apparently exceeded her husband in ability since she was the one who verified Thoth's work.

THE RETURN OF THE HERON

The sacred marriage of Thoth and Seshet served a higher purpose. This purpose is discovered by decoding the common symbol of this couple – the heron bird, the symbol of Dawn.

5. Heron atop the pyramid; symbol of Thoth and his beloved Seshet.

Throughout history the Savior figure has been represented as the Dawn. In Egypt, the opening of the doors of heaven and liberation of the Dawn was sometimes represented by a wading heron or ibis bird.

Egyptian myths say that at the dawn of the world, the Christ, Messiah or head of the Spiritual Hierarchy emerged from the central point in heaven (Tula) and took the form of the heron, radiating light from its outstretched wings perched atop the pyramid. This Teacher delivers teachings that would enable our transformation into the heron, a body of light capable of traveling in higher dimensions of existence.

The heron symbolized the Morning, because, waiting in the water at the seashore, she was the first to welcome the Dawn as it rose from the East. Among the Egyptians the heron – also known as the Bennu bird, 'bird of creation' and the phoenix – was regarded as the symbol of regeneration and resurrection and betokened the coming of light.

The baboon, one symbol of Thoth, was the emblem of the *wisdom* of the Dawn. Because of the baboon's serious expression, almost human seeming persona, and its habit of announcing the sunrise with its chattering, it was revered as the Hailer of the Dawn.

From this we can see the relationship between Thoth and Seshet. She is the first to see the Dawn, the Savior. When Dawn arrives she anoints or awakens her husband who then goes out into the 'world of men' to announce its arrival.

As we can see, these two were far from ordinary people.

Delving deeper into the mystery tradition, we learn Thoth and Seshet were believed to be incarnations of the Biblical Seth and his wife Sahet. Seth, in turn, say early Jewish historians, was the reincarnation of Adam, the model man lambasted as the fool for Christ in the Old Testament.

Many pre-Christian writers believed Adam was no fool. Instead, by listening to the goddess, he surpassed ordinary human beings in every conceivable way. Indeed, the very concept of the Fall was rejected in favor of the belief that Adam was actually a heavenly figure who is successively incarnated in human form throughout history! He has mastered the means to transcend earth life. He incarnates in human form at will, even foretelling his future name and background.

This Adam or 'model man', that is the one we are to emulate or follow, routinely sets up shop in different cultures and civilizations. During his lifetimes, the Sumerian texts tell us, Adam passes along and retrieves the wisdom and possessions he has acquired. As we will see, one item included in Adam's baggage is the Key of Life.

Many ancient writers supposed Adam's son Seth to have been Enoch/Thoth, the Peacemaker. (In Islamic tradition and lore it is accepted as fact that Enoch is a later incarnation of Adam.) This fact is amazingly concurrent in light of our hypothesis that this entity continues to incarnate to fulfill a spiritual mission for humanity.

A most interesting passage from the Jewish historian Josephus points out that the "children of Seth," who were called "the foundation," are involved in a messianic plan for the salvation of humanity before a cataclysm. These Children of Light constructed a massive temple, the Great Pyramid, for all future generations. One day, the heron would land atop this Pyramid and deliver a teaching which would enable us to return home. This prophecy reverberates throughout the books of the Old Testament and tells of the coming of a Messiah, the Lamb slain from the foundation of the world, a divine offering sent to assist a lost humanity, the Son of God, born as a man and dying as a man.

This same soul entity would later be identified by Jewish scholars as the prophet Elijah. Elijah (850 B.C.), whose name means 'Yahweh is God', was seen as one who would in the end bring peace to the world and as one who would be precursor and partner of the Messiah. Therefore, he is called the Peacemaker.

Jesus, himself, identified John the Baptist as the reincarnated Elijah.

This, at last, is the true reason Enoch was roused from his bed and taken on a journey to heaven. This highly trained spiritual messenger, who <u>was</u> Seth, Enoch, Elijah, and John the Baptist among others – fills the office of the Peacemaker, Christ's prophet.

THE GOSPEL OF TULA

The Book of Enoch states that while in heaven Enoch received training directly from the Lord. Proof? Later, over one hundred phrases attributed to Jesus in the New Testament would find precedents in the Books of Enoch. These books are certain to have existed at least two hundred years before Jesus, although the wisdom tradition emphatically states it was written by Enoch before the Flood, which would make them at least 8,000 years older than Jesus.

Christ's beatitude "Blessed are the meek: for they shall inherit the earth" sounds strikingly similar to Enoch 6:9, "The Elect shall possess light, joy, and peace; and they shall inherit the earth."

The Biblical term "children of light" may equate with Enoch's "generation of light." Enoch stated: "And now I call the spirits of the good from the generation of light, and will change those who have been born in darkness."

Jesus' description of the afterlife of the righteous is found almost verbatim in Enoch 50:4: "All the righteous shall become angels in heaven." Matthew records Jesus as saying, "For in the resurrection they . . . are as the angels of God in heaven."

The term "Son of man," often attributed to Jesus, is first used in the Book of Enoch. Enoch himself was called "Son of man" by God.

The list continues. The idea that Jesus' teaching was preceded by Enoch, and was not original to Jesus, has troubled many – especially the nervous ones who banned the Books of Enoch and attempted to destroy all known copies. We might never have known of the secret teachings of Enoch if not for the discovery of a surviving copy of the Books of Enoch by James Bruce in 1773 in Ethiopia.

Christianity finds it troubling that Enoch would claim to have direct access to the Lord. It is not troubling at all if we accept that these two figures are 'working together'. At the least these parallels support the notion that Enoch and Jesus drew their inspiration from the same well. Quite possibly Enoch, as the Peacemaker, was taught by Jesus and sent back to earth as a preview of things to come.

THOTH/ENOCH'S MISSION

For an unspecified length of time after his trip to Tula and return to earth, "Enoch was hidden, and not one of the children of men knew where he was hidden, and where he abode, and what had become of him."

While on the subject it is worth clarifying exactly where home was to Enoch. According to Cedric Leonard (*Quest For Atlantis*), the tantalizing story of Enoch/Thoth's origins emerges from the Egyptian *Book of the Dead* which calls to mind the story of Atlantis. Enoch was born in a distant land to the west which was located across a body of water. Its capitol was by the sea.

This land was referred to as the "Island of Flame which is in the sea" (Hymn of Rameses IV and Pyramid Texts). A terrible cataclysm occurred which darkened the sun and disrupted the gods, but Enoch led the people to the safety of an eastern country. From this we may conclude that Enoch/Thoth, as the mystery tradition upholds, was an Atlantean.

When Enoch finally appeared to the people of Atlantis something strange happened. According to Jewish lore, when men gathered around Enoch and he spoke they raised their eyes and saw the form of a white steed descending to earth within a storm. Then the people told Enoch and he spoke unto them, saying: "This steed has descended for my sake. The time has come and the day when I go from you and from which day forth I shall never see you again. Then the steed was there and stood before Enoch and all the children of men saw it clearly."

Interestingly, the white horse is frequently associated with the Tree of Life which connects the human realm with the upper and lower region of spirit. The role of the Messiah is to connect the souls of earth with the Tree of Life. As a shaman, Enoch would have been the connecting link between heaven and earth.

THE CHILDREN OF DARKNESS

The Books of Enoch reveal that the world neighboring the pristine Atlantis was not a pretty place. It was corrupted when the fallen angels, the Children of Darkness, and their leader, Azazel, who developed an insatiable lust for the "daughters of men." The human-alien hybrid offspring of these extraterrestrials were used as slaves and sex objects by the fallen angels.

These angels were not cuddly, ethereal, winged creatures as the early Church Fathers liked to think of them. The emphatic point the Dead Sea Scrolls make is that these angels were already in human bodies before they came down from the sky, which can only mean they are extraterrestrials. Detailed descriptions of their arrival appear repeatedly, even in the Bible, although now their significance is more fully apprehended. There are bright lights, lightning, fire, smoke, wind, whirlwinds, quakes and thundering that accompany them. All of this leads us to the conclusion that these beings, or "Watchers," are traveling in noisy space craft, or creating warps in the time/space continuum as a result of "crossing through" dimensions. Either way, as G. Cope Schellhorn comments in *Extraterrestrials in Biblical Prophecy*, "it is a safe bet to read 'extraterrestrial messenger or crew member' whenever the word 'angel' appears."

These beings were interfering in ancient human affairs (and may still be today!). Enoch interceded. He went amongst these fallen ones warning them of a coming judgment and the imminent arrival of the Lord. This implies a Christ visitation in the time before the Flood.

If Jesus did not appear to judge the watchers, and the evil of mankind, during the time of Atlantis there is no question that he had this in mind when he appeared some 10,000 years later. Jesus himself said, "Now is the judgment of this world-system [of the Watchers]: now shall the prince of this world be cast out." Jesus' inference is clear: he came to impose judgment upon the fallen angels and upon the offspring of the extraterrestrials as prophesied in the Book of Enoch.

From this rendering of the Book of Enoch, we can deduce two of the great secrets of humanity. One, the offspring of the fallen angels, the Children of Darkness, were still active in the world during the time of Jesus. And, two, Christ made at least one previous attempt to save the souls of planet earth, in the time before the Flood. The man sent to clear the way for his arrival was Enoch.

OPERATION RESCUE

Together, Enoch/Thoth and Seshet set about fulfilling the business of the Lord, spending decades traveling to all four corners of the earth preaching the Gospel of Tula.

Knowing about the impending cataclysm, Thoth and Seshet (like a couple securing their beach front property before a tidal wave) began scattering artifacts and important books of knowledge. These items would be relocated in future incarnations and be used to spiritually uplift the human race.

The enormity of this undertaking cannot be underestimated. Global in scope, psychic and physical in actualization, this was a monstrous effort to preserve what had taken thousands of years to create.

THE SPHINX AND DOG: MARKERS AND POINTERS

One matter of serious consideration to Thoth and Seshet was how to mark their repositories so that when they returned they would be able to easily remember and locate them. To this end, they supervised the construction of 'markers' (typically of cyclopean masonry) that could withstand the immense power of inrushing tidal waves and the passage of time before the earth was ready to be resettled. These markers would trigger soul-level memories in Thoth and Seshet, helping them to recall their mission. Furthermore, they would indicate the time when mankind would once again awaken in consciousness and lay claim to Enoch's secret knowledge. They may also have been pointers indicating where this advanced civilization planned to take refuge during the cataclysm.

The dog was one of the sacred symbols of Enoch/Thoth. This is believed to be an allusion to his connection with the Dog Star, Sirius, the most important star to the Egyptians. Coincidentally, Sirius is also symbolized by an enclosed sun cross, the symbol for Tula.

6. The dog-headed Thoth holding the Key of Life. Does this really mean he was from Sirius?

In the 1930's, Prof. Constantino Cattoi and his wife Maria, both research scientists and archaeologists, discovered that in certain places there is a strange concentration of electromagnetic energy. They further found that where this energy exists there are strange rock sculptures with odd markings and hieroglyphics.

Near Sicily, Cattoi and his wife located a massive stone 'Sphinx'. This sculpture has the head of a dog connecting it directly with Enoch. The Cattois also found archaeological anomalies in Albania, Greece and Libya. Cattoi writes:

> The great rock sculptures are concealing their age-old secrets . . .
> their 'language' (their meaning) is largely unknown because it is the
> 'magic language of animals,' written with symbols representing animal and human forms carved in stone to remind those of a far future
> time of the precepts of the original 'wise men' who received them
> from the messengers of God. I believe that Thoth (Enoch) actually
> travelled to various parts of the ancient world . . . wherever he went
> a gigantic carving was left of his own symbol the Dog. Sometimes
> there are **two dogs** shown. (One for Thoth, one for Seshet?)

THE WHITE HORSE AT THE TEMPLE OF THE STARS

Another artifact widely conceived as the work of Thoth and Seshet is the Somerset Zodiac, a prehistoric earthwork planetarium that has been called the Temple of the Stars. Measuring ten miles in diameter, its hills and artificial waterways depict the signs of the zodiac, and clearly were designed to be seen from the air. Its central and most enigmatic figure is a white horse.

The Somerset zodiac is an 'alarm' set for the beginning of the Age of Aquarius – today. Outside the zodiac is the figure of The Great Dog, presumably put there to guard this Temple of the Stars. I suggest it was erected as a marker and pointer and also as a signature of its builder. Momentarily we will see exactly where this mysterious Dog is pointing us.

THE TEMPLE OF ILTAR

Perhaps following the adage that it is unwise to put all of your eggs in one basket Thoth and Seshet established a repository in the Yucatan Peninsula of Guatemala. Edgar Cayce dates the establishment of the Temple of Iltar as 10,640 B.C., or approximately 1,000 years before the Maya recorded the destruction by flood.

Cayce states:

> *Then, with the leavings of the civilization in Atlantis (Iltar – with a group of followers that had been of the house of Atlan (TULA) the followers of the worship of the ONE – with some ten individuals – left this land Poseidia, and came westward, entering what would now be a portion of Yucatan. And there began, with the activities of the peoples there, the development into a civilization that rose much in the same manner as that which had been in the Atlantean land . . .*

The pyramidal temple constructed by Iltar (also known as the Temple of the Sun or the Temple of Light) was said to have been built by physical and spiritual forces. We are told it will be rediscovered when "the time of changes" is near and the records placed there will be revealed.

These repositories are so numerous that an entire book could be devoted to them. This, in fact, may be an issue up for discussion at the highest levels of the government. Imagine the enormous wealth that may be buried underground within these lost cities of the ancients. A casual estimate would place the value of gold alone at these locations in the trillions of dollars. For those in the know, these lost cities represent the ultimate Easter Egg hunt. Locating these caches is limited only by our ability to believe in them and our ability to physically find them. One technology which would make this search enormously easier and less costly is about to go 'on line'. I speak, of course, of the HAARP.

HAARP

In *Angels Don't Play This HAARP* authors Jeane Manning and Dr. Nick Begich describe the HAARP, a multi-faceted weapons system capable of an extraordinary array of features. The HAARP broadcasts specific frequencies in the form of radio waves bounced off earth's fragile ionosphere.

The HAARP is a mad scientist's dream come true. From their control room atop the world in the Alaskan bush, HAARP scientists literally possess the ability, among other things, to directly program human consciousness. These "angels" would be consciousness deejays, steering humanity as they please by literally playing the human mind like a harp. While we struggle to master the Key of Life, those who wish for humanity to remain ignorant of our true power would have the ability to insure that we never 'hit the high note' by weakening our minds with brain-debilitating frequencies.

At the same time, with HAARP in rational hands, it could be used to assist in the spiritual transformation of humanity. In this aspect it reminds one of the story of Orpheus, the Christ of Greek mythology who played his lyre so gently and beautifully that it tamed the beasts, transforming them into angels. Like the modern day Peacemaker, Orpheus was the forerunner or prophet of another Christ, (Orpheus' divine alter ego) Dionysus. Like Jesus, and possibly our modern day Peacemaker, Orpheus was a teacher of the mysteries of life after death and was killed as punishment for his revelation of the gods' secrets to humanity.

Another feature of this not so human, or even earth, friendly technology (it erodes our precious ionosphere) is called tomography. Simply put, the HAARP makes it possible to peak beneath the earth's surface. Through this technology the earth could become as a drop of water under a scientist's microscope. The HAARP enables scientists to look within the bubble and locate hidden repositories of valuable minerals and resources. It could also enable scientists to more easily locate lost cities.

HAARP has been labeled the most under-reported story of our decade. An enormous government cover-up has been underway to conceal the true capabilities of this technology. The reader can bet if lost cities and ancient caches of knowledge were discovered few of us would know anything about them.

It is thought-provoking that one of the chief images in the myth of Orpheus is the Golden Fleece of Gilgamesh which chronicles the ancient Sumerian king's search for the secrets of the gods. Recently, an intelligence officer involved in the construction of NORAD, the United States military's underground command post in Colorado Springs, told this author an insightful story about the secret scientists and engineers who designed and built this mind-boggling facility. Apparently, these scientists believed themselves to be reenacting the Epic of Gilgamesh. If so, this is astonishing because, according to Zecharia Sitchin (*The Twelfth Planet*), the Epic of Gilgamesh describes the ancient hero's journey to an extraterrestrial space port and command center. In light of this interpretation, is it possible that the scientists at NORAD were not building a facility, but rather rebuilding an ancient lost city?

CHAPTER TWO

TULA: THE SPIRITUAL SUN

Thoth/Enoch had the ultimate human experience. He physically went to the 'top of the mountain', the Promised Land, and received training personally from the Lord. The Book of Enoch does not state how Enoch induced his experience, but we can be assured that he, as a shaman or psychopomp, was highly trained in this aspect of his mission.

Today, millions of people have had an ultimate experience comparable in many ways to Enoch's. I speak, of course, of the Near Death Experience wherein the soul leaves the body and encounters another dimension of existence. Although not 'physical', these experiences affect a person's life and attitude profoundly. If the experience is pleasant, they are not afraid to die again.

Like Enoch's experience, these near death episodes typically involve an encounter with a bright, sometimes frightening, light. Then, a tunnel experience is frequently recounted. From here the experiences vary. Some encounter otherworldly beings, sometimes ascended family members. A few actually experience what is described as a 'city' or a 'hall of learning' in another dimension.

This raises an intriguing question. Do we moderns go to the same place as did Enoch? If so, where is this place?

TULA

According to the wisdom traditions of the Mayans, Greeks, Egyptians, and Asians, among others, the name of the dwelling of the Lord is Tula, the Central or Spiritual Sun.

Since for most reader's this is their initial contact with the concept of Tula, let's begin by taking a mythological journey through the various legends of Tula.

According to the Greeks, the first center for the whole of earth, the sacred island where the first earthlings emerged, was called *Hyperboria*. This was a paradise "beyond the north wind," a "white" or "pure island" where an advanced civilization flourished. Its center, a mecca for learning, was called Tula. This land, according to renowned mythologists Rene Guenon and Joseph Campbell, was the Garden of Eden of our race, now preserved among numerous religions as the City of the Gods or the Holy City.

According to the Greeks, the earthly Hyperboria and Tula was a duplicate of a heavenly original. A common belief held by nearly all the peoples of the ancient world (and believed by many today) was the notion that all the 'waters' or 'souls' on earth originated from the same pure place. This idea is found in the Garden of Eden story in Genesis 2:10: "And a river [of souls] went out from Eden [the center of the universe] to water the garden [earth]; and from thence it was parted and became into four heads." The Nordic Edda confirms the four streams came from a central fountain – in the home of the gods. The Hindu texts describe a fourfold headspring of all waters (souls?) at "the center of heaven."

7. Enclosed sun crosses. The primordial symbol for Tula.

The sun-cross or the enclosed cross depicts these four life streams. Thus, the sun-cross serves as the symbol of the *original* Holy Land, the *Central Sun*, from which our souls are said to have originated. All over the world, people recorded the idea that the world has four corners, four directions meeting at a center point marked by a cross.

From this decoding of ancient myths, we may conclude that from Tula flowed four paths of souls. In myths these appear as four rivers, four winds, or four streams of arrows. Like Eden, the enclosed cross is the original symbol of Tula. This enclosed sun cross, in turn, links with the four-petaled Flower of Life, one of the family of images in the symbolic language of Jesus.

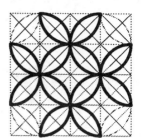

8. Four Flowers of Life form an enclosed sun cross, a symbol for Tula.

TULA: THE WHITE ISLAND

As the moon and earth revolve around the Sun, so does our entire solar system orbit the galactic center of our galaxy (which is believed to be in the constellation of Sagittarius, symbolized by the Centaur, a creature that is half man, half horse). The concept of the Central Sun or Spiritual Sun appears in many different names the world over: the white island, the floating island, the revolving island, the lost isle in the midst of the cosmic ocean. This lost isle is not of the earth. It is the lost isle, our spiritual core, Tula, floating in the sea of heaven.

The *Mahabharata*, the beautiful holy book of India, and the Vishnu Purana (2000 B.C.), the oldest of the Hindu Puranas or books of legend, devote considerable attention to *Atala* , the "White Island," describing it as "an island of great splendor." Atala, with the T-L-A indicators of Tula in the name, is obviously Tula.

Without exception this white island of the ancients – floating, revolving and shining – is esteemed as the center point from which humanity arose and spread into the galaxy. Mythologists find recollections of this heavenly Tula in the story of the cosmic egg found in Egypt, Indonesia, Iran, Phoenicia, Latvia, Estonia, West Africa, Central America and South America.

The Chinese, the Japanese, the Egyptians, Indians, Fijians, Mayans and others believed in the existence of an island associated with immortality. This island is called the Island of the Blest, Fortunate Isles or Scilly Isles. All three names refer to Tula.

These islands, in the Chinese legend, are thought to be inhabited by those who have won immortality or by those who have come to earth to inhabit human bodies in order to pass on to higher realms of existence.

Remarkably, each of the cultures that preserve a memory of Tula also possess techniques for traveling there temporarily. These techniques include the automatic inducement of what we in the West call the Near Death Experience. Additionally, the religions of these cultures also developed the means to permanently return to Tula.

9. The same traditions which preserve the sun-cross depict a columnar stream ascending into the heavens and connecting with a celestial dwelling. The repeated symbol for this link is a pyramid with an enclosed sun-cross at its apex. This image is found throughout history as the Eye of Horus (ancient Egypt) and the Great Seal of the United States of America.

It appears certain times are better than others for the soul to make the extraordinary journey to Tula. Earth's journey around Tula is divided into cycles, 'worlds' or Great Years of 26,000 years. These periods are divided into twelve New Ages of 2,150 years each.

10. 13,000 years of light. 13,000 years of darkness. The Chinese yin and yang symbol, the Mayan Hunab Ku and a Navajo symbol.

The Chinese yin and yang symbol, the Mayan Hunab Ku and the Navajo symbol shown here are the primary symbols of this journey. Because the earth is tilted on its axis it spins towards Tula for one half of the 26,000 year cycle and away from Tula for the other half. What many ancients noticed (including the Mayans, Tibetans and the Hindus) was that, during the spin toward the light, we spiritually 'awaken'. During the spin away, we fall spiritually 'asleep'. For the past two thousand years we have been in the most asleep point. Today, at the beginning of the Age of Aquarius, we are beginning to awaken. The Mayan calender reminds us a 26,000 year cosmic cycle comes to a close in 2012. Conceivably, billions of souls may make the 'jump' to Tula at this time. Where, or more intriguingly, to what, will these souls be jumping to?

TULA: BLACK HOLE OR WORMHOLE?

University of Arizona astronomers, using a new high-speed, infrared camera mounted on a Kitt Peak telescope, believe they have discovered a black hole inhabiting the area *near* the center of our Milky Way galaxy. Theoretically, physicists view black holes as time machines which may open gateways to parallel dimensions. Unfortunately, these celestial bodies, due to their small size and staggering gravitational forces, draw in all surrounding materials on a one-way course toward their centers. Therefore, venturing toward a black hole is dangerous business. Not even light escapes its grasp – hence, the name *black hole*.

Who would want to venture to a black hole? Practically speaking, no one. That's why theoretical physicists invented something else to inhabit the galactic core, something which changes the picture considerably. That something is called a *white hole*, a 'cosmic gusher' of matter and energy. If for every action there is an equal and opposite reaction and if humans are indeed programmed to go back 'home', perhaps this is the reason physicists were driven to discover worm holes leading to Tula.

ANGELS THIS WAY

In physics circles it is said that, whatever a black hole can devour, a white hole can spit out. These white holes precisely conform to the image the ancients held of the center of our galaxy. While the influence of a far-off, matter-gushing galactic core may seem remote to some, I remind the reader that the ovulation and gestation rates of terrestrial animals are directly influenced by the earth and her motion in relation to the Sun. Since our Sun is directly connected to the Spiritual Sun, as Tula is called, this influence is automatically passed to every inhabitant of earth.

White holes are the subject of intense scientific research in America and Europe and have led scientists to ponder the mysteries of interstellar passageways called *wormholes*. In the past few years, the scientifically-rooted concept of worm holes, or Star Gates, has become a popular topic on such television shows as *Star Trek: Deep Space Nine* and *Sliders* and in movies such as *Star Gate*.

Theoretically, these 'gates' are cosmic shortcuts that allow rapid transgalactic travel. Several serious proposals for designing gateways to other parts of the Milky Way have been presented in technical journals within the past few years. What was once the esoteric domain of shamans and religious people is rapidly becoming the exoteric, leading edge of science. It is possible a physicist may soon proclaim the *re*-discovery of a wormhole or cosmic gateway we can follow back to the past, to the origins of the human soul, to Tula. I emphasize re-discovery of this knowledge, for the ancients proclaim that intelligent beings – i.e. mapmakers or time travelers – ventured to earth in the distant past with the mission of connecting us to the intergalactic highway or "bridge across forever."

LORDS OF TIME

The Mayans, for example, record that Lords of Time (nine of them to be exact) periodically emerge from Tula, Tollan or *Azt-lan*. They come to earth to build Tulas, temples which act as spiritual centers for new civilizations. These temples are also learning centers that enlighten entire civilizations and enable some to literally vanish into higher realms of existence.

It is fascinating to follow the chain of meanings of the Mayan word 'Aztlan', by which many believe is meant Atlantis. Aztlan (remember, the key letters are T-L-A) means 'White Place' or 'Place of Herons'. The heron, we know, is the bird of resurrection and ascension or travel to higher realms. The teachings offered at these Tulas are meant to keep us in balance and harmony with the Spiritual Sun and, hence, ourselves. Ultimately, they are meant to enable us to ascend or return to Tula.

In *The Mayan Factor,* Dr. Jose Argüelles, who spent twenty years deciphering the Mayan mythology, makes a fascinating study of the Maya and Tula. Dr. Argüelles describes the original Mayans as diviners of harmony, "galactic masters who communicate information from outside the solar system to our planet." Because Tula is on her own spiral of ascension and therefore 'moving' in relation to the rest of the universe, and because earth is on her own spiral of ascension, periodic adjustments must be made to the bridge linking the two locations. Hence, the Lords of Time are sent to earth make these changes and provide instructions for the soul to travel safely and directly home after 'earth school' is out.

Argüelles clearly shows the Maya were celestial navigators and stellar cartographers who left an intelligent code containing instructions for traveling directly to Tula. This code is built into the elaborate pyramidal temples of the Maya at Tula in Mexico and elsewhere. The Mayan Tula and others were built as receivers of spiritual code from the primal or galactic Tollan or Tulan, the place of origin, as well as the place of entry to this world.

The Mayans, as builders of Tula, are in fact Peacemakers or wayshowers home to Tula. Their descendents, the Hopi Indians, still call themselves 'the peaceful ones' and believe their role is to keep the earth in balance. Today, the Hopi believe the return of the Peacemaker is imminent. He will restore balance to the world.

Dr. Argüelles describes 'tula' as not just a place but as a process of becoming, a point of entry from one world-realm into another. (The Key of Life, which we will examine momentarily, is the symbol for the teaching through which one enters this expanded world.)

The mythical Shambhala, which Argüelles equates with Tula, is described in similar terms by the Buddhists, many of whom believe an earthly Tula can still be found hidden in a remote valley somewhere in the Himalayas. Other legends say that the kingdom of Shambhala disappeared from the earth hundreds of years ago. At that time the entire society became enlightened, and the kingdom vanished into another, higher celestial realm. As we will see, those who involve themselves with the Tula legend, including the builders of the Great Pyramid and Moses, have a habit of mysteriously vanishing or making a mass exodus from the earth plane.

Author, mystic and painter Nicholas Roerich led an expedition to Outer Mongolia in 1934 in search of the fabled city of Shambhala/Tula and its king. Astonishingly, Roerich equated Christ with the King of Tula, believing He had reincarnated and was living on earth. Mr. Roerich traveled to Mongolia as a representative of President Franklin D. Roosevelt, who himself believed this legend. They were in a race against Adolph Hitler, who also subscribed to this belief. It is my belief Roerich and President Roosevelt were correct. They were simply sixty-five years too early.

Today, Tibetans believe the King of Tula will soon return to lead humanity into a new era of peace and light. This prophecy corresponds with that of the pre-Christian Mandaeans (modern day Nazarenes), an offshoot of the Essenes. The Mandaeans cherished a closely guarded prophecy which concerns Tula. This prophecy states that the Secret Adam (who is equated with Christ), will return to earth to construct a machine to transport the souls of earth back home. This eternal machine may be an actual device, but more likely it is also a *process* within each of us represented in concrete form by the temple or machine.

JESUS AND TULA

With these prophecies in mind, many may be wondering where Jesus fits in with all of these Tula legends. Based on the early Christian texts found at Nag Hammadi, Eygpt and elsewhere, there is good reason to believe that Jesus came to earth to build a new Tula and to restore the connection between the heavenly Tula and human civilization at the beginning of the Age of Pisces.

It is important to note here, as does Margaret Starbird in her provocative book *The Woman With The Alabaster Jar*, that the Greek New Testament originally calls Jesus not "carpenter" but *tekton* (Mark 6:3). The word for carpenter, *najjar*, was applied to a sacred brotherhood, the Nazarenes, who made a living by woodworking.

A *tekton* was a construction engineer, a designer of houses (presumably for the Lord) or a bridge builder (presumably across forever to 'Home'). This interpretation places Jesus squarely in the role of cosmic contractor sent to build the most direct route or Way to Tula. Following Jesus' Way home would enable a soul not only to escape earth life, but also to avoid entanglement in the theoretical labyrinth of worm holes permeating our galaxy.

JESUS: THE TULKU

Again and again Buddhist and Hindu scholars document Jesus' journey to India and his spiritual initiation by Buddhist and Hindu masters in his quest for the Key of Life, the means to improve and purify the soul and ultimately transcend earth life and return to Tula.

In Tibet, the highest order of Buddhists are called *tulkus*, or precious ones. These are masters who, compelled by a super-human compassion for the suffering of humanity, voluntarily choose rebirth in a limited human body to help lead others to Enlightenment. If Jesus were a Buddhist, it is virtually certain he would have been a tulku. If so, this is very interesting and worthy of serious consideration.

Tulku is a word composed of the root *tul*, meaning 'what binds' or Tula. *Ku*, in numerous traditions, means 'shining one' and is a reference to soul or spirit. In Egypt, the word *khu*, Great Hu, meant the 'shining, translucent, transparent, intangible essence of man'.

By this rendering, Jesus would be a 'shining one of Tula', the Central Sun, sent to earth to build a bridge for souls to travel from an earthly Tula to the divine Tula at the center of heaven. Remarkably, the shining ones of Tula may correspond to the "Kings of Light" described in the Hindu texts and echoed in the Kings of Light of Chaldea. Noah and Moses were said to have had dazzling faces. Jesus is invariably shown with a crown or halo of light surrounding his face.

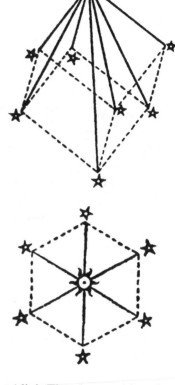

11. **In his tremendously superb book Jesus Christ: Sun of God David Fideler discusses Jesus' relation to Tula, the Spiritual Sun or the Sun behind the Sun. The spiritual number of Jesus, says Fideler, 8 or 888, is the same number as the Spiritual Sun. Fideler offers the illustration shown here, a cube in its isometric projection, to illustrate his point. Six rays fan out from the seventh inner point of the cube. These 'seven stars' are the same seven stars of the constellation of the Pleiades which are the gateway to the Central Sun or Tula. The key to the ancient mysteries of Tula is revealed in the upper cube. Through this perspective an eighth, hidden Spiritual Sun, is revealed from which all souls flow. According to early Jewish philosophers, God resides in the "Sun behind the sun" – Tula.**

There is more. These tulkus typically do not 'die'. They have achieved what is called the Rainbow Body in the Buddhist tradition and practice what is called *powa*, the 'transference of consciousness', a technique whereby their consciousness takes up a new existence in a new body. At the moment of their 'death' the tulkus leave signs or indications of where they will reincarnate and a name by which they can be identified. These signs enable search parties to locate them. Once located, extensive tests are given to insure that the person located is the reincarnated tulku. Personal possessions may be hidden among identical objects which only the reincarnated tulku can identify. Once identified, tulkus are taken to the monastery for training. These tulkus then take up their former possessions and teaching positions, continuing their 'mission' where they left off.

TAXILA

It is fascinating to examine the early life of Jesus from the perspective that he was a reincarnated Buddhist tulku. Mary and Joseph were Essenes (or *therapeutae*, as the Greeks called them), a mystical, possibly even Buddhist order, which existed on the shores of the Dead Sea. The Nazarenes were an offshoot of the Essenes. Interestingly, German writer and researcher Holger Kersten (*The Original Jesus*) traces the origins of this order to a north Indian Buddhist enclave called *Taxila*, a place name in which, perhaps not so surprisingly, the T-L-A indicators of Tula are evident. This detail fits in perfectly with our rendering of Jesus as a tulku, an agent from the heavenly Tula sent to build a new earthly Tula.

Taxila was hailed far and wide in the ancient world for its university where ancient sciences were taught. It has been compared to Alexandria, Egypt, where the massive Library of Alexandria contained over 500,000 volumes of ancient, possibly even antediluvian (pre-Flood), texts. Taxila is practically a lost city, and its influence on the unification of East and West has been almost completely ignored. However, in Jesus' time Taxila and Alexandria were linked. The Buddhist missionaries in Alexandria kept in constant contact with Taxila.

Among those 'in the know' were the Jewish Essenes, whom Kersten documents were in contact with the nearby community of Buddhist monks. In fact, the similarity of their teachings makes it obvious that there was considerable interaction. Attentive investigators have noticed that many of the parables and stories found in Christianity are direct copies of earlier Buddhist works, including the Parable of the Mustard Seed, the story of the Prodigal Son, the Sermon on the Mount and the Temptation in the Desert by evil. (It is quite apparent that the scribes we know of as Matthew, Mark, Luke and John were highly influenced by earlier Buddhist authors.)

Undoubtedly, the Essenes were aware of the prophecies of the return of an enlightened being. In India, this being was called Krishna, in Asia, Buddha and in Egypt, it was Horus. Following the signs in the heavens concerning the return of this being (a rare astrological conjunction in 5 B.C), the "Three Wise Men" set out to find him.

Jesus fulfilled the prophecies of the birth of a sacred king to many religions and nations. The Essenes gave him the title *Christos*, the literal meaning of which is 'healing moon man'. From the Egyptians he received the title of Good Shepherd after Osiris. From the Persian Mithra he was given the title Light of the World, Sun of Righteousness, Helios the Rising Sun. From the Greek Dionysus, he received the name King of Kings, God of Gods. Vishnu and Mithra were the Son of Man and Messiah until Jesus came along to claim these titles. 'Savior' was applied to each of these teachers before Jesus. Mystery schools the world over believed at certain times in human history, particularly at the beginning of each New Age, ordinary children or men could be 'possessed' by the Holy Spirit of God. The children were called the Sons of God.

The Buddhists recognized the baby Jesus as a reincarnated tulku, therefore the Three Wise Men escorted the child and his parents East with them. Since Jesus was recognized as a reincarnated enlightened one, it made sense to return him to his homeland. As the events unfold, the Magi are warned in a dream not to return to Herod for fear of the child's murder. Jesus was immediately taken to Egypt.

Was the baby Jesus taken to the Pyramid as the Egyptian prophecies of the return of the heron describe? We cannot say for certain. However, if there is one place on earth that could protect the Christ child it is the Great Pyramid. Built to resist earthquakes, floods, wars, and probably even a nuclear attack, it is believed by many that the Great Pyramid was designed as a cosmic communications device, a temple of initiation, a Bible in stone. Whatever its true intent, the Pyramid is the perfect place to place the vessel of Christ. By its brawn and its cosmic aura, how could Herod possibly even think about penetrating this fortress?

After his stay in Egypt, Jesus returned to the area we now call Galilee for a short time before beginning his travels. During his so-called missing years it is believed Jesus was raised and trained by Buddhist priests first in Egypt and then in India. As Taxila was the place where students of the Buddha went to learn the Dharma ('wheel' or 'way'), it is likely this is the place where Jesus spent the 'missing years' of his youth.

TULA: THE LOST KINGDOM OF JESUS

When he returned to Jerusalem as an adult, Jesus was a full tulku, or shining one of Tula who had a clear vision for a new Tula centered in Jerusalem, and for a new world order based on spiritual (not economic, political or religious) ideology. His idea was to tear down the existing temple and replace it with a "temple made without hands," a phrase which had a specific meaning to the people of his time, and which we shall attempt to elucidate today.

Jesus' vision was based on his perception of the intimate relationship between human and human, human and earth, and human, earth and heaven. It was rooted in extensive training which he received studying ancient Tula complexes in his travels in Egypt, India, and America (a journey which we shall revisit in a later chapter). His teachings, which would unite humanity with the angels and transform us into herons, would be embodied in the new Tula. Once opened, the principles taught at Tula would revolutionize life on earth, transforming it from wasteland to garden. In particular, his discovery of a limitless source of energy had many practical applications, most of which are only now being developed.

THE GOLDEN NEEDLE

I give you the end of the golden thread
only wind it into a ball,
it will lead you in at heaven's gate
built in Jerusalem's wall.

– William Blake
"Jerusalem"

Jesus, the Tekton's, plan for the Tula would require utilizing hundreds of tons of gold, which had relatively recently been stored at nearby Solomon's Temple, the fortress atop Mount Mariah at the center of Jerusalem. 138 tons of gold (worth billions of dollars today) were housed at this location along with the secret geometric plans for the construction of the Tula.

The gold would be used as a 'golden needle' which would tie the 'thread' between worlds. By building the Tula, the Tekton was constructing a connecting link to what the ancient Egyptians called the *Shu* (a soul pipeline or bridge for souls) and which modern physicists call a 'wormhole' to travel through the galaxy to the central point in heaven or Tula. Throughout history people of faith or no faith at all who have had Near Death Experiences tell of going towards a light, being met by loved ones, and seeing beautiful places. The Shu may be this 'white light' or 'tunnel'. Tula, say the ancients, is the otherworldly place they experience.

In a later book we will explore this concept in detail. For now, we simply need to understand that the Shu, or white light worm hole, is connected to a web on earth composed of Tulas constructed at strategic sacred locations (each of which is a repository of enormous amounts of gold even in modern times). Periodically, these Tula complexes are activated with the result that the spiritual vibration of the earth is altered to allow for effortless mass translation or evacuation of souls from earth to heaven.

To activate the web of spiritual vibration for the new Tula across the earth, Jesus hinted he was going to tear at the social fabric of earth life by sewing onto it a new cloth, "for no man also seweth a piece of new cloth on an old garment: else the new piece that filled it up taketh away from the old, and the rent is made worse" (Mark 2:21).

Jesus was very deliberate in his wording in this regard. He was clearly going to use his golden needle to thread the way, or bind, earth to heaven. The spiritual vibration of the souls on earth could be raised. If they so chose, millions of souls could then escape earth life. This is described in the mythology of the ancient Greeks and the Hopi Indians as escaping the Labyrinth of earth life into which the souls had been woven or entrapped. In this scenario, the Tula is a 'docking station' for the mating of two worlds.

The sacred symbol or logo for his enterprise was the butterfly, the primordial symbol for Tula. The butterfly is one of a family of ancient symbols for ascension and resurrection which includes the six-pointed "Star of the Magi" or Star of David, and the ancient four-petaled Flower of Life symbol.

THE FISH

We will return to the butterfly in a moment. First, we need to clear up a few misconceptions surrounding Jesus' well-known alternate symbol to the butterfly, the *vesica pisces* or so-called fish, which is one component of the Flower of Life.

Early Christians believed that the fish symbol was derived from the idea that *ichthys* (Greek 'fish') was an acronym for "Jesus Christ, Son of God." This name, like much of the rest of Christ symbolism, was copied from earlier pagan originals.

Ichthys was the name of one of the sons of the ancient Sea-mother Mari, who was universally depicted wearing a blue robe (the attire of the beings from the Pleiades). *Delphine* , meaning 'dolphin' or 'womb', was the Sea-goddess's name when depicted in mermaid form. This is quite fascinating in light of the fact that in Christian art a dolphin pierced by a trident represents Christ on the cross. Also, in Greek tradition the dolphin is a psychopomp, a guide of souls to the Blessed Isles, otherwise known as the Scilly Isles or Tula.

Synchronistically, the fish symbolizes three additional important aspects of Jesus' mission as a Tekton. One, the fish or *vesica pisces* was a master mason's mark. Two, it originated in ancient Egypt and symbolized 'tying the knot' between earth and Tula. Three, it was the astrological symbol for the Age of Pisces the Fish which Jesus came to introduce.

  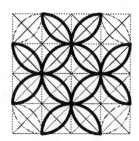

12. Overlap the two cosmic fish, often shown as triangles, and you have the Star of David. The Star of David, in turn, 'morphs' into a butterfly and back into a Flower of Life.

Why is a full and correct understanding of this symbolism so important? By learning to find and correctly interpret images of this nature, we find the secret images or sacred language of Jesus, and the priesthood he represents. Speaking in this language will enable a correct analysis of Jesus, in the past and the present.

For instance, all of this symbolism was best rendered in Jesus' personal sacred number and 'signature', the figure 8, the symbol for infinity which is derived from the sacred marriage between two 'fish'.

Traditionally linked with Saturn – the planet of boundaries, gateways, endings and transitions – this influence pervades the eight's meaning, and expresses the potent influence Jesus was to have on earth, then and now. Four is traditionally the number of earth symbolized by the four seasons, elements, winds, and archangels. (Please take note: the significance of Saturn and the number four will continue to influence our story.) As two times four, eight reflects the idea of two complimentary worlds meeting each other. This is why the two fours appear in the symbol on the cover of this book. The two hands shaking and joining conveys the idea of two worlds meeting each other, or the act of sacred marriage between earth and heaven, the *hiero gamos*.

THE RETURN OF THE HERON

What we today readily identify as a fish is one of a catalog of ancient Egyptian hieroglyphs for resurrection and for tying the bond between heaven and earth. Significantly, the *vesica pisces* is also the Egyptian hieroglyph for the heron, predating Jesus by millennia. By invoking the fish, Jesus was, in effect, proclaiming himself the Heron.

Egyptian myths say that at the dawn of the world, the Christ, Messiah or head of the Spiritual Hierarchy emerged from the central point in heaven (Tula) and took the form of the heron, radiating light from its outstretched wings perched atop the pyramid. This Teacher delivers teachings that would enable our transformation into the heron, a body of light capable of travelling in higher dimensions of existence. Once again, the fish is the Egyptian hieroglyph for the heron.

As Wallis Budge states in *The Gods of the Egyptians*, "the heron was certainly a sacred bird, and that its body was regarded as a possible home for a human soul is proved by the 84th Chapter of the *Book of the Dead*, which was composed with the view of helping a man to effect a transformation into a heron."

For certain, the sacred geometry of the fish contained the essence of Jesus' teaching for leading a balanced life. Following this teaching led to integration with Tula or what he called Salvation. To the ancients, the fish symbolizes a cosmic knot or bond with Tula.

Indeed, thousands of temples have been constructed based upon the sacred geometry of the *vesica pisces*. Known as the "geometry generator" for its ability to spin off sacred geometric shapes, this pattern was used functionally and symbolically in the construction of doors or portals between earthly and heavenly places. In other words, the fish embodies the sacred geometry used in the construction of star gates. Today, in fits of misunderstanding, the fish is used in the design of corporate logos, such as CBS and Mastercard.

What became of the Tula Jesus was to construct? As we will see, Jesus' plans for an earthly Tula were given to his closest confidant, Mary Magdalen, and constructed as a twenty-one square mile Flower of Life in Southern France in an area called Rennes-le-Chateau.

A NEW TULA, A NEW SACRED SIGN

The Age of Pisces is finished. Today, the sign of the fish is due to be replaced. Religious worship will soon take the form of the New Age of Aquarius, symbolized by the water-bearer (water is the symbol for wisdom). This is interesting because astrologers tell us Aquarius is an air sign.

As has happened at the beginning of virtually every recorded New Age, the faithful will likely wish to cling to their old images. Moses, for instance, had to destroy the image of the golden bull to introduce the Age of Aries, the Ram. Jesus, came as a shepherd (never referring to himself as a fish or a fisherman) to transform the sheep of the Age of Aries into the New Age of the Fish.

In the Age of Aquarius we will be transformed from 'fish' into something else. What will that be and how shall we symbolize this New Age? I will suggest two possible symbols here and a third later in this work. Like early Christians drawing fish in the sand, these symbols are designed not merely to identify the 'faithful', but rather to act as psychological mandalas which trigger deeply embedded soul memories and instructions for linking us with the galactic Tula.

The first symbol I propose for the New Age of Aquarius are the letters "MM." These letters are rich in connections to Tula, and even to Jesus. To begin, the letter 'M' is based on the symbol of the twin peaks or double mountain, which is an ancient epitaph for Tula. The twin peaks are seen as the breasts of the Tula, the Great Mother, from whence our souls originated.

The letters MM are also the Roman numerals for the year 2000, the initials of Mary Magdalen and, coincidentally, the two wavy lines of the astrological symbol for Aquarius. The 'resurrection' of Mary Magdalen as the symbol of our New Age would reflect the unprecedented resurgence of goddess consciousness and a recognition of the feminine aspects of god in our world. Without question, the patriarchal system which has dominated human affairs for the past 2000 years has led us to the brink of the Promised Land. However, as evidenced by the myths of the sacred marriage, the only way the Peacemaker can take us into the Promised Land is through the anointment or illumination of the goddess energy.

This ancient belief is reflected in its most uncanny form in the beloved Disney film, *The Little Mermaid*. As Margaret Starbird points out in *The*

Woman With The Alabaster Jar, in the opening moments of this hugely popular movie the little mermaid girl, Ariel, resurrects a painting from a long submerged galleon. This painting is *The Penitent Magdalen* by the seventeenth-century French artist Georges de la Tour.

Children (and more than a few adults) world wide fell in love with the story of a little mermaid girl's search for her prince. Coincidentally, the marriage between the aqueous princess Ariel and her earth-bound prince is precisely the 'story' of the Peacemaker and his search for his beloved. As in the *The Little Mermaid*, once the two are joined in sacred marriage the 'kingdom' is renewed.

Before leaving this subject it is worthwhile to note that the name Ariel is another name for none other than Jerusalem, the City of Peace. It is also worth asking why Disney went to such pains to implant these ideas in the consciousness of millions of children? Could it be some 'enlightened' storysmith at Disney knew the symbols of our New Age and sought to anchor these core ideas in the emerging thoughtsphere of humanity?

This idea may sound a little far-fetched, but it must be remembered that in an animated movie which costs millions of dollars to produce nothing is done by chance. Every detail, right down to the inclusion of an obscure painting of Mary Magdalen is intentional.

The second possible symbol for Aquarius emerges when we dig deep into history. To the ancients, Aquarius was symbolized not by the water-bearer, but by the phoenix or the heron, the bird of resurrection and ascension, carrying the 'cup of immortality'. This cup contains the water ('wisdom') which will enable our transformation into herons, beings of light capable of travelling in higher dimensions of awareness.

The theme of the Peacemaker finding his beloved rings in the symbol MM and in the symbol of the heron atop the pyramid. The voice of the heron's beloved (MM), who sat at his feet drinking in every word (Luke 10:39) will soon be heard. Once again, she will anoint him and the bond between earth and heaven will be renewed. According to the Book of Revelation, it is the marriage of the Lamb with his bride, Ariel, Zion or Tula, that will cause the water ('wisdom') to flow, bringing peace and abundance to earth.

CHAPTER THREE

THE KEY OF LIFE

The wisdom tradition states the Peacemaker will recover the esoteric training called the *Key of Life*. Nostradamus affirms he will use this to lead humanity to a new beginning. It is the focal image of the Book of Revelation. What, exactly, is the Key of Life?

The key has long been a mystical symbol of knowledge about the 'greater' life after death. Indeed, the Key of Life is based on two things: one, remembering that our goal in life is to co-create heaven (Tula) on earth. Two, transforming ourselves into a heron, a being of light capable of travelling in the higher dimensions, to return to the heavenly Tula.

THE STORY OF THE KEY OF LIFE

It is important to realize the Key of Life is a pre-Flood technology and body of knowledge. An old Jewish legend unearthed by Zecharia Sitchin tells of the staff of miracles, or Key of Life, used by Moses to perform many miracles (including the Red Sea's parting) and originally brought out of the Garden of Eden by Adam. In one version, the Key of Life was carved out of a single stone; in another, it was made from a branch of the Tree of Life, which grew in the Garden of Eden.

Adam, says the legend, gave the Key of Life to Enoch; then Enoch gave it to his great-grandson Noah, the hero of the Deluge. Then it was handed down through the line of Shem, son of Noah, from generation to generation, until it reached Abraham. Abraham's great-grandson Joseph brought it with him to Egypt where he rose to the highest rank in the Pharaoh's court. There, the Key of Life remained among the treasures of the Egyptian kings until it was passed on to Moses. Later, Jesus acquired the Key of Life, using it to perform many of His miracles.

In this legend humanity had reached a high degree of civilization and then, due to a cataclysm, 'forgot' its own past. As frequently happens, what was misunderstood was destroyed or swept under the rug. Up until the middle ages, ancient spiritual beliefs (including those of pre-Flood days) were widely practiced throughout the world. With the widespread persecution and assassination of spiritual beliefs in medieval Christian Europe, the keepers of the wisdom of the ages went underground and formed secret societies to preserve the relics and knowledge of the ancient world. Devices such as the Key of Life would have only been known and understood by a few initiates privy to its secrets. Stories about Tula would also have circulated within these secret priesthoods.

The secrets these priesthoods possessed were encoded in myths (such as the Holy Grail) and into works of art, including those of Mozart and Leonardo da Vinci: two masters involved in the perpetuation of ancient mysteries. Amidst these works of art the images and symbols of the Key of Life and Tula circulated undetected (like the painting of Mary Magdalen in *The Little Mermaid*) by all but the 'enlightened'. What secret symbols were these?

In all ancient myths of lost paradises, the land of peace (Tula) sits like a flower atop a cosmic pillar or staff – "earth's highest mountain." Strangely, this mountain has twin peaks, one to the left and the other to the right of the central pillar. Since the word *tula* means 'balance', we can presume one of these peaks is on earth and the other in the heavens. This presumption is backed by myths which tell us Tula is the place of the double mountain.

13. Tula, the twin peaks, sits atop the Key of Life. Later, it will be revealed that this same symbol was a hieroglyph used by none other than Moses to represent the means whereby all men might unite with the God force.

The Egyptian Mount of Glory (*Khut*) is depicted as two peaks between which rests the enclosed sun. The enclosed sun is the spiritual center of the universe, or Tula. This depiction was by no means exclusive to Egypt. The Delaware Indians of America have what is thought to be a myth of a glorious land called "the *Talega* country," where in the beginning "all kept peace with each other." If we carefully reread the word *talega* we notice the letters T-L-A, a tip-off to its origins in Atlantis or Tula. In fact, the Delaware "Hymn to the Flood" tells of the destruction of their lost homeland. "Much water is rushing, much go to the hills, much penetrate, much destroying. Meanwhile at Tula, at that island, Nana-Bush becomes the ancestor of beings and men . . . the beings and men all go forth from the Flood creeping in shallow water or swimming afloat, asking which is the way to the turtle-back [island], Tula-Pin."

The Delaware hieroglyph of this lost land is identical to the Egyptian pictograph for the Mount of Glory. To the Egyptians the Mount of Glory, or Tula, was alternately signified by the scepter of Ra, which was depicted as a twin peak atop a single column. This hieroglyph indicates the Key of Life represents the pillar or the Way to heaven. This pillar is also known as the Tree of Life.

THE SECRETS OF THE KEY OF LIFE

What are the secrets of the Key of Life? From the ancient texts one deduces that the Key of Life is at once a spiritual training and a technological device, a staff of miracles or magic wand with which many extraordinary things have been accomplished including the leveling of mountains, the stunning of intruders and, incredibly, the transfer of souls from one dimension to another.

The Key of Life training encompasses all aspects of yoga, mysticism, meditation, the martial arts, magic and metaphysics. For those who seek it, the Key promises insight into the seeker's true nature and the secrets of the universe, including mind over matter.

Throughout the ages the symbol for the Key of Life has been transformed, the determinative factor being the perspective from which one is viewing the Key. In one instance, it was a circle of life or heaven atop an earthbound *tau cross*. In this form, the Key, or *ankh* as it was called, is often found in the hands of Egyptian gods and pharaohs.

In Egyptian myth, the ankh was seen as a key to the Nile. It is important to understand that Egyptian cosmology (like the Atlantean and Mayan) was dualistic. Earthly phenomenon are correspondent to heavenly originals. For instance, the Egyptians thought of the earthly river Nile as the counterpart of the heavenly Nile, the star-fields of the Milky Way. In another example, the three pyramids of Giza are offset to exactly coincide with the pattern of the three stars in Orion's belt as they appeared over Giza in approximately 10,500 B.C., the reported date of the pyramids' construction.

Egyptologists favor the view that the ankh secretly represents the male and female genitalia combined. This view is echoed in the Hindu tradition. Here, the esoteric aspect of the Key of Life is called *Tantra*, a magic sex act wherein the Divine Presence or Holy Spirit is channeled through the interplay between the male and female energies of a couple.

The object of Tantra and the Key of Life is to produce a specific spiritual vibration. Orgasm, as through Tantra, can liberate the soul and awaken the Divine power within. In theory, an awakened couple's orgasm will attract a Magical Child who leads the human race to the Light. This emphasizes the idea that the Key of Life is an inner spiritual process. This notion of awakening latent spiritual power, especially through intercourse, was 'too much' for certain early religious authorities to discuss publicly. Mention of this was deliberately removed during the Middle Ages in order to assist the Church in its struggle against contenders for its power because in all mystical traditions it was recognized that the female, not the male, held the keys to awakening the inner spiritual power.

14. Caduceus.

Later, the Key of Life was transformed into the *caduceus*, a 'rod of power' with entwined serpents. The caduceus revived the ancient seal of the Ningishzidda (Lord of the Key of Life), the Sumerian name for Enoch/Thoth. Biblical writers renamed it *Nehushtan* and worshipped it as the earliest form of the God of Moses (Numbers 21:9, 2 Kings 18:4).

Many readers will immediately recognize this ancient symbol as the emblem of the medical profession. This idea came from the Greeks who adopted the seal of the Peacemaker as the symbol for their god Asclepius, the god of medicine, who was believed to have been a Peacemaker.

Here we encounter a very interesting detail of the Key of Life. The caduceus has two 'snakes' that face each other and cross *seven* times. These snakes represent the dance between the male and female energies of the universe 'out there' and the universe 'in here', in the mind/brain system. They also represent the 7 electrical points of the body called *chakras*, which are thought of as microbrains or 'seeds' of spiritual potential which require awakening in order to flower.

This symbolism of the 7, the number of creation, links the Key with the seven-branched candlestick or 7 lights before the Holy of Holies in the Jewish Temple (Exodus 25:3) which Moses was instructed to construct. Esoterically, the Holy of Holies is believed to be the female womb or the human aura in which the chakras are sheathed.

Why is there such an insistence on connecting the Key of Life with the number seven? One thought-provoking explanation says the number four represents the male principle and the number three represents the female principle that in its oldest manifestations had three aspects: Virgin, Mother, Crone. Therefore, one reason the ancients so highly revered the number seven was that it united four and three within it.

I believe the real reason for the importance of the number seven is encoded in the story of Jesus curing Mary Magdalen from possession by seven "demons." Uncovering this reason takes us to the core of the Key of Life training.

MARY MAGDALEN: HOLDER OF THE KEY OF LIFE

In the Gospel of John it is told that the first person to behold Jesus after the Resurrection was Mary Magdalen. It is this mysterious woman who holds the secret to the Key of Life and to a staggering and completely new understanding of the man we call Jesus. Decoding her secret offers an extraordinary message for the future of our civilization.

The Gospel of Philip says: "There were three who walked with the Lord at all times: Mary his mother, her sister, and Magdalen, the one who is called his companion." This Gnostic document also records that Mary's closeness with Jesus stirred jealous feelings in the hearts of the other Apostles because he kissed her on the mouth. Of the seven lists in the four Gospels that name the female companions of Jesus six list Mary Magdalen ahead of Mary the mother of the Lord. Obviously, Mary, the Magdalen, came first. She even became known as the 'apostle of the apostles' as attested in the Gospels of Matthew, Mark and Luke. (Only the 'heretical' Gnostic scriptures make mention that Jesus had 12 female apostles to accompany the 12 males and that Mary Magdalen was the ringleader.)

So, who was this woman? Mary Magdalen was a woman of noble birth who resided at the temple at Magdala, a village on the outskirts of Jerusalem with thatched roof homes, magic and enchantment. In Hebrew, Magdala literally means 'tower' or 'elevated, great, magnificent'. The place name *Magdal-eder* translates to 'tower of the flock'. It was known as the City of Doves. The dove symbolizes peace, ascension and the Pleiades star cluster.

In fact, Mary was a Benjaminite, one of the original twelve tribes of Israel. Long before Jesus came along, this family was ostracized for suspicious dealings (including marriage) with beings who, it was reported, came from the stars. At one time, the Benjaminites possessed Jerusalem. King Saul, a Benjaminite, was the first King of Jerusalem. His daughter, Michol, was the wife of King David. From their inception the destinies of the tribes of Benjamin and David were intertwined. A dynastic marriage between a Benjaminite priestess (heiress to her former lands encompassing Jerusalem) and the messianic Son of David would have fulfilled every Jew's millennial wish book. It would have been seen as the time when swords would be beat into ploughshares and all would be balanced with God.

Mary Magdalen was known as the inspirer of Jesus by the Gnostics (Greek for 'knowledge'), the secret disciples of Jesus who purported to possess his most secret teachings about the Universe and about gaining entrance to Tula. This image contradicts the 'official' Church association of Mary as the archetypal whore. Far from being a harlot, Mary Magdalen was a special companion of Jesus, a relationship which blossomed after he healed her of possession by seven demons (Luke 8:2, Mark 16:9).

Mary has been criticized in many ways but her victory over the seven demons illustrates her extraordinary spiritual credentials. It singles her out as one who had received a remarkable spiritual attunement from Jesus. This attunement gave her expanded human abilities and prepared her soul to exit the earth plane.

Early Christians adopted the ancient belief that our souls descended from a central point in heaven (which we have identified as Tula). According to this theory, the earth rested within a series of *seven* crystal spheres or bowls. The soul, in turn, was nested in a human body and energy field, which also contained seven levels called *chakras* ("as above, so below"). As the soul descended onto the earthly level it collected excess baggage from the seven planetary spheres (the origins of the idea of the Seven Deadly Sins) which needed to be cleansed before one could return to the central point in heaven.

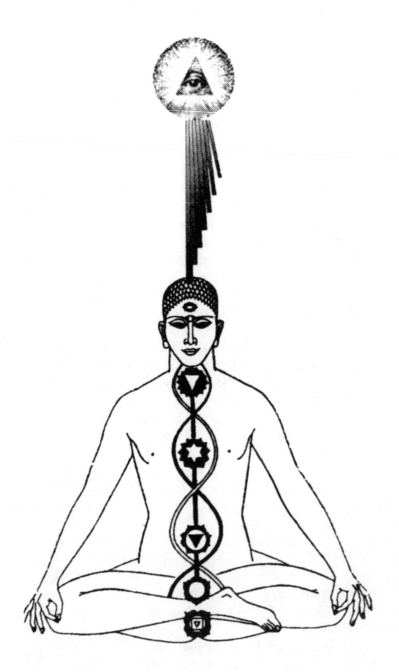

15. Seven human chakras or energy centers. "One, two, three, four, five, six, seven. All good children go to Heaven" (Children's song).

In the Pistis Sophia, a Gnostic text, Jesus told his followers:

Stay not your hand until ye find the cleansing mysteries which will cleanse you so as to make you pure light, that ye may go into the heights and inherit the light of my kingdom.

This "cleansing" (or perhaps 'Christing') was done through an initiation or *attunement* centered around overcoming seven demons. These demons represented the seven planetary spheres of the Pleiades, a star cluster in the constellation of Taurus the Bull which has a tremendous wealth of lore and legend surrounding it. Most of this lore centers around the Mother symbol of the dove (the Pleiades being the home of Dove-goddesses, or Hathors) who guarded the 'gate' to the central point of heaven, Tula.

I refer to this initiation as the *Pleiadean Attunement*. In short, when Jesus cured Mary Magdalen of possession by seven demons, he was attuning her soul with the Pleiades and assisting her in transforming herself into a being of light.

Understanding the Pleiades as the star gate to Tula explains why in many religious traditions the soul transforms into a dove at death. Since ancient times there has been a belief that souls could take the form of birds. Latin *aves* means both 'birds' and 'angels'. It is likely these terms refer to the heron or the body of light that Jesus mentions.

The name 'dove' has been applied to prophets throughout history who enabled this extraordinary transformation. For example, the prophet sent to Ninevah as God's messenger was called Jonah ('Dove'). This same Jonah, you may recall, spent three days trapped inside the belly of a whale. Jonah was actually the Babylonian god *Oannes*, a figure who was part man, part fish (and who we will meet again shortly). John the Baptist was also called Johannes, or the Dove. When John baptized Jesus (or, rather, attuned Him) a dove, signifying the Holy Spirit, descended upon him. Clearly, John was connecting Jesus with the Pleiades. He was also connecting him with Jonah.

Why was this so? The enlightened meaning of Jonah's (and Moses') rescue from water, Oannes' half-man, half-fish incarnation, John's baptizing in the River Jordan, and Jesus' walking on water are all the same: these figures have all achieved enlightenment and have passed over the waters of immortality. They are all tulkus, perhaps even 'shining ones of Tula'.

Furthermore, they are all members of a priesthood (which for the sake of simplicity we will call Doves) who returned to this plane to reveal the means whereby others may learn the Key of Life, the means to "cross over." The knowledge these Doves represent existed before the Flood, during the last Golden Age. Hence, the rescue from water motif. The Doves have been sent to help the rest of humanity remember the Key of Life.

THE KEY OF LIFE AND HUMAN DNA

The attunement the Doves offered triggered a transformation of being which ultimately enabled souls to travel through the 'star gate' of the Pleiades. Many will notice the caduceus model of the Key of Life resembles the molecular models of DNA. This observation reveals an important aspect of the Key of Life. The receptor sites for the energies of the Pleiadean Attunement are designed into our genetic coding. Hence, they are part of our divine birthright. The evolution of the human soul occurs through the unfolding of the two opposing energies of yin and yang, light and dark, matter and spirit represented by the entwined serpents (and simultaneously by the yin-yang symbol).

According to legend, it was Enoch/Thoth who, by separating the two opposing forces with his golden wand or rod of transformation, introduced the third equilibrating or balancing force, symbolized by the Dove. This third, balancing force is the teaching which enabled our return to Tula. This is why the Key of Life (in all its forms, but especially topped by a bird) is the symbol for the teachings which lead to Tula.

In the Greek tradition, Thoth was transformed into the patron of roads, pathways and boundaries, including those of consciousness. Sacred to him, and presumably the brotherhood of the Peacemakers, was THE PATH or THE WAY. This term was not only the signature of Jesus ("I am the Way. . ." John 14:6), but also was the original name of Christianity. This referred to Jesus' teaching of "the path between opposites." Jesus sought to help humanity transcend the polarities of light and dark into a higher dimension, Tula, symbolized by the dove. Once again, in the sacred tradition the name of the dove of peace is *Ionah* or *Ionas* and John the Baptist was called *Ioannes*.

Nowhere in the Scriptures is Jesus said to have or use a staff of miracles or even a magic wand. Yet, as Thomas F. Mathews observes in his *The Clash of the Gods*, in early Christian art the wand (after the scroll of his teaching) is the most popular attribute of Christ. Over and over again Early Christian miracle images present Jesus with the wand. It is meant to convey the magic power of touch. The purpose of showing Jesus performing miracles with the wave of his wand was meant to connect Jesus with Moses, whose words he fulfilled.

16. The Key of Life is called in the Orphic hymns "the blameless tool of peace." Hermes is frequently shown, wand in hand, animating and releasing lifeless shapes, and guiding souls upward, releasing them from the Underworld (earth).

In truth, Jesus *is* associated with the Key of Life in the Bible. We have already witnessed this in the story of Mary Magdalen. This is not, however, the only place in the Gospels where Jesus appears with the Key of Life.

The Book of Revelation tells us that "the book of seven seals" contains Jesus' message for pre-Tribulation personal transformation or apocalypse. *Apocalypse* refers to revealing what is hidden and awakening to a new form of existence when we realize the enormity of our power within. This "book of seven seals" is represented by the entwined serpents giving way to the dove of the Holy Spirit. The seven seals may well be the seven chakras.

THE KEY OF LIFE IN THE BOOK OF REVELATION

The Book of Revelation begins with John in a shamanic trance, likely out of his body on a lower astral plane. As John says "I was in the Spirit on the Lord's day [as was Enoch] and heard behind me [as did Moses] a great voice, as of a trumpet" (Revelation 1:10).

Suddenly, this voice says, "I am Alpha and Omega, the first and the last." John believes this angel to be Jesus (Revelation 1:17-19). In his hand Jesus holds *seven stars*. We recall that the caduceus and the chakras of our own body have seven points or stars. Jesus must be holding the Key of Life! Hermes used this wand to conduct souls from one dimension to another. It appears Jesus is using the seven stars for this same purpose.

If indeed Jesus did use the Key of Life to conduct souls (maybe even himself) from one dimension to another, he would not have been the first to do so. As the Jewish legend states, he was one in a long line of initiates beginning with Enoch who possessed the Key of Life.

Perhaps the most astonishing intimation of the Key's soul transfer capabilities is found in this pre-Christian illustration featuring the Egyptian goddess Isis. She is suckling Horus, the Egyptian Savior. Standing before her, Key of Life in hand, is Ra, the Egyptian Lord of Eternal Light, the Christian Archangel Micha-El. Standing behind her is his brother Thoth/Enoch, the Peacemaker. This is a startling ceremony for two reasons. First, because Isis is receiving the *breath of life*, the soul, from Ra. Horus, we can see, is the benefactor of this spiritual essence. (This may mean that Ra's soul is 'jumping' into Horus' body; or, more startlingly, that Ra and Thoth – like John and Jesus – are representatives of a third figure who was known to the Ancients but has been omitted from Christian dogma: Bot.) The second facet of this puzzle is that Chapter Two of the Book of Genesis offers an identical technical version of the Key in use:

> *And Yahweh fashioned the Adam of the clay of the soil; and He blew in his nostril the breath of life, and the Adam turned into a living Soul.*

These two linkages appear to hold the profound proof that the Key of Life is used to transfer the souls of humanity's greatest teachers to earth. This truth was possessed by the Sumerians whose mythology has been brought to life in the *Earth Chronicles* series of books by Zecharia Sitchin.

17. Isis, Horus, Thoth and Ra using the Key in a sacred ritual whereby the soul of the Savior enters Horus.

ENKI

Sitchin's research on the history inscribed on Mesopotamian tablets yielded proof of the involvement of *Yahweh* (Enki to the Sumerians) in the genetic alteration of mankind. It further shows that this genetic alteration was performed in conjunction with the Key of Life.

A hundred years ago no one knew who Enki was or where he came from. In the 1840's the Germans, seeking to prove their Aryan nation theory and that their god-kings were blond Atlanteans from the Atlantic shores of Europe, began digging for the ancient roots of these god-kings in the sands of Iran and Iraq. They unearthed massive libraries of ancient Sumerian writings. Libraries and museums throughout the world are now in possession of over 500,000 artifacts, drawings and historical texts which reveal that the stories of the ancients were, in reality, actual events. They present a rather spine-tingling version of the beginnings of mankind and are very clear as to what the initial life force, breath of life (or 'Word') was.

About 450,000 years ago, according to the historical accounts of the Sumerians, a group of extraterrestrials called *An-nun-aki* – 'those from heaven to Earth came', splashed down in the Persian Gulf and established a colony called E.RI.DU ('Home in Faraway Built') on its shores in present day Iraq. They were led by ENKI ('Lord Earth' or 'Lord of the Waters') and came to Earth to mine minerals they needed to repair the atmosphere of their home planet, Nibiru.

Nibiru is a massive twelfth planet in our solar system that makes a 3,600-year revolution around the Sun in an elliptical orbit far beyond Pluto. Sitchin's research reveals the Niburian civilization's technological prowess was so advanced they could literally reach out into the stars to purloin whatever resources they required. They busily colonized other worlds including Mars, which Sitchin believes is a "midway station" between earth and Nibiru.

Nibiru is called the "Planet of the Crossing," and is symbolized by an enclosed cross. The enclosed cross, of course, is one of the oldest and most prolific symbols known to man. It belongs to everyone, yet no one today seems to be able to say exactly where it came from. According to the Sumerians, the symbol of the cross originated from Nibiru. As we have seen, its origin is much more profound, symbolizing the our galactic home, Tula. It is worth noting that, according to the Hopi, if the Peacemaker returns with the cross alone it will be a sign of great suffering to come. If, however, the Peacemaker returns with the cross inside a circle (the symbol of the feminine and wholeness) humanity will proceed in peace. According to Robert E.G. Temple (*The Sirius Mystery*) the word Nibiru may be a contraction of the Egyptian Neb-Heru, or Lord Sun, linking it with the origins of the Sun god.

Using the Old Testament as a reference point, Sitchin devoted over thirty years to researching and synthesizing the archaeology and history of this era.

While others read the Sumerian tablets (including *Atrahasis*) metaphorically, Sitchin perceived them as a kind of ancient *New York Times*, believing they recounted factual events.

According to Sitchin, Enki and the gods came to earth to mine gold. When the gods tired of their work, they revolted. As a solution, Enki genetically altered early man to become slave workers. Later, he implanted highly evolved souls in these beings, and put humanity on the path to its present evolutionary stage.

18. Ptah, The Developer.

The Egyptians called Enki or Yahweh *Ptah* ('The Developer') shown here with the staff in hand. He was revered as the Teacher, assisting in the birth of the "white ones" or the "purified," both terms that allude to Tula, the White or Pure island. Here, it is interesting to compare the name Ptah with Peter (from 'petra' or stone), the New Testament disciple who holds the *key* to the kingdom of heaven.

Another interesting connection was made by Plato who called Ptah *Poseidon*, naming him the founder of Atlantis. Posei, or originally, *Potei*, is a title which means 'Lord'. *Don* means wisdom. Potei-don was symbolized by the white horse – a wild, galloping, stampeding, thunderous stallion. Thus, he was known to the Greeks as the 'Earth Shaker', a reference to the pounding of the horses' hooves across the landscape. From this the white horse became a symbol of the Peacemakers and was associated with Enoch, as well as one of the Four Horsemen of the Apocalypse, the white horse in the Book of Revelation of John upon which the Christ figure rides. We can now begin to understand this white horse is the symbol for a man.

19. The serpent symbol of Enki. Notice the similarity with the symbol for our DNA. (Copyright Z. Sitchin, *Genesis Revisited*)

According to Sitchin's research, Enki/Yahweh's additional symbol was the serpent, presumably for its ability to shed its skin and, therefore, to achieve a sort of immortality. Since Enki was a biospiritual engineer, the serpent symbol would have been appropriate for him in ancient times just as it is appropriate today for use by the AMA. In fact, Enki is the 'first healer' of earth.

Enki was assisted by his chief nurse, the goddess Ninhursag, called 'lady of life' or 'lady of the rib' in a series of genetic experiments which resulted in mankind's alteration from *homo erectus* to *homo sapien*. The parallels with the later Eve story are striking. At Eridu, their research lab, the two scientists and lovers conducted extensive genetic research. The Bible calls the serpent who tempted Eve *Nahash*, a Hebrew word meaning serpent and literally meaning 'He Who Solves Secrets'. A related word means soul. Here, there is a startling connection.

Ancient teachings reveal that a serpent (or soul) cannot stand erect of its own accord. By analogy, a serpent needs a tree to wind its way up toward the world of spirit. Thus, the spine represents a tree on which the spiritual life force or soul can ascend; and thus comes the association with the Great Tree of Life. Unless it has a vehicle in which it can ascend, a serpent is doomed to isolation in the lower worlds. Likewise, a body without spiritual animation is a meaningless heap of chemical compounds. Without spiritual fire, nothing can exist; hence, the combined symbols.

The accompanying illustration shows Enki and Ninharsag together. She appears to be standing in front of some laboratory test-tube flasks. Enki is waving his "Exalted Scepter and Staff," which he would later give to his son, Thoth, the entity I call the Peacemaker. This is the so-called staff of miracles or Key of Life that, among other things, legends tell us can be used to infuse lifeless matter with life force and to conduct souls between worlds.

20. Enki and Ninharsag with the Key of Life. (Copyright Z. Sitchin, *Genesis Revisited*)

While this history may seem strange to some, it is wonderful to others. No one really knows where we came from or how our souls got here. Or do they?

Here we see a page from an ancient Mayan manuscript, showing the mythical birth of humanity and illuminating the sacred meaning of the Mayan word *te* (which ordinarily means tree or the letter T). We see a person emerging from a sacred tree, a caduceus of entwined serpents! This knowledge was known to the Maya long before the arrival of the Catholic priests, who brought the Christian concepts of Adam, Eve, the serpent and the tree, but certainly not the staff symbol! The Mayan story must be source material.

Hunbatz Men (*Secrets of Mayan Science and Religion*), a Mayan ceremonial leader, believes that "obviously, the creation of human beings, the tree, and sacred things have been linked since the beginning of time. A transcendental synthesis of human religious experience is inherent in the word *te*, Sacred Tree, which emerged from the words *teol* and *teotl*, the names of God the Creator in Mayan and Nahuatl. These most revered and sacred words of the ancient people, symbolized by the Sacred Tree, were represented in Mayan hieroglyphs as the symbol "T." Additionally, this symbol represented the air, the wind, the divine *breath* of God."

If this provocative analysis of man's beginnings is correct we are dealing with a race of beings who possessed profound genetic and spiritual knowledge. Seemingly, Enki knew how to infuse this 'life force', 'soul force' or 'breath' (word) of God into the human body. So too did Ninharsag. They appear to have literally been able to transfer souls from another dimension to particular human bodies.

Modern spiritual theories cannot even agree that man has a soul, but Enki and Ninharsag were manipulating this spiritual 'stuff' and demonstrating precise knowledge of Cosmic Laws which presently elude modern science. Legends depict Hermes, the Greek name for Thoth the Peacemaker, guiding souls between worlds with this Key of Life. From this we must conclude these Cosmic Laws involve the development of the imagination and awareness of other planes of existence.

There is another illuminating legend surrounding Enki's assistant Ninharsag, whom many in the Western world know as the archangel Gabri-el.

GABRI-EL

The archangel Gabri-el (Gabri = God's Hero, El = Shining One) serves as Heaven's chief ambassador to humanity. She is the only female in the heavenly host's higher echelons. The female character of this remarkable archangel is revealed in popular lore, which tells how she takes the invariably protesting soul from paradise and instructs it for the nine months it remains in the womb of its mother before birth.

Gabri-el is considered the angel of childbirth. According to Biblical legend, it was Gabri-el who brought the news to Mary that she, the Palestinian peasant girl, would be the mother of Jesus. Six months before this event Gabri-el had a similar 'conversation' with John the Baptist's mother, Elizabeth.

The Annunciation by Bartel Bruyn shows a female Gabri-el conducting the soul of the Savior and the Holy Spirit in the shape of a radiant dove into Mary. The Hebrew word denoting a physical virgin is Bethulah, literally 'House of Tula' or 'vessel of the soul of Tula'. Until recently, the exact location of the home world of this Christ or Sun God has gone undetected. If we follow the thread of Sitchin's research, however, we may discover it is Tula, the center of our Milky Way Galaxy which is guarded by Nibiru. We can clearly see the wand with the entwined serpents as the conductive force for this soul. We also notice Mary's head is illuminated, indicating she is an initiate. This scene is a near duplicate of the Egyptian scene depicting the arrival of the Holy Spirit. It appears that whenever a Savior comes to earth there are important staff-centered medical procedures involved.

21. The Annunciation.

In this scene, called the "greatest event in history," Gabri-el tells Mary not to worry: "Ave, gratia plena, Dominus tecum": Hail, full of grace, the Lord is with thee. Coincidentally, in the Roman Catholic celebration of this event, the Alleluia of March 25, this miracle is imaged as the blossoming of a plant or tree: "The rod of Jesse blossomed! A virgin has brought forth God and man. God has given peace, reconciling in Himself the lowest with the highest. Alleluia."

This celebration tells us Jesus epitomizes the 'balancing' the 'People of Tula' had come to teach. With Christ, opposites would be reconciled: "I say to you, Love your enemies" (Matthew 5:44). The presence of the wand with entwined serpents, the dove and Mary (the illuminated initiate) confirms Jesus' affiliation with this group.

CHAPTER FOUR

THE LABYRINTH

The hero's path of the Peacemaker (and the essential predicament of every soul on earth) is expressed in the Greek story of Theseus and the Labyrinth. This story traces back several thousand years, and labyrinths themselves can be traced back over 3,500 years. In our special time of spiritual transformation, the labyrinth is resurfacing as a peaceful space.

According to the legend Theseus, the son of the King of Athens, volunteered to go to the island of Crete to kill the Minotaur, a monster half man and half bull who resided deep underground in a labyrinth. By marking his trail with a string provided by Ariadne, a beautiful maiden with whom Theseus was in love with and whose name means Very Holy One, Theseus was able to find his way out of the labyrinth. Until Theseus, no one had ever escaped the labyrinth.

The universal symbolism of the labyrinth stands for the soul's journey into the earth form, which, from the soul's perspective is perceived as a death and then as a return to life once earthly life is completed. Earth life is completed once we tame the 'beast' within and transform ourselves into angels. The Key of Life is required to effect this transformation.

22. Hopi drawing of Mother Earth.

The Hopi Indians call the labyrinth Mother Earth or Spider Woman. Carved on a rock near Orabai, Arizona are the two Hopi symbols shown here. The square labyrinth represents spiritual rebirth from one world to another. The lines and passages within the circular maze form the universal plan of the Creator which humanity must follow on its Road of Life. It is representative of the womb, the underworld chamber through which the soul emerges in the quest to find its way home to Tula. It is said that those who can escape the maze, the clutch of Spider Woman, reside with God. As you ponder these drawings, it is vital to note that, coinciding with the Pleiadean Attunement, the labyrinths have seven levels and the word 'Minotaur' is composed of the root 'min' (or man) and taur (or taurus), the bull, the constellation in which we find the Pleiades.

23. Mazes are found in all world religions including the Christian cathedral at Chartres.

24. 'Impossible' objects.

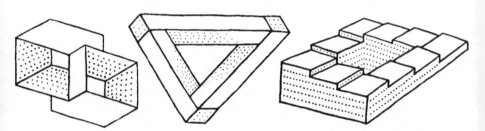

A corresponding idea in the Buddhist tradition shows us that incarnating in human form is like the 'impossible' objects shown here – the ambiguous triangle and the endless stair on which we can mentally walk up clockwise or down counterclockwise, round and round, forever without getting anywhere. A major aspect of initiation is learning to see life as a trick of the mind, an illusion, which can be escaped by building a "bridge across forever" out of this predicament. The ancient Buddhists had a mantra, later converted into a children's song in the West, which captures this philosophy and eases the initiate's mind: "Row, row, row your boat (body) gently down the stream (the River of Life); merrily, merrily, merrily, merrily, life is but a dream (an illusion)."

THE DOUBLE AXE

Significantly, Theseus overcomes the Minotaur (the beastly or lower part of himself) with the double axe, the emblem of the Goddess, at the center of the labyrinth. The double axe is the Cretan symbol for the Key of Life; so here, in Greek form, lies the philosophy of the Key of Life as the solution to ascending from our earthwalk. Central to this is the idea that each of us must go deep within ourselves to seek out and harmonize with our hearts. There, coiled within our inner selves, we will find Ariadne's thread, the lifeline that will lead us safely home.

25. Goddess with the double axe, the Cretan Key of Life.

Theseus personifies the Peacemaker as a navigator sent in to map a way out of the labyrinth of earth. This he does, but only with the help of the beautiful maiden Ariadne. Once again this brings up a crucial point about the Peacemaker. He succeeds only to the degree that he incorporates the goddess into his mission. Thoth was enabled or empowered by his beautiful maiden Seshet. Jesus' female counterpart was Mary Magdalen. The presence of the goddess must always be with the Peacemaker or he is doomed to failure. She completes him: he cannot be whole without her.

THE PANTHER

Ariadne is frequently depicted astride a panther, a symbol of power and protection. Initiates of the Egyptian mysteries were sometimes called *panthers*. Geoffrey Higgins discovered two references in early Jewish commentaries on the Scriptures to the effect that the surname of Joseph's family was *Panther*, for in both of these works it is stated that a man was healed "in the name of Jesus ben Panther," or Jesus son of Panther. The name *Panther* establishes a direct link between Jesus, who was raised by highly trained initiates, and *Dionysus* (Saturn or Enki) who was nursed by panthers, that is, by initiates of the mystery schools.

Pan is the root for a number of other fascinating associations. Among the Greeks Pan was used to mean the All, the Everything, and the Universal. PAN, is also the root of Panacea, the goddess of health, and is equivalent to ban, bon, and ben, all meaning good.

Pan also appears to have been the original culture-bearer of Japan. The Japanese call their country Nippon (on ip pon), and their national slogan is BANZI! – the light of the great fire of life. In modern Japanese Nippon has the meaning of 'fountain or source of light'. Later, we will see that ancient parchments make it clear there is a deep connection between Pan and the 'King of the World' (the King of Tula).

BLACK SAILS FOR WHITE

The story of Theseus has even more valuable information to yield. Significantly, when Theseus began his quest, he set sail in a ship with black sails. He promised his father he would exchange the black sails for white once his mission was successful. If not, his father would launch a full-scale attack on the Minotaur. (In a similar way, says the Book of Revelation, Christ waits in heaven with His army prepared to attack.) Theseus subdued the Minotaur, but forgot to change his sails to white. When his father saw the black sails he assumed the worst and threw himself into the sea.

The reason Theseus forgot to change the sails is because of Ariadne. In the story, Theseus agreed to take Ariadne home to Athens with him in repayment for her assistance. Actually, they were in love. On the first night of their journey, they rested at the island of Naxos. The very next morning Theseus set sail without his beloved, deserting her. He could not stay with Ariadne for he feared that if he did, and consummated their love, he might not complete his mission. On the morning of his departure, out of grief for his love of Ariadne, Theseus forgets to turn the sails. (After Theseus deserted her, the God Dionysus, who is identified as Enki, appeared and made Ariadne his bride. Some scholars believe Dionysus is the alter ego of Theseus rather like Superman is the alter ego of Clark Kent.)

According to the Book of Revelation, once the Peacemaker has accomplished his mission in our time he must gather the Children of Light to build Tula in preparation for the arrival of its king. Allegorically, without the Tula the earth's sail is presently 'black'. Once constructed, the Tula, or New Jerusalem (new 'City of Peace') as it is called in Revelation, will introduce an era of light. This will send a signal to heaven that earth is ready for deliverance. Jewish wise men debate whether or not the Tula will be constructed before the arrival of the Messiah or if the Messiah will build it himself. This debate is further complicated when it is realized the Essenes were expecting the arrival of not one but two Messiahs.

What happens if Tula is not built? The probable answer to that question leads us into waters that, for the moment, I am unwilling to wade in. I will, however, hint that the answer may be found in a remarkable legend which is directly related to the story of Theseus. This legend concerns Lucifer and was cherished by the first initiates of the Holy Grail.

LUCIFER

According to this legend, the crux of the battle between Christ and Lucifer was over the issue of free will. Lucifer desired that man be deprived of the ability of make mistakes, to wallow in perfection, so to speak. Christ desired that man be imperfect, able to make choices for himself, but be redeemed through Him when we sin or forget that the purpose of life on earth is to discover the way to ascend through the star gate of the Pleiades and return to Tula.

Consumed by his own self importance Lucifer fell from light to the darkness of earth (the Labyrinth). During his fall the rebellious Archangel lost a precious stone which had shone like a star in his crown. From this stone was carved the Holy Grail, the cup in which Joseph of Arimathea received the blood of Christ.

In *Parzival*, the Holy Grail is described not as a cup, but as a stone of the purest kind called *lapsit exillas*. In his excellent work *The Grail: Quest for the Eternal*, John Matthews observes this description has been an immense puzzle to scholars. Numerous interpretations have been put forth to suggest what Wolfram meant by *lapsit exillas*. Parzival describes this stone as a jewel, an *emerald*, which fell from the crown of Lucifer during his war with God and was then brought to earth by angels where its power became neutral. Others believe that Seth returned to the Garden of Eden in search of a cure for his father's illness (his soul's entrapment in a human body on earth) and was given – along with a promise that God had not forgotten humanity – a cure not only for Adam, but also for all of humanity: the emerald stone or the Holy Grail.

The legend continues in a most prophetic vein, saying that when his mission is accomplished, the Archangel Lucifer is promised to become God of the planet Venus, which was originally destined for him, and for which he longs. By this time earth will have 'blossomed' with the Christ energy.

Lucifer, having regained his star and his stone, will assemble his legions to begin again on Venus. Attracted by his flaming torch, spiritual beings will descend to Venus, and Lucifer will begin to teach them. Then the torch of Lucifer will signal 'From Heaven to Earth!' and the Cross of Christ will answer 'From Earth to Heaven!' At last, the black sail of earth will be changed to white.

THE GRAIL QUEST

There is a deep-rooted urge in many of us to go on a Grail quest – that is, to find Christ consciousness, our divine alter ego, within us (as did 'Christ' Galahad in the heavenly city of Sarras in the story of the Holy Grail and 'Christ' Theseus in the Greek tale). As souls, each of us enters the earth plane to conquer the labyrinth and to learn what it means to be a human being. Once successful, we must turn our 'sails' from dark to white and leave this plane of existence for new frontiers.

Jesus clearly recognized the true predicament of our souls here on earth. In fulfillment of the word of Moses, who led the Exodus out of Egypt, he began searching for ways for us not only open our hearts, but also to see our way (not out of Egypt or through the Red Sea) but out of earth life altogether into another, higher dimension – Tula.

To this end Jesus spent his entire life travelling the planet, recovering the scattered keys to true knowledge of resurrection and ascension, to release us from our spiritual bondage and to take us Home. As Jesus said in the apocryphal *Gospel of Thomas* 39:

> *The Pharisees and the scribes have taken the keys of knowledge and hidden them. They themselves have not entered* [the Promised Land?], *nor have they allowed to enter those who wish to. You, however,* **be as wise as serpents and as innocent as doves**.

This statement, combined with his appearance in the Book of Revelation with the seven stars, can lead us to only one conclusion: Jesus possessed the Key of Life. He found the 'thread' that would take us out of the labyrinth of earth life and the key to the door that opened the path to Tula.

Jesus may even have written his cosmic theories or the laws regarding the Key of Life in books. Contrary to popular misconception, Jesus was most certainly literate. His book of cosmic theories may even be the *Book of Life* described in Revelation. He is also believed to have passed his teachings orally to a few select students, including Mary Magdalen, and to have modeled/tested his procedures (the Biblical term is *sacrificed* himself) for soul travel to Tula in his own resurrection and ascension, reappearing to Mary with proof that his method worked. What proof did Jesus return with? We shall see in a moment. But first, the ancient artifact which anchors this mystery to earth must be decoded.

THE ALABASTER JAR AND THE ANOINTING OF JESUS

Our earlier identification of Mary as *the* Magdalen, or the primary representative of the temple of Inanna, is important because she was also the bearer of a mysterious alabaster jar. This alabaster jar appears to have some form of miraculous qualities. In this jar, "vessel of light or life," was kept the anointing oil made from a plant that originally grew in India (the sacred domain of the goddess Inanna) that would proclaim God's chosen Messiah. In the religions of Egypt, Sumer, Babylon and Canaan from which Christianity emerged, anointing the head of the king with oil was a ritual performed by the heiress or royal priestess who represented Inanna (Venus). When Mary Magdalen poured this rare oil on Jesus' head, this proclaimed his kingship.

The anointing of Jesus ranks as one of the most important events in the Gospel. Its significance is emphasized by the fact that it is one of the few events which is recorded in all four official Gospels. Whenever anyone else tried to proclaim Jesus "the Messiah," he always silenced them, telling them not to reveal his identity. In an about face, he tells his disciples that the story of the woman with the alabaster jar would be told and retold "in memory of her." This fact is what makes what happens next so important to our story.

The Gospel of John states Mary arrived at Jesus' tomb at first light on Easter morning (John 20:1-3). Here, the Gospel subtly documents that no men announced Jesus' resurrection. Only priestesses, the performers of this ritual/ceremony, were the ones awaiting the resurrection of Jesus. This is so because the springtime festival called Easter is named for the moon goddess *Eostre*, the northern name for Astarte or Inanna (the mother of Thoth).

Fixed as the first Sunday after the first full moon after the spring equinox, what was known as the pregnant phase of Eostre entering the fertile season, this pagan festival was not claimed by the Christians until the late Middle Ages. Easter came to mark the time when the priestesses of Inanna would sacrifice yet another in a long line of men who periodically died and were reborn in an atonement ceremony.

In common language, the purpose of this ceremony was to make sure the bridge between earth and Tula worked. Those sacrificed were highly trained initiates called *tulkus* or *shamans*, who were specialists in working with the 'fire' of higher dimensions or vibrational levels and travel between earth and Tula.

As Lance deHaven Smith comments in *The Hidden Teachings of Jesus*, when Jesus prophesied that his crucifixion would bring "the remission of sins," he meant something different than what is preached today. In the New Testament, the original word for *remission* is *aphesis*, which means freedom.

Jesus had come to bring freedom through linking the bridge to Tula. A by-product of this is the releasing of humanity from the cycle of earthly incarnation and its constant judgment, condemnation and punishment. People would be given freedom from 'sin' because they would never again have to abide by the laws of corrupt men. They would be living in a higher, more spiritual realm.

CROSS, PILLAR OR SPHINX?

While on the subject of the Crucifixion it is worth noting that the word cross does not appear in the original Bible texts. The Greek word stau-ros, which was translated as 'cross' actually means pillar or pole. (Remember this word stau-ros because it will produce startling ramifications later when it is revealed that a similar word was used to describe the Sphinx.) The image of a bloody Savior nailed to a cross did not appear in Christian art until five hundred years after the Crucifixion. Early Christians even condemned this image as pagan.

If not the Sunday School image, what then may the cross (or pillar) refer to? The Tree of Life.

The lower section of the ankh or Key of Life is a cross. It is thought-inspiring to consider that the Key of Life was made from a branch from the Tree of Life which grew in the Garden of Eden. The church claimed the True Cross was made of the same wood as the Tree of Life in the garden of Eden. Like the Key of Life, Adam conveniently passed the cross along his bloodline for the express purpose of crucifying the Savior (who in this case would be himself) whenever or wherever he appeared.

The Egyptian name for the Tree of Life was the *Djed pillar*, a ladder to heaven, sacred to Osiris and Horus, the Egyptian savior figure. This 'ladder' is a symbol of that which must be ascended in order to reach Tula. It was described as the ladder by which souls of the dead made their way to the

Fields of Peace (which, coincidentally, were always said to lie to the north, the same direction as Tula.) The ladder concept appears in between the time of Horus and Jesus in the story of Jacob's Ladder. By this rendering, Jesus' agony in the garden may not be a physical mutilation. Instead, it may be indicative of soul travel to an otherworldly locality, Tula. We shall examine some provocative details concerning this event momentarily.

As the Gospel of John continues, Mary is weeping on this ancient Easter morning, weeping for her companion, Jesus, almost as if he were a test pilot flying a dangerous mission. Suddenly, from within the tomb appear two angels (assistants in this transdimensional experiment) dressed in white. The angels ask her why she is crying. "Because they have taken away my Lord, and I do not know where they have laid him." Upon this answer, she turns around and sees Jesus standing there.

Jesus asks her, "Woman, why are you weeping? Whom do you seek?" At first Mary takes the man for 'the Gardener'. Politely, submissively, or angrily (I can't tell which, but certainly with respect) she says to him: "Sir, if you have carried him away, tell me where you have laid him, and I will take him away."

Jesus says to her, "Mary."

Startled, she turns and says to him in Hebrew, "Rabboni!" (a special Hebrew term for Teacher which denotes God). She rushes to his arms, but he stops her saying, "Do not touch me."

This scene is at once provocative and confusing.

First of all, how could a woman described as Jesus' close companion and partner not recognize him? Was it because it was dark? Was he disguised? Was he in some ethereal form, perhaps cloaked within a body of light (his protective 'bridge-checking' suit)? Perhaps this is why he told her not to touch him.

None of these answers are satisfactory. In fact, each raises the even more important question of why, of all people, Jesus would appear as the Gardener. Today, when we say 'the Terminator' we think not only of the archetypal character of the protector but of a particular actor, Arnold Schwartzeneggar who temporarily represents this archetypal character to us. Likewise, Christopher Reeves is the shape-shifter figure 'Superman'. Why Jesus the Gardener? Could this be his alter ego?

On the surface, Jesus' appearance as the Gardener seems to have no meaning. Why not something 'holier', perhaps an angel or a sphere of light? Meticulous editing went into the later versions of the Gospels, yet this seemingly insignificant yet glaring detail survived in John, the most 'reputable' Gospel.

The significance of Jesus being referred to as the Gardener could not have been underestimated. Nor could it have possibly been misunderstood by the early Christian community who recorded this event. (Nothing in the New Testament symbolism is given by chance.) In the early Christian world people knew exactly who was being referred to when the Gardener was mentioned. This detail deserves further research and clarification by us today. For if we can decode the meaning of the 'buzz word', the Gardener, we likely will learn some astonishing things.

In fact, the historical evidence of the Gardener points to only one (actually the simplest and clearest) explanation. Jesus is not the Gardener. There was another man in the garden that Easter morning. Not some lowly weed puller either. This Gardener commanded Mary Magdalen's respect; and, as we might imagine, Mary kowtowed to no one.

So, who was this Gardener?

CHAPTER FIVE

THE GARDENER:
THE KING OF TULA

Mythologically, the Gardener is an ancient archetypal figure known as the Green Man. He is the forest or garden healer, a fertility hero, who is typically depicted with vegetation (symbolizing the Word of God) spewing from his mouth.

Archetypes are constantly repeating characters or figures which appear in the myths of all cultures. Examples of archetypes are the savior (Jesus), magician (Merlin), pure knight (Sir Galahad), witch, queen, young hero (Luke Skywalker), king (Arthur), warrior (*Star Trek's* Lt. Worf), shapeshifters (Superman), the wise old man (Kung Fu), etc.

The earliest recorded example of the archetype of the Green Man emerged in a collection of stories known as the *Atrahasis*, named after the first name of mankind's first savior. Atrahasis means 'the far wise'. These stories originated with the ancient Sumerians, who lived in the biblical land of *Shumer*.

In the famed *Epic of Gilgamesh*, the story of the ancient Sumerian king's search for immortality, Atrahasis is called *Utnapushtim* which means 'he found life' or, presumably, the way out of limited earth life into a greater spiritual life. He became *Noah* in the biblical story. From then on he would be associated with a rescue from water or, on a deeper level, with the way to cross over the waters of immortality. This places the Gardener squarely in the tradition of the priesthood or tribe of Doves, those who come to teach the means to transcend earth life.

In Islam, the sage *Al-Khidr*, an abbreviation of Atrahasis, guarded the Fountain of Life (at Tula) and gave water (souls or wisdom about souls) from it to the King Sakhr (meaning 'rock') who then achieved immortality. In the Arabian Nights stories (the Islamic *Gilgamesh*) Al-Khidr is known as "the green one," the Green Man. (The next book in this series, *The Gardener and the Tree of Life*, will delve further into the story of Atrahasis. This is the first recorded savior story and provides an answer to the greatest mystery of human history: who created us and why.)

Mentioned earlier was the concept of Jesus' Pleiadean Attunement, a teaching which would enable our return to the central point in heaven. William Anderson, author of the *Green Man: The Archetype of our Oneness with the Earth*, points out that the Green Man, or the Gardener, is in fact the immortal ruler of Hyperboria – a Greek name for heaven. The Greeks recorded that Hyperboria's center, a mecca for learning, was called *Tula*. Therefore, we can only conclude the Gardener is the King of Tula.

A summary is in order. Thus far, we have proposed that Jesus was originally known as a Tekton, a builder of the bridge to heaven called Tula. In the Buddhist tradition, Jesus was known as a tulku, a "shining one of Tula" who worked closely with Mary Magdalen and the priestesses from the temple of Inanna who preserved the oral teachings on attuning the soul for return to the central point in heaven, for return to Tula.

Upon his crucifixion – the test of Jesus' theory regarding the soul's proper alignment with Tula – Jesus left earth for three days and reappeared to Mary Magdalen with the Gardener in tow. Now where did Jesus go to find this Gardener? Since the Gardener is the ruler of Tula at the central point in heaven, it is reasonable to presume this is where the Gardener is most likely to be found at any given time. If this is so, it would seem logical Jesus spent his 'missing' three days returning to Tula and bringing the Gardener back to earth.

WILL THE REAL GARDENER PLEASE STAND UP

Who, exactly, was the Gardener? Probing into the historical 'descendents' of the priesthood of Doves yields an answer – an answer that may be at once confusing and unsettling: the Gardener was John the Baptist.

How can this be? My search for this answer began with *The Sufis*, a book in which Idries Shaw makes a huge contribution toward unearthing the obscure mystery tradition concealing the true identity of the Gardener. He first observes the connections between the Arab Khidr Order and the famous British Order of the Garter:

> *The early records of the Order of the Garter are lost. Its patron saint was St. George, who is equated in Syria, where his cult originates, with the mysterious Khidr-figure of the Sufis. It was in fact called the Order of St. George, which would translate direct into Sufi phraseology as Tarika-i-Hadrat-i-Khidr (the Order of St. Khidr). It became known as the Order of the Garter. The word "garter" in Arabic is the same as the word for the Sufi mystical tie or bond.*

The modern day Order of the Garter (not a 'garter' at all, but the 'Guarder' or 'Keeper' of the sacred secrets) traces its origins to the Knights of the Round Table (c. 516 A.D.) and is attributed to Saint George, who is, by tradition, the patron saint of England. While he is supposed to have lived during the third century, history offers little information on the factual Saint George. Mythologists believe he represents the higher nature of man overcoming the dragon (love energy) of his own lower nature to release the *Christos*, the god-man or ascended alter ego imprisoned in every creature. Releasing, or resurrecting, this 'Christos' within, we have learned, is the Key of Life.

Astonishingly, Barbara Walker (*Women's Encyclopedia of Myths and Secrets*) found that "folklore named the pagan savior, Green George, a spirit of spring (Easter). His image was common in old church carvings, a human head surrounded by leaves." Thus St. George, the bearer of the Key of Life, is the Green Man.

THE RETURN OF THE GODDESS

This leads us into a deeper mystery. Invariably, the Gardener or Green Man is found near the Tree of Life in the company of the goddess with her mysterious alabaster jar. Osiris, for example, was the Egyptian god most closely associated with the djed pillar or Tree of Life. He is usually shown painted green. Therefore, he is a green man or Gardener.

Furthermore, Osiris was a potter and jar maker. This would suggest that the mysterious contents of the alabaster jar were crucial to the success of individuals who ascended through the Tree of Life. Astonishingly, in numerous Egyptian depictions, Enoch/Thoth (Osiris' son) is shown holding what appears to be an ink jar which has led interpreters to label him the Scribe of the Gods. However, on another level, the ink jar is symbolic of the 'heart' or the 'divine essence'.

The threads revealing the vital contents of the alabaster jar, the identity of the Green Man, and, coincidentally, the meaning of the Holy Grail legend may be found in India. The early crusaders (led by the Knights Templar) brought the Holy Grail back to Europe believing that if the grail (the Cup of Christ) were not recovered, then that which befell Saudi Arabia would befall their own homeland: it would become a desert wasteland.

In *The Sufis*, Idries Shaw gives an account of a Sufi named *Khidr Rumi*, the *Cupbearer* of Turkestan. The name Khidr, which is also spelled *Khizr*, is a Moslem name used in reference to the Biblical prophet Elijah.

Now we are getting somewhere. According to Jesus, John the Baptist, *was* the reincarnated Elijah. If John the Baptist is Elijah, logically, he is also Khizr. Khizr is the patron saint of water (a symbol for the wisdom to help the soul escape earth life). Also, Khizr means green!

A mysterious man bearing a vessel of water preceded Jesus on his entrance to the house of the Last Supper. Can we conclude John the Baptist played a role in delivering the miraculous alabaster jar or its precious wisdom to Mary Magdalen and Jesus on the eve of the crucifixion? Did the contents of this jar assist Jesus in the same way it aided savior figures of the past? Furthermore, does this prove John the Baptist was the Gardener? Hang on to this question for a moment while we uncover another piece of information about the mysterious man with the jar.

According to Barbara Walker (*The Woman's Encyclopedia of Myths and Secrets*), the meaning of the man with the jar was preserved in the Babylonian record of a savior-god Nabu. This god was always preceded by a jar-bearer, carrying the vessel of life that indicated the presence of the spirit of the savior. Tradition states the contents of this jar may have been some form of extraordinary oil which enabled contact with the Holy Spirit or the 'divine essence'. This being the case, we must ask if by being anointed by the goddess Mary Magdalen, Jesus' consciousness was being prepared for his voyage through the Tree of Life to Tula in order to connect with the 'divine essence'?

Biblical accounts are clear that whenever the Holy Spirit was upon him Jesus behaved differently. This led to the heretical conclusion that Jesus was 'possessed' by Christ consciousness and was himself not *the* Christ. This observation takes on a thorny crown when it is realized that Jesus was a shaman, which can have the connotation of fire worker or perfume maker.

Is it possible Jesus, or John the Baptist and Mary Magdalen, were brewing some form of cosmic aromatherapy which would trigger deeply embedded receptor sites in the human brain or in human DNA? Is this the means to create a "temple built without hands" which in turn creates a bridge between earth and Tula? Was Christianity meant to be an experience in which the Christ within each of us may emerge? If so, where is that teaching or the means to effect this transformation of consciousness?

Earlier we examined hieroglyphs that were part of the symbolic language of Jesus. Included was the four-petaled Flower of Life. In this regard it is interesting to note that virtually every ancient civilization knew of certain plants which could open the gates of consciousness while allowing the initiates to be in full control of their faculties. It is conceivable this plant was a hallucinogenic. However, it is also possible it was some form of 'super nutrient' which triggered advanced mental capabilities. Throughout history, even to modern times, the human race has been virtually starved nutritionally. If we raised our children on proper diets their abilities would soar. Instead, our world of fast food offers a banquet of brain-numbing 'psuedo-food'.

In Egypt, one substance which could open the gates to clear consciousness, deep insight, and freedom was known as the sacred regenerating Plant of Horus (Horus was the Egyptian 'savior') called *wn-n-wn* , 'essence of being'. Astonishingly, this substance, which grew in "the divine lands," was symbolized by the four-petaled Flower of Life hieroglyph.

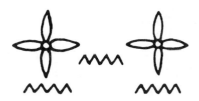

26. The Egyptian hieroglyph for "essence of being."

ALL ALONG THE WATCHTOWER

High on the rocky slopes overlooking the Dead Sea oasis of Ein Gedi (domain of John the Baptist and the Essenes) archaeologists have recently discovered the ruins of a massive watchtower with walls five-feet-thick! Its entrance is sealed with a huge circular stone much like the 'tomb' of Jesus.

"Cursed be they who reveal the secret of the village," warns a centuries-old inscription on the mosaic tile floor of a synagogue nearby. The secret of the long-buried village lies inside the tower, where the Jews of Ein Gedi made a prized *balsam oil used to anoint the biblical kings of Judah* (!), according to Hebrew University archaeologist Yizhar Hirschfield. The balm – apparently grown on terraces around the watchtower – was made from a species of the persimmon tree found only along the shores of the Dead Sea and in nearby Jericho, one of the oldest cities on earth.

Let's remember this discovery and return to another related issue raised a moment ago: what are we to make of the fact that the King of Tula is consistently thought to have been associated not with Jesus but rather with John the Baptist? John is believed to have held the office of the Peacemaker, the forerunner of Christ. According to the Talmud, one of the missions of the Peacemaker is to retrieve the flask of manna and the anointing oil (known as a potion called chrestos to the Essenes). Could this mysterious watchtower at Ein Geidi be the garden in which the sacred plant used in the manufacture of the anointing oil was grown? With walls five feet thick this watchtower was obviously quite a fortress. It tends to remind one of a modern well-secured nuclear missile silo. Obviously, whatever was harvested or housed in this ancient silo was of immense value. No one who didn't belong there could enter.

THE ESSENES

While on the subject of anointing the Messiah we must point out once more that it was revealed in the Dead Sea Scrolls that the Essenes were awaiting the arrival of not one but *two* messiahs or Christs ('anointed ones'). One was the Peacemaker (the forerunner who clears the way) who was called the Wicked Priest by the Essenes. The other was described as a King of Love, Teacher of Righteousness or Man of Destiny.

The origin of the brotherhood of the Essenes is bound up with this mysterious figure, the True Teacher, or Teacher of Righteousness, who was called by the Essenes and by himself 'the Man' and was also revered as Prophet, Priest and King (lawgiver). History has yet to reveal who this person was. Some believe the name Essenes comes from Esnoch, or Enoch, and claim him to be this mysterious founder. Others connect the Essenes with Esrael, the chosen few Moses took with him to (or, as we will see, from) Mount Sinai. Once again, this is a connection with the Peacemaker.

MELCHIZEDEK

Still a third possibility is that this Moreh-zedek (Teacher of Righteousness) comes before us like the mysterious Melchi-zedek (King of Righteousness) in the Epistle to the Hebrews, "without father, without mother, without ancestry, having neither beginning of days nor end of life" (Hebrews 7:3). Melchizedek was the priest to whom Abraham paid a tithe. This was in exchange for an extraordinary teaching (undoubtedly the Key of Life) which Melchizedek bequeathed to Abraham and his family line. As we know, Jesus would later come from the family of Abraham, and was in possession of the Key of Life. More astoundingly, according to Psalm 110, Christ Jesus was "a priest forever after the Order of Melchizedek"!

The Melchizedek Scroll, a rare Dead Sea Scroll, offers an amazing identification of Melchizedek with the promised Messiah. According to the Gnostics, the key difference was that Melchizedek was the savior for angels, Jesus merely came to save humans. Some powerful labels used to identify Melchizedek include: the Messiah, the Anointed One who proclaims Salvation, the Prince, the Judge, the Avenger, the Messenger of God, and Michael the Great Prince.

In *The Bloodline of the Holy Grail*, Laurence Gardner offers an intriguing explanation for the origins of the name Melchizedek. The line of Zadok were priest kings descended from the Archangel Micha-el. (Hence Melchizedek is Michael-Zadok.) Furthermore, this Melchizedek priest had an ambassador who was designated the 'Angel of the Lord', or emissary of Michael. The 'Michael' at the time of Jesus was John the Baptist. This means Jesus is the Peacemaker, the forerunner of John and not the other way around.

In other passages, the Melchizedek Scroll connects the coming of the Messiah with the Year of Jubilee, which ends with the final "redemption of the land." This is in complete accord with the Biblical view of Jesus as the returning great high priest who will announce the Great Jubilee (the Great Year which comes to a close in 2012) and "the restitution of all things." The biblical terms "redemption" and "restitution" refer to a new vibrational frequency which is expected to sweep the earth sometime before 2012. These terms and the acts of Melchizedek make it clear that Jesus is clearly working to clear the way for another 'Christ', the Gardener.

In fact, Melchizedek is seen in the Jewish tradition as the same individual as Enoch and Elijah. Therefore, he must also be John the Baptist. At least one contemporary writer has documented the names by which the Essenes referred to themselves. Among those names are the Sons of Light, the Sons of Truth, the Sons of Zadok, or Zadokites, the Men of Melchizedek (the z-d-k ending being a variation of Zadok) and the Nozrim (the Nazoreans). These groups are all one and the same.

Baigent, Leigh and Lincoln (*The Messianic Legacy*) state that the purpose of the Essenes was oriented towards preserving the teachings and the dynastic legitimacy of the high priesthood of Melchizedek. In the Old Testament, the

High Priest of both David and his son Solomon is called Zadok, reflecting either a personal name or title. This High Priest, they note, is traditionally very closely associated with the Messiah, the anointed one, the rightful king.

As Nazareans, says Hugh Schonfield, the Essenes were regarded as maintainers and preservers of the true faith of Israel, and the Messianic Plan associated with a Davidic Messiah. Their claim was shared by the Samaritans, dwelling in Sumeria, who maintained that they were the keepers and custodians of the original religion of the Israelites (which was not the religion of the Jews). In fact, both the Essenes and the Samaritans were in opposition to the Jews, stating that they had falsified the Law of Moses.

In the chapter on Tula we spoke of the Mandaeans or Nazarenes, an offshoot of the Essenes, who believed that at the end of time what they call the Secret Adam will come to earth. The Secret Adam is a messianic figure who builds a machine that then transmits all the souls back to their hidden source in the All-Father. Schonfield (*The Passover Plot*) states there is good reason to believe that the Mandaeans were the Nazoreans/Nazareans, hence a branch of the Essenes.

According to Schonfield, the Mandaean-Nazoreans have always held John the Baptist in high esteem. In fact, the *Mandaean Sidra d'Yahja* (Book of John the Baptist) and the Aramaic *Genesis Apocryphon* discovered among the Dead Sea Scrolls have direct links. In the Book of John the Baptist Jesus seeks to be baptized by John and is refused as an impostor. John finally receives a message and agrees to the baptism.

THE TULA CONNECTION

Earlier we mentioned the high ground north of Jerusalem, Mount Moriah. An extraordinary revelation awaits when we explore the meaning of the word Jerusalem. Urusalim, the Akkadian name from which Jerusalem originated is derived from two words, *Uru* and *Salim*. Now, *Uru* is derived from the verb *yarah*, meaning 'to found' or 'to establish'. The meaning of the second word, Shalim, has not been as clear. That is until we find that *Salim* – correctly understood by the early Jewish rabbis in the Haggadah, the oral part of the Talmud – means 'peace'.

By this rendering the true meaning of Jerusalem would be 'foundation of peace' or 'establishing peace', an interpretation that is supported by the function of Melchizedek, the priest and king of Salem. According to mythologist Rene Guenon (*Fundamental Symbols*) the place names *Salem* (peace), *Luz* (light) and *Tula* (balance) are interchangeable. (Luz was the name of the place where Abraham's grandson Jacob had his experience with the heavenly ladder.) Thus, this Melchizedek could rightly be called the King of Tula. If so, he is also the Gardener. To paraphrase the psalm, Jesus could thus be a "priest forever after the Order of the Gardener."

IN WHOSE NAME?

The discovery of the Teacher of Righteousness has caused a radical reconsideration of Jesus which will surely draw serious questions to the existing Christian order. Can it be true that there were not one but two messiahs and that Jesus was the forerunner of a radically more secret figure? If so, this fact prevents us from truly understanding our past, and thus, from accurately interpreting the prophecies concerning our future.

We may pose a new series of questions, the answers to which may resolve all the other issues: is it possible John the Baptist was the Gardener and he was with Jesus in the garden that Easter morning? If so, why didn't Matthew, Mark and Luke also record John's resurrection? Would that be admitting they were indeed both Christs? Would this fact have tainted the 'official' story of Jesus as a lone savior? Or, is it possible, as the Gnostics maintain, that John the Baptist was the true Christ and Jesus his prophet? If so, then we are once again forced to dig deeper to answer the questions of who is the Gardener, and who is the real Jesus.

CHAPTER SIX

THE EMERALD TABLETS

While on the subject of the Gardener, it is fascinating to note that the Key of Life is accompanied by a mysterious body of teachings known as the *Emerald Tablets*. These "green writings" are attributed to Thoth and are thought to contain not only God's secret wisdom of immortality but also the Divine Plan for harmonizing and connecting heaven and earth. Since these teachings, and the efforts to preserve and resurrect them at times of crisis in human history, figure so prominently in our story it is worth taking a moment to familiarize ourselves with them.

The history of the Emerald Tablets is strange and beyond the belief of modern scientists. They are believed to be of extraterrestrial origin, possibly brought through the 'Twilight Zone' between material and non-material reality.

Zecharia Sitchin (*Stairway To Heaven*) describes in detail their engrossing early history and uses. In ancient times world wars were fought over (and much intrigue surrounded) the acquisition of these "devices." I emphasize devices as the Emerald Tablets appear to be a highly advanced information storage technology, perhaps surpassing anything available today.

According to Sitchin, the Emerald Tablets were brought to earth by none other than Enki, the Gardener and King of Tula. They were carried as talismans by which certain priests could exercise authority over the less advanced priest-craft. The Sumerians even describe their 'gods' and 'goddesses' affixing these stones to their garments.

The Emerald Tablets are believed to be formed from a substance created through alchemical transmutation. They are indestructible. Upon them are engraved characters in an ancient language which require spiritual vision to perceive. These characters respond to attuned thought waves, releasing the associated mental vibration in the mind of the reader.

In a relevant legend, Alexander the Great connected himself to Adam. The connecting link in the case of Alexander was a unique stone which emitted green light. It was said to have been brought out of the Garden of Eden by Adam, then handed down from generation to generation. (According the Hebrew oral tradition as revealed in the Haggadah, the Ark of Noah was illuminated by a similar precious stone which served to brighten the inside of the ship and made night seem like day.)

Alexander decided to seek out his immortal ancestors. On one such excursions he was given a green stone reputed to have been brought out of the Garden of Eden by Adam. Could this green stone possibly be one of the ME's (the Emerald Tablets containing the Key of Life) which Enki was known to have brought to earth? It seems likely that the stone Alexander, a prized pupil of Aristotle, sought was a ME as opposed to a simple glowing stone.

THE FIRST KEY

The Key of Life offers the way to find the 'light within' and the 'power without'. It offers liberation from earth, connection to higher realms, accelerated evolution and the transformation of body and soul. In short, it offers a key to the door to Tula and immortality. This is a quest suitable to Alexander the Great.

In the Gnostic gospel, *Pistis Sophia*, Jesus gave what may be the first lesson of the Key of Life. He states that our world and worlds in higher realms are intimately connected "from within outwards." This statement refers to a transformation of consciousness which opens the door to other worlds.

Scientists have recently concluded we only perceive ten percent of the universe. The rest is dark: invisible to humans. Our purpose is to open our spiritual vision to see into this darkness. What is our reward for developing such vision? The Biblical version of opening our sacred vision is described by Isaiah: "For look, I am going to create new heavens and a new earth, and the past will not be remembered" (Isaiah 65:17). We will perceive a new reality and hence see a new heaven and a new earth.

Jesus taught the reality of this new heaven and earth when he described himself as a Good Shepherd who alone could lead the sheep out of their fold. In John 10:9 He further stated:

> *I am the door.*
> *If anyone enters through Me, he shall be saved,*
> *and shall go in and out, and find pasture.*

The key to decoding the esoteric meaning of Jesus as the "door" is found in the *Kaballah* – the Jewish system of mysticism revealed to Abraham by Melchizedek. The Kaballah is linked to the Emerald Tablets. In *Art and Symbols of the Occult*, James Waserman writes that the word Kaballah "comes from the Hebrew root *QBL*, meaning 'to receive', and refers to the passing down of secret knowledge through an oral transmission."

In fact, the Kaballah shares an identical history with the Key of Life, originating in the Garden of Eden as a branch of the Tree of Life and being passed from Adam, to Enoch, to Noah, to Abraham, and finally to Moses who enciphered it within the first five books of the Old Testament.

God took compassion on Adam after he had been banished from Eden (and sent to Atlantis/Tula). He sent the archangel Raziel, whose name means 'Secrets of God', to give him a book – *The Book of the Angel Raziel* – so that man might gaze into the mirror of existence, see himself as an image of God (reflecting the Divine Face) and regain entry into the Garden of Paradise. This book "wherein all celestial and earthly knowledge is set down" has been handed down through the ages. An oral version still exists – the Kaballah.

According to lore, *The Book of the Angel Raziel* was inscribed on a sapphire stone and was once in the possession of Enoch (who ascribed the work to himself as *The Book of Enoch*). There is some debate as to what, exactly, Enoch received. In *The Woman's Encyclopedia of Myths and Legends*, Barbara Walker notes that the Bible called lapis lazuli (the Stone of the order of Melchizedek) *sappur* or "holy blood." It was the substance of God's throne (Ezekiel 1:26). The authorized version' inaccurately translates sappur as "sapphire." Therefore, it is possible *The Book of the Angel Raziel* meant to say that Enoch was of the holy bloodline and that what he truly possessed was the Divine Gene.

The Legends of the Jews from Primitive Times has it that, like the Key of Life, Adam gave the stone (or Divine Gene) to Seth, who gave it to Enoch, who then gave it to Noah. From studying *The Book* Noah learned how to proceed building the Ark. Abraham, Moses and Aaron were next in line. Then *The Book of the Angel Raziel* was given to Solomon who was thought to have derived his great wisdom and magical power from it. It's astonishing to note that a sculpture of Melchizedek in the north porch of Chartres Cathedral depicts him holding a cup (with a stone in it) in his hand that, according to some authorities, is the Holy Grail. Abraham and Moses flank this teacher! According to tradition, Melchizedek initiated Abraham into the knowledge of the esoteric teaching of the Kaballah.

Graham Hancock (*The Sign and the Seal*) notes that Melchizedek is intended here to be viewed as the precursor of Christ and the chalice and the object within it were meant to represent the "bread and the wine, the symbols of the Eucharist." Could they also represent the Emerald Tablets of Thoth?

Furthermore, it is possible that when Melchizedek bequeathed upon Abraham the sacred wisdom of the Kaballah he was teaching him about man's true beginnings, about the way to activate the Divine Gene and, more importantly, about the Divine Plan for the spiritual transcendence of humanity. Is the secret wisdom the Kaballah contains the means by which humanity can lift itself out of spiritual bondage?

THE COSMIC EGG

One of the secret teachings of the Kaballah is that man's true nature is immaterial, spiritual. To the Kaballists the universe is a Cosmic Egg in which all elements are contained. There are, however, more than one of these eggs in whole of Creation; there is more than one universe.

The body of man is enveloped in an ovoid bubble-like iridescence, which is called the Auric Egg. This is the causal sphere or the area in which man's intelligence is contained. Each person's egg of consciousness has the same relationship to the universe as the Cosmic egg has to the Creation. Each of our births, lives, deaths and rebirths take place within this egg and what we learn in one incarnation is taken to the next. To quote the Kaballah: "The spirit clothes itself to come down and unclothes itself to go up."

THE HYPERCUBE

The Key of Life, the Kaballah, the Emerald Tablets and even Abraham and Jesus are associated with a shape called the *tesseract*, which is a three-dimensional 'shadow' of a four dimensional hypercube – a figure having yet another dimension at right-angles to the three with which we are familiar.

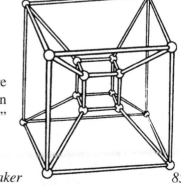

27. Tesseract or 'hypercube'.

The three dimensional cube shown here eloquently demonstrates Jesus' admonition to us to learn to see "from within outwards."

28. The Magic Cube. In Gematria, the secret geometric language of the Christian mysteries, Alpha is represented by the *tetrahedron* and Omega by the *cube*.

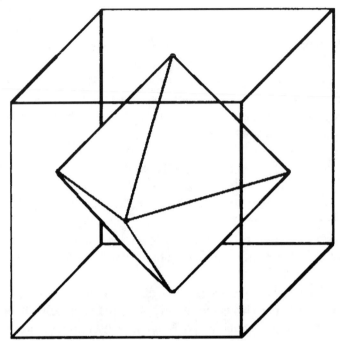

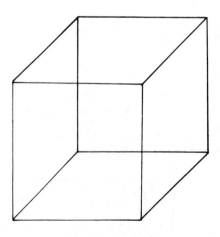

Here we see black lines on a piece of paper that are brought to life in our imaginations as a cube, one with three dimensions. In our minds' eye ("from within outwards"), we can choose to view the cube as if we were looking into it. Yet, by a change of perception, we can view it as if we were looking down into the cube. Everything has changed 'out there', as a result of a change 'in here'. Yet, all we have done is simply altered our perception.

29. The Holographic Cube.

Similarly, the Book of Revelation envisions the complete transformation of perception – "a new heaven and a new earth" (Rev. 21:1). "The world of the past is gone," says Jesus to John. "Look, I am making the whole of creation new."

By simply adding a fourth dimension to this three-dimensional cube we approximate the mind shift from three dimensional to four dimensional thinking, exemplified by the tesseract.

Lionel and Patricia Fanthorpe (*Secrets of Rennes-le-Chateau*) note that members of some ancient mystic cults have been said to meditate for hours upon the tesseract until they experienced a shift of perception: the opening of a gateway to another dimension. Once through this doorway, the individuals are greeted by beings from this dimension.

ABRAHAM

Abraham, the father of the nation of seekers called Israel, was thought to have at one time possessed the Emerald Tablets. His wife, Sarah, wandered into a 'cave' and discovered the Tablets at the feet of Hermes, who at the time was in a state of suspended animation.

This legend gives new light to the Biblical account of Abraham's meeting with the Lord. In Genesis, Abraham is *gazing out the door* of his tent on a hot day. Suddenly, as if out of nowhere, the Lord and two messengers appeared. Instead of gazing out a physical door, could Abraham have been gazing into the emerald tesseract, the doorway to other dimensions?

Abraham apparently did not see the men approaching. He "lifted up his eyes" and they were there, hinting at the possibility of some form of interdimensional travel. Furthermore, Abraham believes one of the *men* is God. How was it that Abraham was able to so easily recognize these emissaries? The only reasonable explanation must be their faces or clothing, their uniforms, or even their weapons. For we learn that in a later incident involving the people of Sodom and Gomorrah the two men, about to be overtaken by the crowd, "smote the people at the entrance of the house with blindness . . . and they were unable to find the doorway." In yet another incident the *malachim* wielded batons that could cause fire to jump out of a rock. The Old Testament word *malachim* means literally 'emissaries'. Perhaps this Sumerian illustration best resolves the issue of how Abraham and others were able to so easily identify the malachim.

30. Malachim. (Copyright Z. Sitchin, *The Twelfth Planet*)

As the story continues, Abraham is informed by the Lord of his impending paternity. Since Abraham is "without seed" and therefore physically incapable of fathering a child this is no small task. Still the Lord maintains Abraham and Sara will bear a child. Not just any child will be born to Abraham. The Lord guarantees the couple will be blessed with a son. Overhearing this patently absurd statement, Sara, who is barren, laughs out loud. The Lord is put off:

The Lord said to Abraham, 'Why did Sara laugh, and say, "Shall I indeed bear a child, now that I am old?" Is anything too hard for the Lord? At the appointed time I will return to you, in the spring, and Sara shall have a son.' But Sara denied, saying. 'I did not laugh'; for she was afraid. He said, 'No, but you did laugh.'

– Gen. 18:13-15

It was then that God marked the pledge by giving Abram the name Abraham and Sara the name Sarah. The Biblical text states that this change signified a change in the meaning of the patriarch's name from 'High Father' to 'Father of a Multitude'. However, the addition of the 'h' sound is also recognized as having a special esoteric meaning.

Esoterically, the 'h' sound is universally associated with *breath* and *spirit*. (Recall that the Key of Life is used to transfer the breath and spirit of God from one dimension to another.) In the Hebrew script, the character for 'h' also symbolizes the number five, symbolic of an initiate. From the point of view of Egyptian hieroglyphics, the insertion of *ha* into Abram's name gives us *ham*, majesty. From this we can conclude that Abraham and Sarah underwent some form of esoteric initiation. As the Jewish legend maintains, they received the Key of Life which is at once a technological device, spiritual technology and, possibly, a Divine Gene.

If this legend contains the true wisdom of Abraham's experience, can we then conclude that what is being passed along this holy bloodline from Adam to Jesus is not just a physical technology but also a secret body of knowledge which included the shamanistic power to communicate directly with the Lord? The first sentence of the Gospel of Matthew declares that Jesus was descended from Abraham. For this reason alone it is worth pursuing Abraham's life story to elucidate the important role of this holy family.

THE BLOODLINE OF THE EMERALD TABLETS

Abraham was born about 4,000 years ago (2,200 B.C.) in the Babylonian city of Ur ('light' or 'fire'), which is in present day Iraq, precisely at the beginning of the Age of the Ram. The New Age of Aries the Ram replaced the Old Age of Taurus the Bull. Centuries before the Christian Era, the pagans revered the constellation of the Ram, calling it the 'Lamb of God'. It was also called the 'Savior', and was said to save mankind from their sins. The lamb was sacred and the priests were called *shepherds*. Among them was Abraham or Ab-Bram (the father of the Ram, or 'he who possesses ram').

Abraham could have been an initiate of any country from Tibet to Egypt. In Tibet ram means 'basis of the world' and is used as the symbol for all that radiates from the Sun: the central spiritual sun, Tula, that is. In Egypt, Ram was also the symbol for fire of the sun and was expressed by the pyramids ('fire within'). In Arabic pyramid is *ahram*.

Because Abraham's family directly continued the line of Shem, (who followed Adam, Enoch and Noah), he has been considered a Semite. The picture that emerges of Abraham is not one of a Semitic Babylonian but more that of a Sumerian. "Abraham," says leading Assyriologist Alfred Jeremias, "headed the Faithful whose reformation sought to raise *Sumerian* society to higher religious levels."

Zecharia Sitchin points out that Abraham identified himself and his family as Ibri, a word the Bible interprets to mean "Hebrew." However, Sitchin and others claim there is no linguistic support for this assertion. Is this an example of Hebrew word play?

Ibri stems from the word Eber, which has the root meaning 'to cross'. If the original Sumerian meaning of the word is used we find that Ibri meant a native of a place called Crossing; and that, says Sitchin, "precisely was the Sumerian name for Nippur: NI.IB.RU – the Crossing Place, the place where the pre-Flood energy grids crisscrossed each other, the original Naval of the Earth, the olden Mission Control Center."

Abraham was a Ni-ib-ri, a man from Nippur, Sumer's religious center. Here was the place where the knowledge of astronomy was kept by high priests. Abraham's father, Terah, was one such high priest. The derivation of his name has an interesting connotation: the cuneiform sign for Tirhu stems directly from that of an object called in Sumerian UG.NAMTAR – literally, a 'Fate Speaker' or an oracle.

Terah's occupation, then, was an Oracle Priest, one who approaches the "Stone that Whispers" to receive the Lord's words and communicate them to the governing class. This highly prestigious function would later be performed by the Israelite High Priest, who alone was allowed to enter the Holy of Holies, approach the *Dvir* ('Speaker') and "hear the voice of the Lord speak unto him from off the overlay which is upon the Ark of the Covenant, from between the two Cherubim." Later, during the Israelite Exodus, the Lord proclaimed at Mount Sinai that his covenant with the descendents of Abraham meant that "ye shall be unto me a *kingdom of priests.*" This statement is the job description of Abraham's family: a royal priesthood.

Not surprisingly, since we are dealing with the descendents of Adam, we once again stumble onto the legendary Emerald Tablets or ME's, the tablets of civilization, which Enki bequeathed to Adam. According to the Biblical Jubilees and more explicitly the *Apocalypse of Abraham*, Abraham and his father are reported to have manufactured the *teraphim* of the Old Testament. These figurines or idols were used for divination: they answered specific questions which were posed to them. Joan Oates, in her work *Babylon*, re-marks that these animated statues which were carried off to war by the kings and priests, were cared for in special workshops by priests who had under-gone extensive training in rituals to endow the idols with "life" and thus enabling them to speak.

Here it becomes obvious that if Abraham's bloodline or priesthood is not that of the Peacemakers, then it is at least a very close offshoot. Recall that the Peacemakers are surveyors and mapmakers establishing the coordinates for the heavenly Tula. Abraham appears at the very beginning of a New Age, a time when earth's position is shifting. It was time for a new earthly Tula to be constructed. Naturally, the Peacemakers would have brought walky-talkies or other similar communications technology along with them. That the people writing these Biblical stories were of a pre-technological level is obvious to us by the way they admire the simplest technology we take for granted today.

31. Teraphim (Copyright Z. Sitchin, *The Twelfth Planet*)

Shown here are drawings of these teraphim. As the reader can plainly see they look like toy doll telephones. The exact nature of the emerald stones embedded in the teraphim came to light shortly after the death of Abraham's grandson Joshua. The story is told in *The Biblical Antiquities of Psuedo-Philo* and is attributed to Philo of Alexandria. Philo describes how after the death of Joshua the tribes sought a leader. Kenaz was elected and he held an inquisition interrogating each tribe about its sins against Mosaic Law. From the tribe of Asher comes this relevant confession:

> *We have found the **seven golden idols** whom the Amorites call the sacred nymphs, and **we took them along with the precious stones** set upon them and hid them. And behold now they are stored beneath the summit of **Mount Shechem**. Therefore send, and you will find them.*

Kenaz immediately dispatched to Mount Shechem a search party that discovered the stones and brought them to him. These stones were described as "light green in color." "And these are the precious stones," he was told, "that the Amorites had in their sanctuaries, the value of which cannot be estimated." These stones (that had been embedded in the hollow eye sockets of the teraphim) match the description of those that were on Noah's Ark which Alexander later sought – they were green and emitted a bright light. Kenaz learned that "for those entering by night the light of a lamp was not necessary, so brightly did the stones shine forth."

Kenaz further learned that these stones were indestructible. Out of desperation, according to Philo, Kenaz finally offered them to the deity, placing them on an altar. That night they were mysteriously removed by an angel.

As we will discuss momentarily, the original Emerald Tablets of Thoth were believed to have been stored underneath that magnificent structure known as the Great Pyramid. Suppose that the "strange cave in the wilderness" Abraham and Sarah entered is actually the Great Pyramid. Suppose their purpose was to claim ancient books, crystals or even the Key of Life (that Jewish legend tells us Abraham possessed). Did Abraham, a man of immense wisdom, return to the 'cave' and recover the Emerald Tablets along with remembrance of who he and Sarah were in past incarnations?

If this is the case, then is it also possible Abraham and Sarah are yet another incarnation of Thoth and Seshet, the husband and wife team of Peacemakers?

If Abraham and Sarah are identified in this way something even more profound was going on. A cursory analysis of global history reveals that the entire earth was preparing to blossom. Egypt, Israel, Syria, Tibet, India, South America, Mexico were all experiencing growth as if the planetary mind was somehow waking up.

The ancient connection between Mexico and Egypt is expressed in the technology, geographical knowledge, and observational astronomy the Mexicans employed in the construction of Teotihuacan, which scholars date to 4,000 B.C. It is no coincidence that Jose Arguelles (*The Mayan Factor*) has called Teotihuacan a Tula. The Teotihuacan complex is a mirror image of the Giza plateau. Here, as in Egypt, there are three principle pyramids: the Pyramid/Temple of Quetzalcoatl, the Pyramid of the Sun and the Pyramid of the Moon.

From this point of view, what we are seeing in 2,200 B.C. is nothing less than the reactivation of the planetary grid. Melchizedek had arrived as the wayshower of this planetary transformation – a transformation sparked by activation of a vast energy network of sacred sites. The most sacred nodal point on this grid was Israel, the place of incarnation.

What we are witnessing here is called the 'quickening' of the earth, an increase in the vibratory levels of man and earth which is thought to spark higher intelligence and increased linkage between minds. Under the guidance of the Order of Melchizedek, the Peacemakers, this was accomplished.

Working in conjunction with Melchizedek, Abraham founded a 'nation of sons of God' which we call Israel. The true Israel is not physical, historic or ethnic. The true Israel is a spiritual nation of seekers of the light, of the higher vibrations within themselves. This nation is also known as the "Children of Light." They are the people who fulfill the plan of the Peacemakers for the spiritual upliftment of humanity.

Under the guidance of Melchizedek the Children of Light brought the new teaching to Qumram, Alexandria, Egypt, Tibet, and likely to America. The true teaching they possessed was the coordinates or codes used to connect earth with the Jerusalem or Tula. These teachings offered ways for the Children of Light to raise themselves, or ascend, to the spiritual level of the Peacemakers or the Sons of Light.

The Sufis refer to the people of Israel as the "People ahl al-Dhimnah," the People of the Covenant of Light. This covenant was administered by the Essenes. From this we may deduce that the true founder of the Essenes, the Sons of Z-D-K, are the sons of Melchizedek. It is interesting to observe, as did John Allegro in *The Sacred Mushroom and the Cross*, that the term *therapeutae* used to describe the Essenes originated from the Sumerian term dara, 'beget' or 'giver of life'. Dara was an additional Sumerian name for Enki, the 'giver of (the key of) life'. From this we may, once again, venture that the mysterious Melchizedek is none other than Enki, the Gardener and King of Tula.

Today, the world has something to look forward to. According to Jewish tradition, the Key of Life must be located by the Peacemaker in advance of the arrival of the Messiah, the Gardener or King of Tula.

The Peacemaker will also return Moses to life. Moses, the Jewish mystery tradition states, encoded the secret instructions that God gave him in the Books of Moses of the Bible. It is also stated that when the Peacemaker returns in our present era he will interpret these Books of Moses: he will reveal the secrets of the Kaballah.

Similarly, according to Hopi Indian tradition, the Peacemaker will also recover something which sounds astonishingly similar to the Emerald Tablets and, through them, create a divinely inspired world of peace and harmony.

What if there is some hidden truth in these legends?

THE RETURN OF ENKI – THE GARDENER

In 1981, just five years after the publication of Zecharia Sitchin's first book, *The Twelfth Planet*, astronomers from NASA and the US Marine Observatory in Washington DC were actively searching for the Gardener's mysterious planet Nibiru. Simultaneously, geneticists backed by billions of dollars in research money, began decoding the Book of Life, our DNA, possibly in search of Enki's 'signature'.

One year later, in 1982, the space telescope IRAS (infrared astronomical station) saw what had not been seen for perhaps two thousand years. On December 30, 1983 the world press reported that the advanced space telescope:

> *discovered a celestial body in the direction of the constellation **Orion**, which possibly is as big as the gigantic Jupiter and perhaps so close to the Earth that it could belong to our solar system.... When IRAS researchers saw the mysterious celestial body and calculated that it was possibly eighty billion kilometers away from Earth, they speculated that it is moving towards Earth...*

In 1987, NASA confirmed what the ancient Sumerians knew: "an eccentric tenth planet orbits the Sun." (It is the twelfth planet if you count the Sun and moon.)

During this same time period (1988-1993) mysterious crop circles or pictograms began showing up in the barley fields of England. One of the pictograms, shown here, has been interpreted as lettering from a mixture of Phoenician, Hebrew and Iberian languages. The inscription is thought to read as "Ptah/Enki, the Creator, wise and kind." These events may not be directly connected, but there is little doubt they are part of a larger picture which is presently developing. In December, 1996 NASA launched a new spacecraft to Mars that will begin sending back data on July 4, 1997.

32. "Ptah/Enki, the Creator, wise and kind"

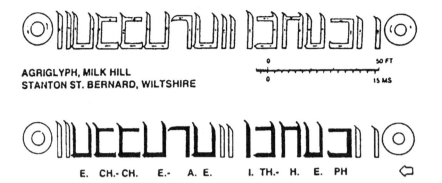

AGRIGLYPH, MILK HILL
STANTON ST. BERNARD, WILTSHIRE

E. CH.- CH. E.- A. E. I. TH.- H. E. PH

Even more startling than the confirmation of ancient knowledge was the reaction to this information by world leaders. The entire political philosophy of President Ronald Reagan, for example, changed overnight. Reagan, who previously taunted the Soviet Union as 'the Evil Empire' and led a five hundred billion dollar plus Apocalyptic escalation of the Arms Race with Russia, suddenly and dramatically became political allies with Russian leader Mikhail Gorbachev, a man who, because of a birthmark on his forehead, many fundamentalist Christians (including several in the White House) were certain was the biblical anti-Christ. Could news of a potential discovery of Nibiru and the possibility that it is inhabited by a technologically advanced civilization have been the trigger for Reagan's complete and total 'enlightenment'?

For those who were unaware of the discoveries in space, Reagan's statements at the Summit talks with Gorbachev soon after the revelation of the existence of the twelfth planet might sound like the meanderings of a space case. Said Reagan:

> How easy his task and mine might be in these meetings that we held if suddenly there were a threat from some other species from another planet outside in the Universe. We would forget all the little local differences that we have between our countries, and we would find out once and for all that we really are human beings here on this Earth together.

This New Age (and, according to Christian religious authority Jerry Falwell, anti-Christian) message would be repeated by the Presidential Guru Reagan at a Summit in Geneva in 1985, at his address before the United

Nations in 1987, at the Summit in Washington DC in 1987, at the National Strategic Forum in 1988 and at the Moscow Summit that same year.

All of this Presidential talk about space aliens and efforts to obtain up close information about Mars leads one to wonder: is Nibiru on its way to earth? Why now? Is this what is meant by the 'time of the Messiah', the 'dawning of the Heavenly Kingdom on earth', the Apocalypse which many associate with the year 2,000 and the appearance of celestial 'signs' (including the Grand Cross, the sign of the Son of Man) in the sky?

CHAPTER SEVEN

TULA:
HEARTBEAT OF THE HUMAN SOUL

Legend tells us that after travelling the world, Thoth and Seshet, the husband and wife team of Peacemakers, went to Egypt; and it is here that our story takes an astonishing turn.

In ancient times the Nile River was bordered by lush meadows, palms and an Edenic plain – a wilderness. Reeds, rushes, desert flowers of pink, lavender and white thrived along its sacred banks.

Standing with Seshet, Thoth beheld for the first time the breathtaking, spectacular grid, the artificially raised and leveled 12 acre platform called the "Egg of Creation" upon which they would supervise the building of the Great Pyramid (then called 'Enoch's Pillar') and the Sphinx.

The task of building the Great Pyramid would be overwhelming even to the modern mind. We can put a man on the moon, but our modern engineering cannot even come close to duplicating the Great Pyramid. Enoch, however, simply stuck his staff, the Key of Life, in the ground and went to work.

On this spot would stand a 45 story structure history wishes did not exist. Gleaming too brightly to look at in the morning Sun, the immense temple would stand like a great, silvered mirror. Inscriptions of the arts and sciences of the advanced civilization that built it would cover its surface.

Upon this magnificent structure would land the heron or phoenix and with its outstretched arms would radiate light. The word phoenix is supposed to have come from the Egyptian word *Pa-Hanoch*, which means 'House of Enoch' (i.e. family of Enoch). The Great Pyramid was often called the "Pillar of Enoch" by the ancients.

It is worth noting that the Great Pyramid was built at the head of the Nile Delta at the point where Upper and Lower Egypt meet. Egypt is the country which lies at the geographical center of the earth. Since the heart was believed to be the seat of the soul, the Pyramid can also be seen in a special way as the heart of the collective human soul. As goes with the Pyramid, so goes with humanity. That is, as we increase our understanding of the Pyramid, we increase our understanding of ourselves,

33. Great Pyramid: constructed as the 'heart' of the earth?

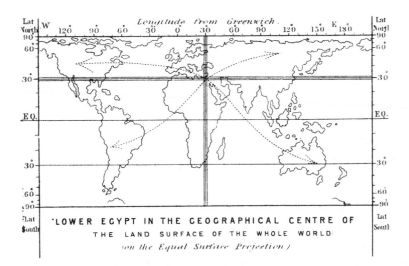

'LOWER EGYPT IN THE GEOGRAPHICAL CENTRE OF THE LAND SURFACE OF THE WHOLE WORLD
(on the Equal Surface Projection)

Scientists point out the Great Pyramid is the center of the ley/gridwork system that covers the earth. Ley lines are invisible rivers or highways of electromagnetic energy. The Chinese system of geomancy, *feng shui* (pronounced *fung shway*) is the science of understanding these magical "dragon currents" which exist beneath the earth. These same energies prompted our pagan and Christian ancestors to precisely locate Chartres Cathedral in France, Glastonbury Tor in England, the Ziggurats in Mesopotamia, and the Washington Monument in Washington DC at exact focal points where they could accumulate the dragon currents some called "prayer energy."

34. Dragon energies atop the pyramid.
(Copyright Z. Sitchin, *The Wars of Gods and Men*)

The serpent is well known to cult worship all over the world. In China its expression presents an interesting twist. Rather than despising or fearing the serpent as the corrupter and destroyer of mankind, the Dragon is seen as an instructor. There is not a single story of a Chinese saint or angel struggling to slay a dragon, but rather there are many stories in which they cultivate or neutralize it – and thus transcend it. The symbol of strength and kingship in China is still the Dragon.

The Great Pyramid appears to be the heart of a giant, global high-tech machine, a grid system engineered by the use of pyramids and obelisks that served as acupuncture needles at sacred centers all over the earth, designed for at least two purposes:

> 1. as a psychotronic instrument capable of receiving 'off-world' cosmic energies and changing them to frequencies capable of influencing the human brain.

> 2. as a means to establish and rearrange the energy flow lines that create the electromagnetic energy that facilitates a way to adjust the earth's frequency or 'heartbeat'.

Today, modern scientists have rediscovered this grid system and, to their horror, realize that humanity's ignorance may have destroyed it. If humanity is to remain on this planet, the grid system must be restored and maintained. This grid system is the key to raising and stabilizing the vibratory frequency of the planet.

THOTH, THE PEACEMAKER

According to Egyptian history, Thoth had more than an engineering miracle to perform when building the Pyramid. Egypt was a land fraught with challenge, a multi-racial society in the throes of a civil war. The image of ancient Egypt that emerges from the remarkably consistent and cohesive Edgar Cayce psychic readings is one of a new nation disintegrating under the stresses and strains of planetary changes, earthquakes and sinking continents, mass migrations of people, the shifting of the poles and an impending Great Cataclysm.

If prophecies and forecasts are correct it was a time very much like our own.

Something or *someone* had to stop the civil war and unite the people, bringing together men and women from the white, the yellow, the red and the black races of Atlantis and elsewhere. If there were ever a time for a great messenger to appear and bring to mankind an important vision for the future, this was it – and his name was Thoth. His role as Peacemaker is shown most movingly in a hymn in Chapter 183 of the Egyptian *Book of the Dead* where he is referred to as Thoth, the Peacemaker.

We now know the true reason Thoth was called the Peacemaker. His soul was charged with clearing the way for the arrival of the Earth Teacher. The vision which held the people together in anticipation of this arrival was the construction of an earthly connecting link to Tula (a symbol of man's unity and unified will to survive) and, quite possibly, a teaching frozen in stone that enabled the Children of Light to escape this plane of existence before the flood.

Archaeologists are now beginning to present proof that construction of the Great Pyramid was started, but not finished, before the Flood. There is compelling evidence to suggest it was completed in two stages. To begin, the lower concourses (up to a height of 30 feet) are made of cyclopean limestone. Above this level, however, the remaining 450 feet of the Pyramid is formed out of much smaller two to three ton blocks.

It was revealed by Robert Bauval's (*The Orion Mystery*) astronomical calculations that the Giza pyramids as a whole were arranged to provide an exact terrestrial diagram of the three belt stars in the constellation of Orion as they looked at precise times in history – 36,450 B.C., 26,000 years later in 10, 450 B.C., and 2450 B.C. Bauval concludes that the Pyramids were designed as a 'star clock' to mark these epochs and the movements of Orion and Sirius, the Dog Star.

If this were so, it pinpoints the initial construction of the Pyramids at the time just before the Flood. This bit of evidence is supported by the discovery of John Anthony West (*Serpent in the Sky*) that the desert monuments of the Sphinx, the Valley Temple at Giza, the Pyramid and the mysterious Osireion at Abydos all show scientifically validated signs of *water* erosion.

West has shown that such erosion could only have occurred before the last Ice Age, placing the construction of the Sphinx and the Pyramids before 10,000 B.C. The geology which proves the antiquity of the Sphinx was provided by Professor Robert Schoch, a Boston University geologist and a specialist in rock erosion, who has shown the weathering of the Sphinx was caused by thousands of years of heavy rainfall occurring long before the 2500 B.C. date provided by Egyptologists for the construction of the Sphinx.

Of course, conservative scholars scoff at such notions. "Where are the skeletons of this supposedly advanced civilization?" they ask. The evidence of this civilization may be found along the banks of the ancient Nile, which are miles inward from the Nile's current banks. In November, 1981 scientists, using imaging radar photography aboard the space shuttle Colombia, discovered a whole system of lost river valleys underneath the desert sands of Southwest Egypt. Amazingly, some of these buried valleys, which are estimated to be over 10,000 years old, are over nine miles wide and could have supported large population centers which we may soon unearth.

Another possibility is this civilization rests at the bottom of the Mediterranean Sea, which was dry during the last Ice Age. Unfortunately, by order of the Greek government, this area is forever off limits to archaeologists. What is the Greek government afraid we will discover there? (There are over 250 known sunken cities in the Mediterranean.)

THE MACHINE

Robert Bauval speculates that two different cultures lived in Egypt circa 10, 450 B.C under the aegis of one cult or brotherhood (that he refers to as the cult of Osiris). They were still there in 2450 B.C. and it was they that supervised the construction of the Pyramids.

Bauval further speculates that the Pyramid is a temple of initiation, a machine or computer. Realizing they could not be here for us, this cult whom I associate with Peacemakers, built the Pyramid as a means to force us to ask questions. In *Fingerprints of the Gods* Graham Hancock quotes Bauval: "they knew that they could do this by creating an eternal machine, the function of which was to generate questions....We're in the hands of real magicians here," states Bauval, "and real magicians know that with symbols – with the right symbols, with the right questions – they can lead you into *initiating yourself*." (I remind the reader that the purpose of initiation is to leave the earth.)

This brings to mind the Mandaeans, an offshoot of the Essenes, who carried a prophecy that the Secret Adam would come to earth and build a machine to transport the souls of the earth back to the heavenly Tula.

In this regard Bauval makes some startling statements.

First, he believes the Pyramid Texts, the ancient Egyptian documents on resurrection and ascension of the pharaohs, may contain the key to the mathematics and geometry of the Pyramids. If so, this is the software from the Pyramid computer. This is the sacred code for returning to Tula.

If the Pyramid is a form of mechanical heart, which raises the frequency of the planet and the *Pyramid Texts* are the software, what is the output? Strange as it may sound, the answer appears to be a way to initiate souls for travel to Sirius!

Once again, I show the heron, the symbol of Thoth and Seshet, perched atop the pyramid. In *Beyond the Blue Horizon*, Dr. E.C. Krupp shows the heron as representative of the star Sirius. In one connection, the heron atop the pyramid symbolizes the returning of Osiris or Christ, who emanates from Tula. Another ancient Egyptian myth showed the heron as the first transformer of the soul after death. Is it possible the Pyramids are pointing us to Sirius as a transshipment point for metamorphosed souls en route to Tula?

35. The heron.

MASS MIGRATION OF SOULS?

This observation takes the meaning of the Great Pyramid a step beyond. The Great Pyramid is not only the heart of the earth, it is also a doorway home. 100,000 or more slaves were supposed to have spent 20 years crafting this machine, honing it to precise measurements matched only by engineers crafting the intricate (and life-saving) tiles for the space shuttles' heat shields. From our perspective, we can see that these 'slaves' (read: unsurpassed master craftsmen) did not build the Great Pyramid as a tomb for a Pharaoh. They built it as a *womb* in which they could transform themselves into a vehicle, perhaps a body of light, capable of traveling the Cosmos.

When Thoth returned from his training with the Lord, he brought with him a secret teaching – the Key of Life – which would enable a segment of the population to attune their soul vibrations to Christ and the heavenly Tula. Hence, they could escape the Cataclysm and the cycle of earthly incarnation (another way of saying living in sin). By having this teaching embedded in its billions of tons of stone, the Great Pyramid is a machine for transporting souls back to Tula. In the next chapter, we shall explore the sacred symbol of this teaching, the tetrahedron.

CHAPTER EIGHT

THE SHAPE OF THE HEART

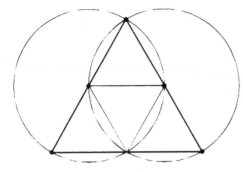

When Enoch travelled to the heavenly Tula, he partook in the ultimate human experience. Like those that followed – Ezekiel, Gudea, Moses, John and Mohammed – he brought something home with him. Enoch was given a vision, a sign from heaven, promising his people's deliverance. In fact, each of these prophets made trips to heaven and returned with a sacred geometric pattern, design or architectural plan for a temple which would attune earth with Tula.

The Pyramid Texts confirm that Thoth discovered a pattern or shape called the *tetrahedron*. Thoth received this pattern during his journey to Tula.

36. Tetrahedral forms.

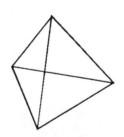

Numerous authors have expressed the opinion that there is a close connection between the Great Pyramid and what are known as the Egyptian mysteries of immortality. These mysteries center on secret knowledge possessed by a hierarchy of initiates. This secret knowledge, in turn, is centered upon the *pattern* for the Great Pyramid or Tula which is derived from the tetrahedron.

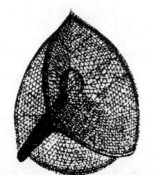

The proper way to view the Pyramid is as if you were looking in. This secret view is expressed in the following diagrams:

37. The 'Solomonic Pentacle' used in casting spells. The quotation from Psalm XVIII indicates it was designed to invoke an earthquake.

38. The Triune Godhead or Trinity.

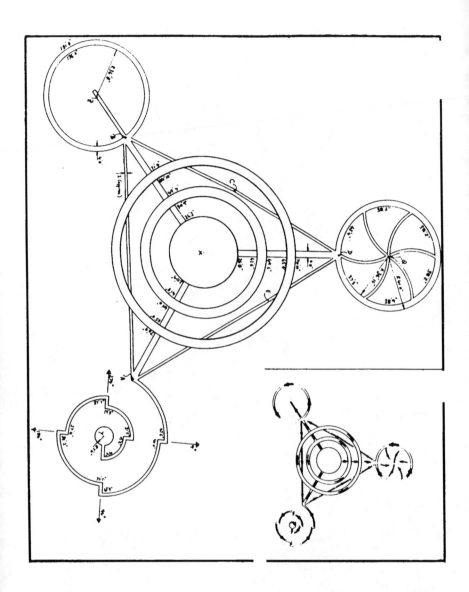

39. A tetrahedron has four triangular faces, four corners, and six edges. This three-dimensional tetrahedron was etched into a corn field by an as yet unidentified intelligence at Barbury Castle, England.

The ancients recognized long ago that all physical patterns of existence, including the human body, emerge from one or a combination of five primordial forms. These five forms are:

1. Tetrahedron
2. Hexahedron (cube)
3. Octahedron
4. Dodecahedron
5. Icosahedron

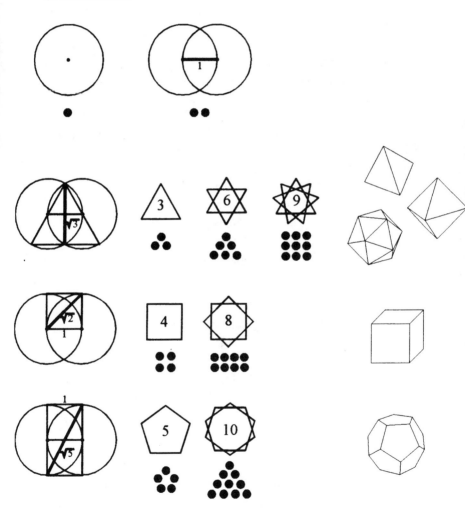

40. Five platonic volumes.

In the mystery schools of Egypt the principles of these five solids were taught. Many books have since been written about these fascinating volumes which are the basis for the science of sacred geometry.

Metaphysically, the tetrahedron is a doorway through which matter enters this universe because it contains the three dimensional patterns of four of the five Platonic solids. These five geometric figures are of immense importance. They have been called the building blocks of the universe or the 'codes of the creator'.

All phenomenon on earth can be reduced to the geometric-energetic constructs of the tetrahedron. It is the fundamental shape out of which everything on earth is constructed. This is why the Great Pyramid is the centerpiece, or heart, of the earthly Tula. The revelation of this very special pattern is perhaps as important as its embodiment in the millions of tons of stone of the Great Pyramid.

In his superlative work, *A Beginner's Guide to Constructing the Universe*, mathematician Michael Schneider makes some important observations about the tetrahedron. Regardless of the culture, he notes, the tetrahedron was the preeminent symbol for the Mother Goddess, the earth. The number four is intimately associated with the guiding values of creation. The Mother gives birth, clothes her creations with material substance (earth, air, fire and water), and encourages their growth. The word *nature* comes from the Latin for 'birth'. *Mater*, the Latin word for 'mother', is the origin of the word matter. *Mater* makes matter. Thus, creation, birth, matter are all wrapped into the mystery of the tetrahedron.

The word 'hedron' offers its own rather interesting chain of meanings. Hedron is derived from a proto-Indo-European root sed, which implies seat, sitting down or settling. Sed also means 'to go', and words such as episode and exodus are derived from it. Cathedral comes from 'sed' and is, therefore, both a seat (a place) *and* a way or a journey. Tetrahedron can therefore be 'four ways' or 'Place of four ways' which may refer to Tula as the place of four winds.

The innermost secret of the tetrahedron is revealed if you interlock two three-dimensional tetrahedrons. This creates the Star of David, sometimes called a star tetrahedron or the octahedron. The two interlocking tetrahedrons represent male and female energy, heaven and earth, in perfect balance. Here, again, is the union of opposites.

41. Star of David or Seal of Solomon. (Copyright Z. Sitchin, *The Wars of Gods and Men*)

This symbol is sometimes called the Seal of Solomon ('Peace'). We know we are on the right track once it is realized that Moslem legend recounts Solomon using this symbol or its process to capture nature spirits!

The star tetrahedron was often depicted by the ancients in its stylized form – the butterfly. The butterfly, a primordial symbol for resurrection and ascension, was the ancient symbol for Jerusalem (the city of Peace) and for Tula in Mexico. It was also an alternate to the fish symbol used by the early Christian faithful to identify themselves.

42. 'Atlantean' Statue from Tula, Mexico with the butterfly emblem emblazoned on his chest.

Astonishingly, if we connect all the lines of the star tetrahedron you end up with a tesseract. As I stated earlier, ancient legends say the tesseract was used as a means to communicate with beings from other dimensions.

In this regard it is fascinating to consider that the Pyramid Texts tell us Thoth not only discovered the tetrahedron, but that he also was a *psychopomp*, a conductor of souls between dimensions. He is depicted with staff or *ankh* in hand, directing souls from one realm to another.

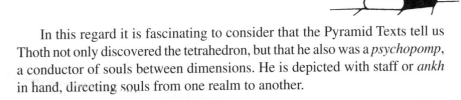

The Peacemaker 109

REDEMPTION

Today, the Key of Life (the Christian secret of redemption) is the same as it ever was. Essentially, it is becoming aware of the existence of Tula and taking steps to return there.

According to Bob Frisell (*Nothing In This Book Is True, But Its Exactly the Way Things Are*) and Drunvalo Melchizedek (who derived his teachings from Thoth), the way to this is by learning to counter-rotate two interlocking tetrahedrons within the body. The energy field created by counter rotating star tetrahedrons in the body is called the Mer-Ka-Ba.

In Egyptian, Mer-Ka-Ba translates literally to: Mer (Light) Ka (Spirit) Ba (Body). When the ancient Hebrews referred to the Mer-Ka-Ba they were referring to a vehicle called the Divine Throne-Chariot: a space/time/light vehicle supposedly powered by cherubim or angels. Abraham, for example, ascended in a Mer-Ka-Ba and heard the voice of God. Since Enoch/Thoth was known to have possessed the Key of Life, it is likely the Mer-Ka-Ba was his mode of transport as well.

43. Star Tetrahedron. "He who understands this symbol may unlock the mysteries of the Universe." – Captain W.M. Morgan, 33rd degree Mason (1827)

Later, the vision of Ezekiel became the central image of Jewish Mer-Ka-Ba mysticism; the description of the Mer-Ka-Ba was the focal point or target of an open-eye meditation. Ezekiel called it a "chariot of fire" with a "great cloud of brightness about it." This, presumably, was similar to the cloud Enoch/Thoth rode during his ascension to meet the Lord.

In the Gnostic manuscript called the *Apocryphon of James*, discovered at Nag Hammadi, Egypt, we learn that Jesus ascends in a Mer-Ka-Ba type vehicle after speaking with James and Peter:

> *'But I have said my last word to you,' says Jesus, 'and I shall depart from you, for a **chariot of spirit** has borne me aloft.'*
> – Apochryphon of James 14:30-34

Is this 'chariot of spirit' a state of mind, a hypnotic trance for instance, or should we take these descriptions to mean Jesus ascended in a literal, physical vehicle for the spirit? Or are they two facets of the same diamond? If so, how does one go about acquiring a Mer-Ka-Ba?

Before the reader begins to worry about their Mer-Ka-Ba, it should be noted that everyone has one. It's our birthright. Once formed at conception, this Mer-Ka-Ba vehicle surrounding the first eight cells remains fixed at the base of the spine, the geographic center of the body, until we choose to activate it. Activation of the Mer-Ka-Ba is achieved through the two-step process of resurrection and ascension and is called rapture. This process centers upon apprehension of the Key of Life and the raising of one's own spiritual vibration. I will leave it up to the reader to discover the most appropriate, individual way to accomplish this. Whether one is just beginning, or well on their way, the ancient texts make it clear that a good starting (or resting) place in such a quest is the well-worn path through the Sphinx.

CHAPTER NINE

THE SPHINX:
GUARDIAN OF THE HALL OF RECORDS AND TULA

Deep neath the image lies my secret,
search and find in the pyramid I built.
Each to the other, is the Keystone;
each the gateway, that leads to LIFE.
Follow the KEY I leave behind me,
seek and the doorway to LIFE shall be thine.
Seek thou in my pyramid,
in the passage that ends in a wall,
use thou the KEY of the SEVEN,
and open to thee, the pathway will fall.

–The Emerald Tablets of Thoth
Tablet V

Man fears time.
But time fears the Sphinx.

–Arab Proverb

The Sphinx, as the guardian of Tula, has many names including 'Father of Terror', an allusion to its prophetic purpose as an indicator of change.

44. The Sphinx: Guardian of the Double Mountain. This extraordinary illustration of the Sphinx shows the Pyramids in perspective in the background, a technique which Dr. Joseph Jochmans describes as "very rarely seen" in ancient Egypt. (Copyright Z. Sitchin, *The Stairway to Heaven*)

After the Flood the Sphinx was re-carved into its present form, interpreted by modern man as a prophecy in stone. The front paws and upper body were molded into a lion. The back paws, lower body and tail became a bull. The head, as always, remained human. And, in what must have been a spine-tingling sight, fires were lit (in stone boxes built on the Sphinx's flanks) to give the appearance at night of the Sphinx having the flaming wings of an eagle, representing Scorpio.

Lion. Bull. Human. Eagle. Anyone who has casually read the Book of Revelation will recognize these creatures from the vision of the prophet John. They are also the Four Beings before the Throne of God, the Mer-Ka-Ba of Ezekiel. Delving deeper, we can also see them as celestial keys; these four beings represent the Four Spokes in the Wheel of the Zodiac, the four fixed astrological signs of Leo, Taurus, Aquarius and Scorpio.

In numerous ancient texts, it is pointed out that our world is guarded by four angels or Watchtowers. These angels prevent the chaotic forces of *Coronzon* (thought to be the true heavenly name of Satan) from entering our world. It is crucial to realize that in ancient times the term 'world' was not synonymous with Earth, but actually signified a *sector of space*. More precisely, a sphere with a circumference defined by the four constellations which mark off the points of intersection of the plane of the ecliptic and the celestial equator of the Earth.

The four constellations marking the boundaries of our 'cube world' are (if you haven't already guessed): Leo (the Lion), Taurus (the Bull), Aquarius (the Man or the Heron), and Scorpio (the Eagle or the Phoenix). Here, once again, are our four beasts. These four angels are also known as the four Guardian Stars of Heaven. They form a cross in the sky. This is why the Bible speaks of the four corners of the Earth, and why ancient cosmologists thought of the world as a square with a dome-shaped roof. The Christian Church later used the four Guardian Stars which define the borders of our world as symbols for the Four Evangelists: Matthew, Mark, Luke and John. This is also why the Sphinx is a composite beast of these same four guardians: Lion, Bull, Man and Eagle. These four beasts represent four astrological ages that were significant in humankind's development: Leo, Taurus, Aquarius and Scorpio.

The Sphinx's prophecy in stone was designed to point backward and forward to these four ages, to these times when mass migrations of souls left the earth and this sector of space altogether. The Age of Leo, 12,000 years ago, saw the last great cataclysm. The Age of Taurus the Bull, between 6,000 and 4,000 years ago saw the rise of ancient civilizations along the Nile, Tigris and Euphrates rivers. The Hall of Records is thought to contain spiritual knowledge which will lead the way to this New Age and will take humanity into the distant Age of Scorpio, when in A.D. 9,000, humankind will rise like the phoenix into a new dimension of existence.

Today, we have come full circle and are entering the Age of Aquarius, prophesied to be the beginning of a new era of planetary awareness and Oneness of humanity. Jesus prophesied that this Kingdom of God would be established in three days. These "days" have been interpreted as stages lasting a thousand years each.

Stage one involved the initial preaching of the Gospel.

The emphasis during stage two was spiritualization of the law.

Many believe the year 2,000 marks the transition into stage three, which is called the Harvesting of Souls. Stage three would be initiated by an Apocalypse: a final battle between the spiritual kingdom and the temptations of the material world. The Kingdom of God (Tula?) will appear after the Apocalypse when the entire earth comes together as one. In the world today, we can easily see the battle lines being drawn for this great conflict.

It may be disturbing, yet it is a fact (one unfortunately unknown to most preachers, priests and rabbis) that the Apocalypse is not God's wrathful way of destroying humanity. The Apocalypse is actually going to be a man-made event.

Furthermore, while most consider the horrific, destructive vision of Saint John in the Book of Revelation to be presaging a purely physical event, most evidence suggests it to be a spiritual process that may become manifest either as a dark or light event, depending upon the input of humanity. The Apocalypse boils down to a battle between the Children of Light and the Children of Darkness inside each human being on the planet.

THE HARVEST

Throughout the document which communicates the instructions for manifesting the end of the world (the completion of a 26,000 year cosmic cycle), the angels responsible for this procedure explicitly refer to the Apocalypse as "the Harvest."

From our human point of view Apocalypse means 'lifting the veil or gate'. From an ascended point of view, the Apocalypse includes the possibility of the earth being conquered by a group of malevolent beings if the veil is not properly lifted. A transcendent point of view also reveals that the one and only way to open the locked gates for these harmful spirits is from the *inside*. The wrathful angels of Armageddon must be invited to earth.

The keys to opening these gates for ethereal entities must be initiated through an elaborate magical procedure. Many believe this same procedure was delivered to Dr. John Dee (private astrologer and magician to Queen Elizabeth) and the famous scryer Edward Kelly in the 1600's. The system is known as Enochian Magic, after the Old Testament prophet and Peacemaker.

The record seems to show that Dee never attempted to use the Keys. Kelly, on the other hand, tried to use the Keys to unlock the secret of manufacturing gold (which by some accounts he succeeded in doing). Both men appear to have been ignorant of the true power of their work.

Dee's library of personal notebooks was ultimately burned. Only the Keys survived. Two hundred and fifty years later, in 1904, Dee and Kelly's Keys were dusted off and implemented by the infamous magician Alestair Crowley. Crowley not only believed he was the reincarnated Edward Kelly, but also the "Great Beast" of the Book of Revelation. He saw Armageddon as a practical matter of opening the gate to the souls or spirits of Coronzon. Fortunately, most do not believe Crowley was entirely successful in opening all four gates of Earth.

This is the understatement of the millennium. For let us suppose, as is reasonably so, that in 1904 Crowley was successful in opening just one of the gates just a tiny bit. Could this explain the atrocities of World War One? Does it help to explain the sick horrors of Hitler, the Cold War, the insane stockpiling of bacteriological and thermonuclear weapons?

The tree of our culture is withered, and vultures sit in its branches.
–Lance deHaven-Smith
The Hidden Teachings of Jesus

The chilling connotations of the Harvest cannot be overlooked. Is this the reason why the principles of resurrection and ascension were discredited early on by the Church Fathers? Or, is this why the Sphinx is called the Father of Terror? Let's take a realistic look at the Sphinx.

THE SPHINX: BOOK OF REVELATION

The ancient name for the Sphinx, as found in the *Pyramid Texts*, was *Rwty*. Author and archaeologist Mark Lehner in his book *The Egyptian Heritage* observes that Rwty is akin to Re-stew, Ra-sheta, Re-tau and Rosta, all variations on the name of the secret sanctuary located in Am Tuat, the underworld described in the Egyptian *Book of the Dead*. Extraordinarily, this sanctuary is related to the deepest mysteries, "the passage of the soul into realms of immortality." This sanctuary was directly associated with the rites of initiation, the means of resurrection and ascension, which the Sphinx was guardian over.

Since the four beasts of the apocalypse seem to combine in the composite image of the Sphinx, it would appear that John was given information of a very high order that had something to do with resurrection and ascension. In ancient pagan symbolism (which John and Jesus were masters of) the Sphinx always guarded both sides of doors or gateways to treasuries of mysterious knowledge or especially to the underworld.

45. The seal of Ningishzidda, the Sumerian name for Thoth. Notice the two cherubim guarding the doorway to the other world.

More significantly, whenever new revelations were received for the Peacemakers, they were deposited in secret vaults somewhere near the Sphinx. Knowledge was never permanently removed from this Hall of Records, only added to.

46. Stele of Thutmose IV. (Copyright Z. Sitchin, *The Stairway to Heaven*)

The famous Stele of Thutmose IV (situated between the paws of the Sphinx) depicts the Sphinx lying upon a sanctuary, with a doorway clearly visible. According to legend, this doorway leading to the Hall of Records was to remain sealed for a future time – a time when man would once again enter an age of resurrection or a Golden Age. The Sphinx, as we have just seen, is the link.

The mystery traditions state that the Hall is sealed to all but the one who matches a particular 'soul vibration'. This man, say the Freemasons, is a 'chosen man of Enoch'. Someday this chosen one (and presumably his wife) will locate this vault and bring its secrets to the world.

What will be discovered upon the opening of the Hall?

Some believe there are working models of ancient advanced technology preserved in the Hall. Included in this cache is the Ark of the Covenant and the Key of Life. We will discuss the Ark in a later chapter. Suffice it to say, the acquisition of these devices is on the Peacemaker's 'to do list'. Together, these devices would give him the power to infuse lifeless matter with life force and to conduct souls from one dimension to another.

Also, the Hall is thought to contain the records of Jesus. Presumably these were placed there by Enoch, giving an account of his future returns. According to Edgar Cayce, "those records are yet to be found of the preparation of the man, of the Christ, in those of the tomb, or those yet to be uncovered in the pyramid [of records]." These will be found before His Second Coming, which Cayce places in 1998. The reopening of the Hall, according to prophecy, necessitates the reappearance of Thoth and Seshet.

Records of Christ or not, it has been observed by more than one author that, once discovered, this underground repository will considerably over-shadow the pyramid as a wonder. Is it possible this will occur in our life-time? Nostradamus certainly believed so.

NOSTRADAMUS AND THE HALL OF RECORDS

Nostradamus predicted the discovery of the Hall of Records. Dr. Joseph R. Jochmans was first to point out that in Century VII, 14 Nostradamus pre-dicted the opening of the Hall:

> *They will come to discover the hidden topography of the land*
> [at Giza, as occurred in 1993]
> *The urns holding wisdom within the monuments* [the Pyramids] *opened*
> *up,*
> *Their contents will cause the understanding*
> *of holy philosophy to expand greatly,*
> *White exchanged for black, falsehoods exposed, new wisdom replacing*
> *the established tradition that no longer work.*

Exactly as has been thought, Nostradamus is here stating that the sacred knowledge hidden underneath the Pyramid will greatly expand our conscious-ness. His description "white exchanged for black, falsehoods exposed" is the most telling, describing a much needed realignment of humankind's con-sciousness. As a result of this discovery Nostradamus tells us in Century I, Quatrain 53:

> *Alas, we shall see a great nation sorely troubled.*
> *And Holy Law in utter ruin.*
> *All Christianity taken over by other laws.*
> *When a new source of gold and money is discovered.*

Today, we have come full circle and are entering the Age of Aquarius, prophesied to be the beginning of a new era of planetary awareness and One-ness of humanity.

The question is, when (and by whom?) will the Hall be opened? In the next chapter, we find out.

CHAPTER TEN

NOSTRADAMUS
AND THE KING OF TERROR

In one of his most specific and least understood prophecies Nostradamus predicted that in July of 1999 the King of Terror will come out of the sky and resurrect the King of Angolmois.

The discovery of this was, for me, spine-tingling for one reason. The Sphinx – a composite creature of the four beasts of the Apocalypse: lion, bull, man and eagle – is called the *Father of Terror*!

Century X, Quatrain 72 states:

> *In the year 1999 [and] seven months,*
> *From the sky will come a great King of Terror,*
> *He will resurrect the great King of Angolmois,*
> *Before which Mars rules happily.*

Let's start deciphering this prophecy by decoding the King of Angolmois. Who or what is Angolmois? Without the final 's', this place name would be an anagram for Mongolia. The first Mongolian most interpreters of Nostradamus think of is Genghis Khan. Thus, say the experts, the King of Angolmois must be the reincarnated Genghis Khan (the *Washington Post's* "Man of the Millennium") who will lead a massive final slaughter of humanity.

I have a different take on this King of the Mongols. In the Buddhist tradition Mongolia is the location for Shambhala, a paradise which is equated with Tula. Furthermore, the myths of the Maya, Toltecs and Aztecs tell of bearded, blond white men who came from a kingdom in Mongolia called Tollan located near Lake Baikal and the river Tula. These Mongolians said they had come from Atlantis and sailed around the world founding new Tulas along the way and naming them after their homeland. From this we may deduce Nostradamus' 'King of Angolmois' is actually the King of Tula.

Who, then, is the King of Terror? The King of Terror has been interpreted as an asteroid or an alien invasion in July 1999 which will result in the destruction of millions of human lives. Still others interpret Nostradamus' use of the phrase 'King of Terror' in a metaphorical sense. For example, Elvis is the 'King' in the same way Michael Jackson refers to himself as the 'king of pop'.

The truth about the King of Terror and the King of Angolmois is far different and more extraordinary than we have previously expected. These two are nothing less than the two anticipated messiahs of the Essenes: the Peacemaker and the Earth Teacher, the King of Tula.

How can a person described as the King of Terror be a Peacemaker?

To understand the meaning behind Nostradamus' epithet the 'King of Terror', it is helpful to recall that both John the Baptist and Jesus were despised and hated as over zealous revolutionaries by the Roman government and the Sanhedrin, the Jewish elite who condemned Jesus. After stirring things up, John was declared a terrorist and decapitated by Herod. Jesus was, of course, crucified. They could kill Jesus, but that wouldn't stop his association with 'terror'. In chapter 21 of the Gospel of Luke, Jesus eloquently predicted the days of terror to come in Jerusalem after his death. By terror many have assumed Jesus meant a world of chaos and confusion, crass commercialism of his image, disease, pollution, urban crowding, etc. If the reader has seen the news reports from Jerusalem lately, they might tend to agree that terror reigns in the City of Peace. However, we have not yet penetrated the inner meaning of terror

TERROR IS ENLIGHTENMENT

Terror can certainly mean chaos, degeneracy. This, however, may not be quite what Jesus or Nostradamus had in mind. Both men, fearing persecution by authorities, chose to conceal their most important teachings in code. In Nostradamus' time, the most terrifying image one could conjure was the Holy Grail. Growing up in southern France, Nostradamus assuredly knew the story of the Holy Grail and the Cathars, who preserved its teachings. What was the Grail and what terrifying secrets did the Cathars possess? The Grail was believed to be housed in a sanctuary – perhaps a cathedral, a mountain peak, the treasury of a castle, or even underneath the Great Pyramid. Those who suddenly came upon the unconcealed Grail suffered a terrifying shock. They became enlightened.

In her book *The Holy Grail*, Norma Lorre Goodrich tells of an anonymous French author who recounts his traumatic first viewing of the Grail in his work the *Grand-Saint-Graal*. In 717 A.D., this Frenchman was paid a visit one morning by a beautiful young man. After a brief interview, the beautiful young man bent down and *blew in the face* of the Frenchman causing his 'vision' to become one hundred times stronger. His vision enhanced, the author was able to recognize the young man as none other than Jesus. (This is curious for the fact that whenever Jesus performed the "Pleiadean Attunement," in which the soul was given instructions for travel through the star gate of the Pleiades, it involved him breathing on his subjects. In modern times, an identical procedure is followed in Reiki attunements that enhance the ability to heal oneself or others.)

Jesus then proceeded to give the Frenchman a tiny Book, no bigger than the palm of his hand. When the author looked at the Book he saw that it read: "Here Commences the Reading concerning The Holy Grail." Then he read: "Here Commences Terror." As he pondered this title, the Frenchman saw a flash of lightning. From this point forward, at least in Southern France, terror and enlightenment were linked.

The Frenchman locked the Book in his altar. The next day when he went to get the Book he discovered to his amazement that the Book had disappeared. A voiced appeared and told him not be to be dismayed. It ordered him to walk along a path until he came to the Junction of *Seven* Roads. (Could this be a stellar journey, the Seven Roads being the seven stars of the Pleiades?) Soon thereafter, he would come to the Great Cross that rises from the Fountain. (Again, the enclosed cross is the symbol of Tula, the central point in heaven in which is found the fountainhead of souls.)

On an altar near this Great Cross, the Frenchman found his priceless, disappearing Book. It was Christ (The King of Tula) himself who now ordered the Frenchman (now transformed into the King of Terror/Enlightenment) to make a copy. The Book became known as the *Grand-Saint-Graal*.

The author of the Grand-Saint-Graal may never be known. He is, however, astonishingly like Sir Galahad. As a sacred king, Sir Galahad was the pure knight who was the last to observe the Holy Grail. Sir Thomas Mallory, one of the most celebrated of all Grail writers, thought Galahad was a direct descendent (through Guinevere) of Jesus himself. (Hence, Galahad also is a descendent of Abraham, King David and King Solomon.)

In a Grail episode corresponding directly to the Pleiadean Attunement, Galahad battles and defeats *seven* knights who had overtaken the Castle of Maidens and held the maidens captive within it. It is revealed that the seven knights are actually the Seven Deadly Sins and the castle is Hell. Here, Galahad is reenacting Christ's descent into Hell in order to set free the souls of the just, represented in this story by the maidens.

Astonishingly, after his discovery of the Grail, Galahad was believed to have lived for a year in the palace of the Goddess, at the hub of the spinning wheel of the Milky Way. This place at the center of our galaxy we now know to be called Tula. Does the *Grand-Saint-Graal*, the story of a young man's journey through the Pleiades to the central fountain in heaven, chronicle Galahad's journey to Tula?

Interestingly, the *Grand-Saint-Graal* contains long passages from the Gospel of John, the only one of the four gospels to document the appearance of the Gardener, or the King of Tula, on Easter morning. Especially in Southern France, in the region of the Pyrenees Mountains, the Holy Grail was equated with a Christ-consciousness which anyone might possess. Many undertook the Grail quest; they called themselves the *kathari* or 'pure ones'. Their name derived from Katherine, the Goddess once portrayed as the Dancer on the Fiery Wheel of Karma at the center of heaven (Tula) and considered the female counterpart of God. Is it fair to ask if Galahad returned to earth from Tula with this Goddess? Perhaps she represents his beloved, his female counterpart who makes him whole and complete.

The Cathars' quest was for the instructions left by Jesus for transforming oneself into a being of light capable of travelling through the stargate of the Pleiades, and then onward to the central point in heaven. The symbol of Katherine's Wheel was their central image. This is not surprising since the goal of the Cathars' quest was to escape the cycle of incarnation on earth. As we know, these Cathars, whose numbers many believe were in the millions, were exterminated by Pope Innocent III. Every one of them, including women and children, were burned to death by the Church because of their true understanding of the Gospel of John, and the Gardener or King of Tula. It is no wonder Nostradamus encoded his knowledge of the King of Terror and the Gardener in such obscure language. (It is worthwhile to note that the spiritual descendents of the Cathars were the Puritans who, as we will see, came to America to found a new Kingdom of Tula.)

THE PEACEMAKER: KING OF TERROR

One of the first of Nostradamus' interpreters to correctly pursue the King of Terror was, appropriately, the Frenchman Jean-Charles Pichon. He declared the King of Terror was not an asteroid but a human being. Pichon further stated that he is an American of Germanic origin who comes to power on the strength of his earlier reputation, or perhaps past life, as a *peacemaker*.

Ancient prophecies predict the Peacemaker will once again enter the Hall of Records and retrieve 'lost knowledge'. The Hall is sealed to all but the one who matches a particular 'soul vibration'. The effect of the revelation of this lost knowledge will be devastating. It is thought to be of such an explosive nature that it will bring terror and chaos to the world's religions and financial markets, the likes of which have not been witnessed since Jesus threw the money changers out of the temple. When this enlightenment occurs, humanity will realize it has been relentlessly persecuted for a very long time by disinformation designed to keep us spiritually deprived.

Furthermore, according to author Joseph R. Jochmans (*Keys of Giza*) the next most auspicious time astrologically for the Peacemaker to open the Hall of Records is in August, 1999 precisely coinciding with the arrival of the King of Terror and the appearance of the sign of the Son of Man in the sky!

From this we see a perfect match between the title King of Terror and the knowledge stored within the Father of Terror, the Sphinx. The connection is clear: the Peacemaker is Nostradamus' King of Terror.

THE GRAND CROSS

On August 11, 1999, a rare astrological alignment of the planets called the Grand Cross will form. The Grand Cross is formed by an opposition of Venus (in Scorpio) to Saturn and Jupiter (in Taurus), lying at a 90 degree angle with the opposition of Neptune and Uranus (in Aquarius) to the Sun, Moon and Mercury (in Leo). This Cross is the sign of the Son of Man.

These four zodiacal signs – Taurus the bull, Leo the lion, Scorpio the eagle and Aquarius the man – are the four beasts of the Apocalypse, the four beasts of Ezekiel's Mer-Ka-Ba vehicle and the four beasts of the Sphinx. They are also, significantly, the last card of the Tarot – the World, or the Wheel of Time.

There are amazing correspondences not only between Jesus and Nostradamus' King of Terror, but also with Buddha. In particular, all three are proclaimers of the Wheel of Teaching (which may be similar to Katherine's Fiery Wheel of Karma). Furthermore, in Hindu, the Peacemaker is called *Rudra Cakra*, 'the wrathful one of the Wheel'. This term could easily be rendered as 'king of the terror/enlightenment contained within the Sphinx, the composite beast of four animals (lion, bull, man and eagle) contained within the wheel of time'.

On August 11, 1999, a total eclipse of the sun will accompany the appearance of the Grand Cross. Nostradamus states in Century III, Quatrain 34:

> *When there is an eclipse of the sun in broad daylight,*
> *the monster will be seen.*
> *Many will interpret it in different ways.*
> *They will not care about money or make provision for it.*

The Jehovah's Witnesses and the Seventh Day Adventists believe this will be the end of the world. Actually, it is the very beginning of a new world.

GREAT TRIBULATION

Nostradamus' prophecy directly corresponds with a prophecy given in the Book of Matthew for the introduction of a New Age of peace and plenty as described in Isaiah. In Matthew 24:29-31 the signs of the arrival of this New Age are given:

> *Immediately after the tribulation of those days shall the sun be darkened and the moon shall not give her light, and the stars shall fall from heaven, and the powers of the heavens shall be shaken;*

The stars falling from the sky poetically describes the appearance of crop circles in grain fields around the Earth. An ancient Native American prophecy states that the beginning of the next world will be heralded by the appearance of the moon on earth. When a crop circle in the shape of a crescent moon appeared in England it was said to have brought tears to the eyes of Native American Elders.

> *and then shall appear the sign of the Son of man in heaven:*

The "sign of the Son of man" is clearly the August 11, 1999 eclipse during which the Grand Cross will form.

> *and then shall all the tribes of the earth mourn, and they shall see the Son of man coming in the clouds of heaven with power and great glory.*

In the antediluvian Book of Enoch we learn the Son of Man refers to Christ's prophet, the Peacemaker: "And he shall send his angels with a great sound of a trumpet."

The "great sound of a trumpet" refers explicitly to the changing vibrational frequency of the Earth. (For a thorough treatment of this subject I refer the reader to Gregg Braden's *Awakening to Zero Point: The Collective Initiation.*)

Humanity is beginning to understand that we perceive as little as ten percent of the observable universe. Visualize, for example, a Universal Grid operating somewhat like cable television. At one time an increase from 10 to 30-40 channels was considered a breakthrough, making new programming perceptible to us. Soon, 500 cable channels will be standard. An increase in channels (energy) widens the 'waveband', allowing more energy to appear on our screens. Expanding the waveband of the Earth will enable previously imperceptible beings, thoughts, and other forms of higher vibrational consciousness, including angels, to become readily apparent to all with decoders capable of interpreting their signals. Most will perceive them as new discoveries; but, for those who have had eyes to see, it will simply be confirmation of what we know has been there all along.

Nostradamus states clearly that earth goes 'on line' or gets plugged into the Universal Grid in July, 1999, with the arrival of the King of Terror which is timed with the appearance of the sign of the Son of Man, the Grand Cross, in August, 1999.

> *and they shall gather together his elect from the four winds, from one end of heaven to the other.* (In Mark it states "from the four winds, from one end of earth to the uttermost part of heaven.")

What has not been previously recognized by interpreters of Biblical prophecy or Nostradamus' Quatrains is that this prophecy directly relates to the Hopi Indian and Iroquois Indian legend of the Peacemaker as a figure who will gather the four races in a sacred circle to create a divinely inspired peace.

For nearly three thousand years, the world has looked for the coming of this Peacemaker. Malachi's prophecy that God will send them "Elijah the prophet before the coming of the great and dreadful day of the Lord" (Malachi 4:5) has prompted Jews to offer a cup each Passover as an invitation to the prophet to appear and usher in the Messianic New Age.

Maimonides, the great Jewish philosopher, wrote that Elijah will arrive before the coming of the Messiah: "Before the War of Gog and Magog, a prophet will arise to rectify Israel's conduct and prepare their hearts [for redemption]" (Mishneh Torah, Hilchos Melachim 12:2).

It is believed this Peacemaker will return either three days or three years before the Advent of the Earth Teacher. Correspondingly, Nostradamus prophesies the arrival of the Peacemaker in July, 1999 and that of the Christ figure three years later in June, 2002.

In Century 6, Quatrain 24 Nostradamus writes:

Mars and the scepter will be in conjunction, [June 21, 2002]
A calamitous war under Cancer.
A short time afterward a new king will be anointed
Who will bring peace to the earth for a long time.

Nostradamus makes clear that this Messiah (or the enlightened being of any of a dozen religious and mythological traditions) will come to earth to take us Home. Century 9, Quatrain 66:

There will be peace, union and change,
Estates and offices [that were] *low,* [are] *high*
those high [made] *very low.*
To prepare for a journey torments the first [child].
War to cease, civil processes, debates.

According to Jesus' own prophecy in Matthew 24:32-34 the generation that saw Israel become a nation will live to see the return of Christ. When Israel was recognized as an independent state on May 14, 1948, and her exiles returned home, it was a signal to many that "the age of redemption had begun."

The Iroquois Indians place the Peacemaker's return in 1996. Edgar Cayce presages the return of the Messiah in 1998. Nostradamus predicted the Peacemaker's return in 1999.

As we can see, the cosmic bond between earth and heaven is about to be tied once more.

THE MARS CONNECTION

Speaking of heaven and earth, it is interesting that the tetrahedron, the Pyramid, the Sphinx, the Peacemaker and Nostradamus all share a connection with Mars. What is it?

In 1976, NASA's *Viking* Mission to Mars sent back some amazing pictures which, under the appraisal of computer scientists Vincent DiPietro and Gregory Molenaar (notice the initial letters D and M in their last names), appear to provide startling evidence that a monumental, Egyptian-styled 'face' approximately 1.6 miles long, 1.2 miles wide and between 1,650 feet and 2,600 feet high sits on the dusty Cydonia plain of Mars. Recent color enhancement techniques used by the D & M team have revealed an eyeball feature in the one visible eye socket and the presence of sculptured teeth in the mouth area.

Nostradamus made a previously undiscovered prophecy in which he foresaw the discovery of the Face on Mars or at least, perhaps, the initials of those related to its discovery. In Century VIII, Quatrain 56 Nostradamus wrote:

When the inscription D.M. is found in the ancient cave,
revealed by a lamp.
Law, the king, and Prince Ulpian tried,
the queen and duke in the pavilion under cover.

In his book *The Monuments of Mars*, physicist Richard Hoagland postulates that the "Pyramid City" and the Mars face found in the Cydonia region of Mars are part of an enormous extraterrestrial message constructed by a group of extraterrestrials called the Annunaki 500,000 years ago. According to Hoagland, the "Mars City" was the first base of the Annunaki before they came to earth. An-nun-aki literally translates to 'those from heaven to earth came'. This group of space travellers was led by Enki, the father of Thoth, who was the founder of the Peacemakers. It was Enki, according to Zecharia Sitchin, who genetically altered humanity, and taught us the secrets of sacred geometry – the universal language of the gods.

As Hoagland's breathtaking research continued, he discovered that the Mars face was not the most important celestial message in the Cydonia region. These structures are 'flags' which are meant to attract us to something much more important – a five-corner, bisymmetrical pyramid whose top points to the face, which Hoagland calls the "D & M Pyramid" in honor of its discoverers DiPeitro and Molenaar. Contained within the geometry of this pyramid was an astonishing discovery: Leonardo da Vinci's ancient sacred proportions of the human form. If da Vinci's famous "man in a circle" is superimposed over the outlines of the D & M pyramid the two conform! As Hoagland writes in *The Monuments of Mars* : "The D & M seemed to be *a striking geometric statement of the humanoid proportions* arrayed on an alien landscape almost in the shadow of the central 'humanoid' resemblance..."

Nostradamus seems to have been on top of this discovery in 1555. Century X, Quatrain 63 states:

> *Cydonia, Ragussa, the city holy to Hieron,*
> *the healing help will make it green again.*

This Quatrain either alludes to Sedona, Arizona or Sedona, USA (Cydonia, Ragussa) and the surrounding desert becoming green again or perhaps Nostradamus was prognosticating the greening of Mars. Considering 150,000 years ago Sedona was underwater, it is possible that one day soon it will blossom. If indeed Nostradamus is referring to the Martian city, he seems to be indicating that it too will soon be terraformed, perhaps for human inhabitation: "the healing help will make it green again." This process has been extensively explored by scientists including James Lovelock who wrote *The Greening of Mars*. Lovelock promotes the Gaia hypothesis, reaffirming the ancient belief that earth is a sentient being.

Nostradamus tells us Cydonia Ragussa is sacred to Hieron. Who is Hieron or Heron? The heron is the bird of resurrection and ascension who waited in the water for the first sign of Dawn. A related word, *heru*, also means 'face'. Heru is not only close to *hero,* but also it's close to the Indian *vira*: "applied to the king [pharaoh] as the representative of the sun-god on earth." Interestingly, the Egyptians told us the Sphinx (and by extension the person who reenters her sacred repository) was not only the King of Terror, but also "Fair of Face."

TETRAHEDRAL METAPHORS

Something astounding happened when sacred geometers including Erol Torun and Stan Tenen decoded the geometry of the Cydonia region. They discovered that the geometric code in the Cydonian geometry is identical to the sacred geometry of ancient Tula complexes including Teotihuacan in Mexico, the Great Pyramid in Egypt, and Stonehenge in England. Again and again they found "tetrahedral metaphors" matching those of Cydonia. Geometers discovered that if one fits a tetrahedron inside a sphere so that its apex coincides with the sphere's 'north pole', the tetrahedron's other three corners touch the sphere at a latitude of 19.5 degrees South. This is a remarkable discovery. Not only do many earthly temples lie at this latitude (North or South), but so do the highly volatile Hawaiian volcanoes. But that's not all. The gigantic, swirling red spot on Jupiter, the Schild volcanoes on Venus, the enormous Mars volcano Olympus Mons, the mysterious dark spot on Neptune and the central area of sun spot eruption are all located at a latitude of 19.5 degrees North or South. Some universal message is being illustrated here.

M.I.T. physicist Bruce Depalma has offered an explanation of the significance of 19.5. He believes that the rotation of these heavenly bodies, including earth, opens a 'gate' and that energy flows in from the 'void', a higher plane, another dimension or even from hyperspace. This energy is in a coherent form and it is exchanged between the dimensions at a latitude of 19.5 degrees.

With the discovery of this apparently naturally occurring phenomena, physicists maintain we have found a spigot of free energy. The proof comes from Neptune. In the autumn of 1989 when the Voyager II space probe passed this planet, scientists presumed it was made of ice. Astrophysicists were astonished to learn that, instead, it was a marsh of methane gases with erratic weather patterns and winds of up to 1,250 mph. Furthermore, Neptune radiates three times as much energy as it receives from the Sun! The only way to explain this is through tetrahedral geometry.

From these observations Hoagland and others concluded that the Cydonia structures appear to have encoded knowledge of a primal energy or light which is now a secret, but could potentially provide unlimited, free energy and revolutionize life as we know it.

Hoagland makes the astounding observation that the Martian pyramids could in fact be an intricately designed series of self-contained living environments plunked down in the middle of the "hostile" Martian atmosphere. In this scenario the Martian Pyramids are markers concealing a subterranean colony or base.

Hoagland based his theory on the work of "environmental architect" Paolo Soleri, who was among the first to propose the creation of *monumental architectural constructions* as a solution to urban crowding. Soleri envisioned enormous structures called "arcologies" or architectural ecologies capable of supporting entire populations and all the life support systems in a single subterranean structure. One of the design criteria for such a city (if it were solar heated) would be an orientation toward the rising sun. This is precisely the intelligent design behind the D & M Pyramid on Mars! If the Hermetic adage "as above, so below" applies to Mars, it would be reasonable to expect that the Martian Pyramid (Tula?) also contains a Hall of Records.

THE HALL OF RECORDS AND MARS

Zecharia Sitchin (*Genesis Revisited*) points out that the ancients attributed communication functions to the Sphinx (and the Hall of Records underneath it):

> *A message is sent from heaven;*
> *it is heard in Heliopolis and is repeated in Memphis*
> *by the Fair of Face.*
> *It is composed in a dispatch by the writing of Thoth*
> *with regard to the city of Amun . . . .*
> *The gods are acting according to command.*

The reference to the Sphinx as the "Fair of Face" and its role as a transmitter of messages makes us wonder what exactly the role of the Face on Mars may turn out to be. Is it possible there is a sister Hall of Records on Mars, just as there are pyramids nearby both the earthly and Martian faces? Perhaps this hypothesis will be proven in 1999.

CHAPTER ELEVEN

THE CAPSTONE AND THE PYRAMID PROPHECY

More proof that the return of the Peacemaker is imminent is contained in the Great Pyramid.

According to Peter Lemesurier (*The Great Pyramid Decoded*) and other authors, a Divine Plan and timetable for man's spiritual upliftment is spelled out in the Great Pyramid. This timetable of prophecies has a different specific emphasis than that of most prophecies. Prophecies usually state that an event is going to occur, but are vague about when it is to occur. The Pyramid, in contrast, indicates specific dates but not what the events occurring on those dates will be.

So much of the Great Pyramid's chronological prophecy has now been realized in history that the scale 1 inch = 1 year has been incontrovertibly proven. The evidence confirms a six thousand year system of prophetic dates, beginning in 3999 B.C.E, (the Age of Taurus the Bull) and ending in 2001 AD.

Max Toth (*Pyramid Prophecies*) projected that the end of the Pyramid's recorded time falls between July 1993 and September 2001. According to Toth, a Kingdom of the Spirit will emerge between 1995 and 2025 and higher spiritual goals and ethics will guide humanity. An entirely new civilization will emerge in 2025.

The Pyramid holds another explosive secret. The sides of the Great Pyramid were once covered with a fine surface of shiny, white limestone. Its four sloping sides originally merged at a point 481.4 feet above the limestone plateau of Giza. Today, the top (including the gold-covered capstone, or pyramidion) is missing and the Great Pyramid is 31 feet shy of its original height.

Where is this capstone today? Why do we care?

All fingers point to Thoth as the keeper of this secret. He was the one who held the plans and he knew who or what the capstone was. He foretold the completion of the pyramid in a chronology in its passageways.

THE PYRAMID PASSAGEWAYS

According to Robert Menzies of Edinburgh, Scotland, the passageways and chambers in the Great Pyramid hold the secrets of God's Divine Plan and its progression through the ages. In 1865 Menzies first proposed the theory that the proportions and measurements of the passage system in the Great Pyramid were a chronological representation of Scripture prophecy. Included in this prophecy was the birth and ministry of Jesus, 11,000 years before the fact.

Before Menzies' time, Scripture scholars had already noticed that the Bible revealed the purpose of the Great Pyramid. To support their idea that the Pyramid was a Bible in stone or even the House of the Messiah, they referenced many verses in the Bible containing allegorical references to the Pyramid.

The focus of the Pyramid chronology is the return of the Earth Teacher. The key Scriptural reference, which incontrovertibly upholds the divinity of the Great Pyramid, is found in Ephesians 2:20: "And are built upon the foundation of the apostles and prophets, Jesus Christ himself being the chief cornerstone."

This is but one of many scriptural text references to Jesus Christ as the living cornerstone, foundation stone, top stone, or capstone, and the Pyramid itself.

It is recorded in Matthew 21:42 that Jesus uttered these extraordinary words: "The stone which the builders have rejected [the one that isn't there] has become the chief corner-stone," and is yet to become the "head of the corner" (I Cor. 3:11, Eph. 2:20-22, 1 Pet. 2:4-5). The author of Matthew must have been directly referring to the Great Pyramid: it's the only type of structure that has a chief cornerstone. Furthermore, the most famous building in the world with a Divine purpose is the Great Pyramid. The missing cornerstone they are referring to is the capstone of the Pyramid.

According to Peter Lemesurier, the Messianic significance of the final placement of the capstone on the previously incomplete Pyramid is referred to in the book of Zechariah:

> How does a mountain, the greatest mountain, compare with Zerubabel? It is no higher than a plain. He shall bring out the stone called Possession while men acclaim its beauty . . . .

Zerubabel with his own hands laid the foundations of this house and with his own hands he shall finish it. So shall you know that the Lord of Hosts has sent me to you. Who has despised the day of small things? He shall rejoice when he sees Zerubabel holding the stone called Separation.

Later, Zechariah 4:9: states: "The hands of Zerubabel have laid the foundation of this house; his hands shall also finish it..."

This extract, says Lemesurier, suggests that the building will be completed by the same person who laid its foundations – which, in the case of the Great Pyramid, would necessarily involve his reappearance. We know this person as the Peacemaker. As the precursor of the Earth Teacher, does this mean he will introduce the Earth Teacher's reappearance by putting the capstone on the pyramid, the Tula? Or is the capstone a reference to the return of the heron, who, perched atop the pyramid (the mass of humanity), will radiate light from its outstretched arms?

Zechariah refers to the Peacemaker by the title, 'Zerubabel' (*Bab-el* means 'the gate of God'). We recall that Thoth was the patron of gates, roads and pathways. Zerubabel is an exceedingly mysterious figure who appears prominently in the Old Testament as the supervisor of the rebuilding of the Temple of Solomon (the name Solomon means 'peace'), and in the New Testament as an ancestor of Jesus.

Current scholars say Zerubabel is nothing less than the first Messiah of the Jews. We have established this as the role of the Peacemaker. His partner in building the Temple is Joshua, in whom many have no trouble seeing Jesus. Zechariah (4:11-13) describes them as joint leaders of the Jewish community after the exile: ". . . a government divided equally between priest and prince." The relationship between them is exactly the same as that between Jesus and John the Baptist. Later in Zecharia, we learn they are "the two anointed ones who stand before the Lord of the whole world." (This statement reinforces the notion that the Peacemaker and the Gardener work on behalf of the third concealed figure.)

From Zecharia it becomes clear that Zerubabel's mission was to construct a physical Temple which would exemplify the covenant or bond between heaven and earth. In our words, he was sent to build a Tula. It would be an outward symbol of the inner spiritual process or teaching that created this bond. Judaism, however, according to the prophets, took this physical symbol too literally. Thus, Zerubabel failed in his mission to create a spiritual bond with Tula. After Zerubabel's death Joshua took on the title of princely-messiah and attempted to make a go of it on his own.

Later, when Jesus and John the Baptist appeared, they took up where Zerubabel and Joshua left off. The failure of Zerubabel to create an 'Empire of the Spirit' led to Jesus' assumed insistence on not building an earthly Temple and the reinstatement of an ancient ideal: a new world order ruled by priest-kings or a priest in tandem with a king.

After John the Baptist's execution, Jesus attempted to fulfill their mission single-handedly. Here, we are reminded of the prophecy of the Mandaeans which stated that a secret Adam would one day return to earth and build a machine to transport the souls of earth back to the All-Father, or the King of Light as he is sometimes called. The Savior emanated from the King of Light. He is called *Manda d'Hayye* ('the Knowledge of Life') from which arose the sect's name. The Mandaeans are better known as Nazarenes. Jesus, we know, was called the Nazarene. They claim descent from John the Baptist and maintain that the soul is in exile on earth, a speck of light temporarily trapped in matter.

Jesus' attempts to introduce this new world order, based upon releasing souls from earth, aroused deep hatred and hostility from the ruling Roman governors and the orthodox Jewish establishment. Such feelings led to the death by crucifixion of at least three conspirators in this attempted fulfillment of God's longstanding plan for man.

THE NEST OF THE HERON

These Scriptures make it clear that there was a deep awareness among the ancient initiates that the Divine Plan for human evolution and spiritual upliftment was tied to the Great Pyramid. The secrets of the exterior symbolism, the interior layout and the missing capstone of the Pyramid were known and apparently guarded by many cultures.

This awareness spans cultures. The heron, the bird of resurrection perched atop the Pyramid, symbolizes the returning Christ and appears throughout the globe. The capstone of the Great Pyramid, as depicted on the Great Seal of the United States of America, even depicts the return of the heron. Is this symbol a prophetic warning or some sort of reminder for the Peacemaker? The Latin phrases on the Great Seal are ANNUIT COEPTIS meaning "He has looked with favor on our beginning" and NOVUS ORDO SECLORUM, which means the "new order of the ages."

47. The Great Seal of the United States.

CHAPTER TWELVE

MOSES

According to Jewish legend, the Peacemaker will bring Moses and the 'generation of the desert' (the Children of Light) back to life. The Peacemaker must also recover the Ark of the Covenant in anticipation of the arrival of the Messiah. The Ark of the Covenant is a communications device associated with Moses in the Old Testament. What's the connection between the Peacemaker and Moses?

It was Moses, we recall, who led the original Children of Light in the direction of the 'Promised Land' during the Exodus. Going beyond the Sunday School version of this story, we now realize the term 'Promised Land' is secret code for the ultimate human experience, the soul's return to Tula. Is there evidence that Moses led the 'Children of Light' to Tula and that this past experience is the true reason Moses reappears in our time?

In the next several chapters we will explore the connections (perhaps chilling at times) between Moses, the Peacemaker, the Ark of the Covenant and Tula. The astonishing revelation contained herein reveals that Moses worked on a Tula project in the past.

MOSES?

Poet, artistic innovator, madman, visionary, reactionary, law giver, instigator of monotheism and forerunner of Christ – all roles played by Moses, you say? Think again: this is *Akhenaten*, king of Egypt.

Akhenaten is the first person in recorded history to worship one God. The Bible assigns this distinction to Moses, but they are not rivals. Controversial but strongly supported archaeological and historical evidence (see especially Ahmed Osman's *Moses: Pharaoh of Egypt*) supports the contention that Akhenaten and Moses are one and the same.

48. Akhenaten.

This very ancient controversy was ignited in the 1930's by no less a personage than Sigmund Freud, the Jewish psychoanalyst. Freud began with the fact that *mos*, the source of the name Moses, is not Hebrew but is an Egyptian word meaning 'drawn from water' or 'a child'. It's interesting to note that a related Hebrew verb *maschah* means 'to anoint' and its derivative word, *maschiach*, means 'anointed' or 'Messiah'. The word 'moses' when understood in its esoteric Egyptian sense, means an anointed one who had been admitted into the Mystery Schools of Wisdom and the mysteries of life.

RESCUE FROM WATER

The story of the birth and childhood of Moses, in particular his rescue from water, directly links Moses with the priesthood of Doves. This story element is repeated in many myths relating the early lives of some of the greatest heroes in ancient times. Graham Hancock (*The Sign and The Seal*) noticed this mythic element is part of an overall pattern in the lives of great Teachers or Civilizers.

Hancock concludes that the meaning of the 'saved from water' element is to connect the hero of the myth to a lineage that existed before the Flood and that these heroes – including Moses, Jesus, Jonah, Sargon and others – are preservers and disseminators of antediluvian knowledge which would otherwise have been lost. More emphatically Messianic is the belief that the 'saved from water' element intimates a previous life in which these initiates had escaped the waters of mortality and were then returning to earth to liberate certain 'chosen ones'.

Hancock proposes that these individuals were members of an ancient brotherhood formed to disseminate sacred knowledge. He further proposes the name of the brotherhood to be the Cult of Thoth, a.k.a. the Peacemakers or the Doves!

Thoth/Enoch, we know, was the Atlantean priest-scientist who possessed the Key of Life, constructed the Great Pyramid as a Tula and built the Hall of Records. This leads us to the conclusion that the knowledge this brotherhood sought to preserve and disseminate originated in the days before the Flood: hence the 'saved from water' motif. If this is the case, the knowledge they preserve is the Key of Life and its repository is the Hall of Records.

This Atlantean dynamic I added to Hancock's truly brilliant hypothesis became even more plausible when we realize that many of the 'saved from water' figures also possessed the Key of Life, which was first given to Adam in the Garden of Eden/Atlantis. Thoth, Moses, Jesus, Sargon all carried the staff as a symbol of their authority as members of the Cult of Thoth, or the Peacemakers.

THE COMPANY OF 8

I am One that transforms into Two,
I am Two that transforms into Four,
I am Four that transforms into Eight.
After this I am One again.

–Egyptian creation myth attributed to Thoth

Before Thoth and Seshet left the earth they gave their wisdom and authority to their children, Tat and Isis, who formed a line of guardians to preserve and protect the secrets of the Hall and to continue their family's primary task – guarding the Key of Life. This is the cult of Thoth or, more properly, the Company of 8.

The Company of 8 preserves the ancient sacred knowledge contained in the Hall of Records beneath the Sphinx and Pyramid. Secretly, there is a ninth keyholder in this company: the Nameless One, the Earth Teacher.

This Company of 8 plus one appears throughout history.

The Maya called the navigators from Tula the Nine Lords of Time. This group was comprised of eight members plus a ninth nameless one. Arguelles clearly shows that these Lords of Time were navigators or mapmakers who left an intelligent code. This code is built into the elaborate pyramidal temples of the Maya at Tula. The Mayan Tula and others were built as receivers of a spiritual code from the primal or galactic Tollan or Tulan, their place of origin and the point of entry to this world.

Heliopolis (which, as we will see in a moment, is actually an ancient Egyptian Tula) was called the City of Eight. Here was the home of the *Ennead*, the company of nine gods and goddesses (8 plus the ninth member Horus, the Egyptian Savior) who represented the archetypal principles of the universe.

The number 8, the Ogdoad in Egyptian, symbolized the new world order of Christianity. According to Jewish tradition, when the Messiah returns, he will set up an eight member cabinet that will include the reincarnated Elijah. Eight members plus the Messiah makes nine members. Obviously, we are talking about the same eight member group of wayshowers who come to earth from time to time to introduce New Ages and to prepare the way for the ninth member, the Earth Teacher, Messiah or Christ, whose mission is to bring Tula (or 'balance') to earth.

I find it interesting that Buddha said that balance is the key of life. In his sermon at Benares (near the Deer Park at Isipitana) Buddha taught that the way to attain balance, liberation or enlightenment is through the 8-Fold Path. "It is the holy eightfold path which leads to the cessation of suffering: that is to say, Right belief, Right aspiration, Right speech, Right action, Right livelihood, Right effort, Right mindfulness, Right meditation."

Correspondingly, the Greeks honored 9 *muses*, who represented or preserved the arts and sciences. From muse comes our word *museum,* which may be thought of as a miniature Halls of Records. The invention of the seven-tone musical scale is credited to the Muses and was based on their 'music' of the seven spheres corresponding with the seven stars of the Pleiades. Interestingly, the Muses were led by Thalia, whose realm of expertise was music in general. The name Thalia rings of Tula and of a related word, Thule, which is Nordic for Atlantis or Tula.

In his book *The Mysteries of Chartres Cathedral*, Louis Charpentier suggests that Chartres is a repository for an ancient wisdom equal to Stonehenge, the Temple of Solomon or the Great Pyramid. He further claims that special knowledge about the Temple in Jerusalem was acquired by a group of nine knights who lived at Solomon's Temple. Charpentier goes on to say that in the year 1118 nine 'French' knights presented themselves to King Baldwin I of Jerusalem and explained that they planned to form themselves into a company with a plan for protecting pilgrims from robbers and murderers along the highways leading into Jerusalem. This Company also asked to be housed within a wing of the palace located near the Dome of the Rock mosque which was built on the original site of Solomon's Temple. The King gladly fulfilled their request and the Order of the Knights of Solomon's Temple (or Knights Templar) was born.

Charpentier describes this company of nine knights as a band of commandos who infiltrated the Temple of Solomon, decoding its engineering secrets and recovering the Ark of the Covenant which was believed to be hidden deep within its underground passages. These nine knights then went on to build the incomparable Chartres Cathedral, concealing the secrets of sacred geometry and possibly the secrets of Tula within its masonry.

CHAPTER THIRTEEN

MOSES: THE PEACEMAKER

In 1937, Sigmund Freud published an article titled "If Moses was an Egyptian." It dealt with the strange issue of why the Hebrew lawgiver, if he were Egyptian, would have demanded that his followers subscribe to a monotheistic God rather than the ancient Egyptian roster of gods. Simultaneously, Freud pointed out near identical points of contact between the new Egyptian religion introduced by Akhenaten and the new teaching concurrently offered by Moses.

Freud wrote: "The Jewish creed says: 'Hear, O Israel, the Lord thy God (Adonai) is one God.'" Freud argued that the 'ai' can be removed from the word 'Adonai' since it is a Hebrew pronoun meaning 'my' or 'mine'. Doing so, we are left with 'Adon' (Lord), which as Freud demonstrated, is the Hebrew word for the Egyptian 'Aten' (the Egyptian 't' becomes 'd' in Hebrew and the vowel 'e' becomes 'o').

The proof that Moses is Akhenaten is now right before our eyes. The name of the God of Moses, Adon, is identical to the name of the God of Akhenaten, Aten.

This is only the beginning, however. When we turn the pages in the life of Akhenaten the Anointed One, stunning revelations await.

THE LIFE OF AKHENATEN

Akhenaten was born in 1394 B.C. at the frontier fortress city of Zarw. He was of mixed Egyptian-Israeli descent, being the son of an Egyptian King, Amenhotep III, and Queen Tiye, the daughter of the Patriarch Joseph (of the multicolored dream coat). Akhenaten was also the grandson of Isaac (who was sold into slavery) and the great grandson of Abraham, who himself, as we have seen, may have a connection to the Peacemaker.

Abraham's bloodline is nothing short of sacred. Remember, Jesus was a descendent of Abraham. Because of his lineage, Akhenaten posed a threat to the Egyptian dynasty. His father had given the midwives attending Queen Tiye orders to kill the child if it were a boy. Upon learning this, Tiye sent her son to the safe hands of her Israelite family at nearby Goshen.

The Bible tells us Moses was raised as a virtuous prince by the Egyptians. A private tutor attended him at all times; and he also attended the great schools of the land, including the school at Heliopolis (City of the Sun). In fact, says the wisdom tradition, Moses became a High Priest of Heliopolis. In Acts 6:22 we learn that "Moses was trained in all the wisdom of the Egyptians." This is one of those 'simple' statements the Bible makes which upon further decipherment is absolutely astonishing.

Moses, the Bible is telling us, knew how the Great Pyramid was constructed, understood the mysteries of the Sphinx, and knew where the Egyptians (who seemed to have appeared from out of nowhere) actually came from. Moses knew the true reason why the Egyptian temples are aligned with Sirius. He could read the sacred writings from before the Flood. He was trained in the Key of Life, even using it to part the Red Sea.

It seems clear that Moses is not the doltish shepherd (who suddenly heard God speak to him from behind the bushes) that the editors of the Bible, that Hollywood and that our Sunday School teachers want us to think he is. Moses was a High Priest of Heliopolis. To appreciate the significance of this, a survey of Heliopolis will be helpful.

HELIOPOLIS – THE CITY OF 8

Heliopolis is one of the most mysterious places on earth, known in the Bible as On. It is also known that Thoth had a sacred sanctuary at Heliopolis. In fact, the Greek name for the city is Hermopolis after Hermes, the Greek name for Thoth. However, according to Rene Guenon (*Fundamental Symbols*), the true ancient name for Heliopolis was *Luz* (light), *Salem* (Peace) or *Tula* !

Now we are getting somewhere.

Heliopolis is a place just strange enough to be an ancient Tula. As if to confirm this fact, Thoth mentions in his Emerald Tablets: "Deep neath the rocks (at Heliopolis) is buried a ben-ben, waiting the time when man might be free." The key in this statement is the ben-ben.

What is the ben-ben? The ben-ben was a mysterious conical stone which was credited with cosmic origins. It was the "celestial chamber" in which the gods landed on earth. This relic of immense value was housed in the Holy of Holies of the Temple of the Phoenix in Heliopolis (the city of the Sun, again Tula). The ben-ben was the forerunner of the phoenix or heron, the legendary cosmic bird of regeneration, rebirth and calendrical cycles. It was believed that the phoenix came to Heliopolis, Egypt's oldest center of worship, to mark important cycles and the birth of a new age.

49. Ben-ben stone. (copyright Z. Sitchin, *The Twelfth Planet*)

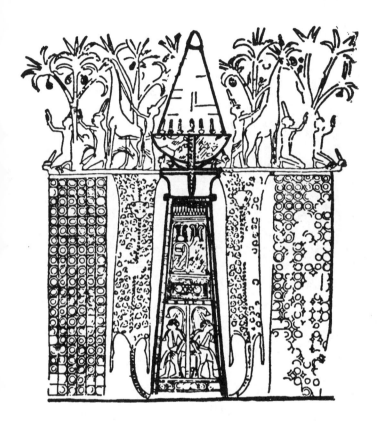

In ancient times Egyptians made pilgrimages to the shrine at Heliopolis to view and pray to the ben-ben. The ben-ben was thought to be the soul of Ra, who was the brother of Thoth. Later, this figure would be known in the Christian tradition as the Archangel Micha-El. What is most interesting about this is that the many illustrations of the opening of the mouth ceremony, the Egyptian ceremony of resurrection and ascension, show the mummy standing with its back to a small shrine topped by a ben-ben. In the Christian tradition, Micha-El guards the gateway to Heaven; Jesus shows the faithful to the gateway.

50. Opening of the mouth ceremony. (copyright Z. Sitchin, *The Stairway to Heaven*)

As Zecharia Sitchin points out in *The Twelfth Planet*, the most authoritative text on the subject, the hieroglyphic depiction of the "Temple of the Benben" looked like a massive launch tower. The original ben-ben has long since disappeared. However, it was depicted on Egyptian monuments as a conical chamber within which a god could be seen.

51. Ancient astronaut in command module? (copyright Z. Sitchin, *The Stairway to Heaven*)

Archaeologists have uncovered a small-scale stone replica of the ben-ben, depicted here with a god (or is it a goddess?) at its open hatch door beckoning with a welcoming gesture. The striking similarity in appearance and, no doubt, function to today's command modules is certainly thought provoking.

If the ben-ben was a command module, it only makes sense that there would be more than one. This would help explain an ancient mystery that today is surprisingly relevant. Around 2,000 B.C.E (about 700 years before Moses) the ben-ben was clandestinely removed from Heliopolis and an obelisk was built in its place. An obelisk is simply a pyramid on a long shaft. At this time a sage-priest to the pharaoh made the mysterious, offhand remark that "something was concealed within the pyramid."

Did Moses/Akhenaten learn what was concealed within the Pyramid?

In *The Sign and the Seal*, Graham Hancock observes, "as a High Priest of the Egyptian Temple Moses would undoubtedly have had access to a substantial corpus of esoteric wisdom and magico-religious 'science' that the priestly guilds kept secret from the laity." According to the wisdom tradition, Moses/Akhenaten discovered what was concealed within the Pyramid. He may even have made use of it.

Is it possible Moses located the secret sanctuary of Thoth, otherwise known as the Hall of Records? Did he remove a ben-ben and travel to the heavens, perhaps to Tula? The Bible does not say so in so many words; but, as we shall see in a moment, there is startling linguistic evidence to support this notion. While we cannot place Moses in a ben-ben, we can, however, link him with another mysterious, otherworldly 'transportation device' or time machine: the Ark of the Covenant. It is toward this that we now turn.

THE ARK OF THE COVENANT

The priests of Heliopolis preserved the legends and the artifacts of the gods of Egypt. Among these artifacts was a certain golden box into which Ra placed for safekeeping his most treasured (or perhaps most powerful) earthly possessions – his staff, a lock of his hair, and his Uraeus, a golden cobra topped headdress which symbolized mastery over time and space (his ability to incarnate and reincarnate at will). Many believe this 'golden box' was, in fact, the Ark of the Covenant.

In the Bible, the Ark is described as a golden throne built so that a person could sit in the 'mercy seat' between the cherubim and communicate with the Lord. The cherubim catch our attention. These winged guardians often appear in religious contexts, especially around the Tree of Life, the link between heaven and earth.

52. Ark of the Covenant

In Genesis cherubim were placed by Yahweh east of the Garden of Eden "to keep the way of the tree of life" (Gen. 3:24) – meaning they were to act as intermediaries between the human and divine realms. In other words, the cherubim guard the mysteries that lead us to Tula.

Coincidentally, two winged beings are featured on either side of the seal of Ningishzidda, (whom the Egyptians called Thoth) as shown on King Gudea's cup. These cherubim guarded the secrets of heaven.

53. Seal of Ningishzidda, the Peacemaker

54. Assyrian 'angels' guard the Tree of Life.

Outrageous stories and legends surround the Ark (some even more powerful than its depiction in *Raiders of the Lost Ark*). The Old Testament shows this cranky device blazing with fire and light, causing cancerous wounds and radioactive burns, leveling mountains, halting rivers, devastating whole armies and wiping out entire cities. It was eventually placed in Solomon's Temple (and subsequently stolen from here) without its purpose being fully understood.

Or was its purpose known and, like the modern day discovery of the atom, concealed to all but a few?

The word used in the Old Testament to describe this sacred coffer is *aron*, which is similar to the Hebrew word for enlightenment. Is this the meaning of the two cherubim? Are they the guardians of enlightenment? Was the Ark, as the ancients maintain, a source of enlightenment?

There is an additional non sequitur involving the Ark which is worth mentioning here. The sole purpose of constructing the Temple of Solomon (which, by the way, no one has conclusively located) was to house the Ark. Over a period of a thousand years this Temple – built by a man whose name, SOL-OM-ON, contains three ancient names for the Sun – was destroyed, rebuilt, and destroyed again. During this entire period, the Ark of the Covenant was missing. Even though it is the single most important artifact in the Bible, its disappearance isn't explained therein. Where did it go?

We cannot be certain. At this point it is worth noting, however, that the volume of the empty sarcophagus in the King's Chamber of the Great Pyramid is identical to that of the Israelite's Ark. Since Ra is reputed to be the engineer of the Pyramid, his 'golden box' would likely fit these dimensions as well. Is it possible the ancient High Priests reclaimed their magic golden box and returned it to its original home in the King's Chamber of the Great Pyramid?

THE KING'S CHAMBER

The King's Chamber is one of the most powerful places on earth. In the esoteric sense it was treated as both a womb and a tomb. It is believed that the Ark of the Covenant was setup in this room and used for the most sacred of ceremonies, the transfer of souls to Sirius. By this rendering, the Ark was a device which opened gateways in space and thus facilitated easy access to other worlds. The initiates of ancient Egypt, including Moses, passed through this mystic chamber. They entered as men and women; they exited as something more.

In *The Secret Teachings of All Ages* Manly P. Hall provides insight into the mystical use of the Great Pyramid and the experience shared by the illumined ancients. An unidentified entity called "the Illustrious One" or "the Initiator," dressed in gold and blue vestments, carrying in his hand the *sevenfold key of eternity* (the Key of Life), is said to dwell in some undiscovered chamber of the Pyramid. This being is also referred to as "the Holy One," and "the lion-faced hierophant" and is thought to have never left the Pyramid.

The mystery of mysteries was unfolded to the neophyte by this teacher. The process whereby the individual divine spirit is separated from the material body was revealed as was divine name, the Ineffable Name of God. This "most high secret and unutterable designation of the Supreme Deity" is the knowledge through which man and God are made one. With the receiving of this name, the initiate became spiritually enlightened. This name is also needed to gain entrance into the Hall of Records.

Manly P. Hall describes the ritual enacted in the King's Chamber. "The King's Chamber was . . . a doorway between the material world and the transcendental spheres of Nature . . . Thus in one sense the Great Pyramid may be likened to a gate through which the ancient priests permitted a few to pass toward the attainment of individual completion."

Does this explain how Moses and, perhaps, the early Peacemakers, including Enoch, traveled to the heavenly Tula?

According to the legends of the Hebrews, the present-era Peacemaker must recover the Ark of the Covenant in anticipation of the arrival of the Messiah. Could it be he does this in order to 'soul travel' to Tula as did the ancients?

Moses, reputedly, received instructions for the construction of the Ark after his journey atop 'Mount Sinai'. What if, as the Egyptians maintain, the Ark already existed and it was the means to travel to Sinai and Moses located this transportation device within the secret chambers of the Pyramid?

If this were the case, a reevaluation of Sinai is in order.

SINAI

In the biblical book of Exodus the tale is told of Moses ascending 'Mount Sinai' to meet Yahweh. This is another Sunday School fairy tale. Two facts reveal what was truly occurring in this episode.

First, Sinai means 'twin mountains'. Twin mountains, say the Egyptians, is another name for Tula. It was often represented as two cones or two tablets.

Second, the Greek and Latin word for tablet originated from the Sumerian TAB-BA-LI, 'twin cone'. In Hebrew and Muslim thought 'the mountain of paradise' is a double mountain.

As we have already noted, the symbol of the twin cones or twin mountains is global, if not universal. From ancient Sumeria to Mexico, the central sun, the Tula, rests upon twin peaks. The Delaware Indians of America call this land the **TaLegA** country. The Delaware pictograph for Talega is identical to the Egyptian symbol for Tula.

If the two tablets refer to a journey to Tula, this leads to the vital question of what, exactly, Moses brought down from Mount Sinai (Tula). Tradition says that when Moses went to the top of the mountain he was given *stone tablets* with a *body of teachings* inscribed upon them *including* the Ten Commandments. These commandments are a clue meant to guide the seeker in the direction of ancient Egypt for these ten laws – abided by the Hebrews – had been in existence for millennia. They first appeared in the Egyptian *Book of the Dead* which is thousands of years older than Moses. Spell 125 contains the following negative confessions which are spoken to the god at the gates to heaven:

> I have done no falsehood,
> I have not robbed,
> I have not stolen,
> I have not killed men,
> I have not told lies.

The Ten Commandments are identical to these confessions, only they are phrased as "thou shalt not" admonitions such as :

> Thou shalt not steal,
> Thou shalt not kill.

When Moses came down the 'mountain', he found the Israelites were worshiping a golden calf. In itself this is not unusual. These people lived during the last breaths of the Age of Taurus the Bull – an age which began around 4,000 B.C. The bull featured prominently in the rites, religions and cultures of this era.

If one reads between the lines, it is easy to see the Israelites did not want to go stampeding into the new Age of Aries the Ram, a situation not unlike present-day Christians resisting our own change of Ages. Nor is it unlike the time of Christ, who came to lead humanity out of the Age of Aries into the Age of Pisces.

Unable to convince his 'chosen people', it is said that Moses was so angry that he smashed the tablets containing the 'divine blueprint'. Later, according to Exodus, the Lord told Moses to make two new tablets to re-place them and to build an Ark of the Covenant to house these new tablets. Then, once again, Moses revisited the peak of 'Sinai' and returned with a new set of tablets. If not commandments, then what exactly did Moses bring down the mountain with him on these new sacred tablets of stone? We are told these 'tablets' contained a 'divine blueprint'. As we have established with Enoch, whenever a prophet journeys to Tula his purpose is to return with the pattern for the new Tula.

If Moses followed the pattern of this ancient myth, we may conclude that, when he ascended 'Sinai' the *first* time, he went to the heavenly Tula and was given a plan or pattern for a new earthly Tula. When he returned, he sought to build this temple and to establish a new world order during the Age of Aries. However, the Israelites were deeply entrenched in their worship of the golden bull, the symbol of Taurus the Bull, and of the previous Age. He smashed this set of tablets and had to get a new set.

TIAMAT

On his second trip, Moses may have returned from 'Sinai' with something other than tablets. An explanation for what this might have been is recorded in the legends concerning Tiamat. According to the Sumerians, a thirteenth planet called *Tiamat* once existed in our solar system. The subsequent destruction of Tiamat resulted in the creation of earth and the asteroid belt (which is unexplainable by astronomers). In mythology, Tiamat was the Goddess Mother from whose body the earth sprung. In the Bible she appears as the Deep (Genesis 1:2) and was personified as a womb.

By most accounts, Tiamat was the victim of a planetary holocaust: she was destroyed by another planet, Marduk. The myth relates that Tiamat had chosen as her king the ruler Kingu rather than Marduk. Hence, Marduk destroyed her out of jealousy:

> *She (Tiamat) exalted among the gods, her sons, that she had born, Kingu, and made him greatest among them all ... placed him on a throne, saying, by my charm and incantation I have raised thee to power among the gods. The dominion over all the gods I entrusted to thee. Lofty thou shalt be, thou my chosen spouse; great be thy name in all the world.*

Tiamat then gave Kingu the Tablets of Destiny and the authority to rule over all the other gods.

It is important to realize Kingu, like Thoth (the Peacemaker), was identified with the moon. Myths say that it was from Kingu's blood, or "living waters," that the first man on earth was created. The Chaldeans called Kingu *Sin*, the Moon-god of Mount Sinai. Like Thoth, Sin was born of Inanna. In *The Woman's Encyclopedia of Myths and Secrets*, Barbara Walker writes, "The god Moses met on Mount Sinai claimed to be the god of Abraham, though he said Abraham knew him by a different name (Exodus 6:3). In fact, Abraham may have been the same deity. Very ancient documents used the name Abraham or Ab-ram as a synonym for Ab-Sin, Moon-father." Jesus, a descendent of Abraham, was called Christ, or literally "healing moon man."

These seemingly disjointed connections form a startling picture if we ponder what association there may be between the Emerald Tablets of Thoth, the 'tablets' Moses received on Sinai and the Tablets of Destiny which Marduk murdered Kingu in order to possess. It is also worth shining this light on the tablet of the Hopi Indians, a piece of which the returning Peacemaker possesses. Once the Peacemaker's piece is joined with the rest of the tablet a divinely inspired world peace will ensue. What do these 'tablets' represent?

One extraordinary explanation may be found in the work of Rabbi Yonassan Gershom whose book *Beyond the Ashes – Cases of Reincarnation from the Holocaust* documents stories of those who died at the hands of the Nazis and have now, he believes, returned with a special mission. According to Rabbi Gershom, the real reason behind the imprisonment and persecution of the Jews in World War II is far more cosmically significant than has been previously apprehended.

Gershom believes that the Jews were a group of souls called *Tikkun Olam*, which translates literally to: Repair the World. It could also be translated as 'planetary healers'. These planetary healers have the job of keeping time and space in balance. They raise the vibrational quality of the earth in anticipation of the arrival of the Messiah. By another rendering, the Planetary Healers are, in fact, a 'collective messiah' or 'collective Christ'. Showing the lesser evolved souls the way to the Tree of Life is the task for which they are chosen.

Gershom maintains that the Covenant on Sinai (Tula?) was a cosmic event in which the Planetary Healers pledged their allegiance to God and to uphold this world. After this pledge, they achieved victory over the Children of Darkness. Throughout history, whenever evil attempts to assert itself on earth, the planetary healers are the first to intervene. This is the reason why Hitler and other dictators have sought to persecute or destroy the Planetary Healers first. If they can first be eliminated, then the forces of evil can break down the spiritual energies or 'thoughtsphere' protecting the planet.

If this rendering is correct, when Moses/Akhenaten ascended Sinai/Tula his purpose was to renew the agreement between one group of souls, the Planetary Healers, to come to earth to uplift the spiritual vibration and show the way home for their brethren – those souls who suffered the destruction of Tiamat. In this scenario, the green stone or Emerald Tablet of the Peacemaker may well be a remnant of the exploded planet Tiamat. If so, the stone's energy would likely contain powerful memories of this destruction and the fateful course chosen by this civilization. Given that souls, no matter how advanced, are thought to take the vow of forgetfulness before reincarnating on the earth plane, reacquiring this hunk of green stone would serve as his wake-up call, triggering the most deeply embedded soul memories.

I will go further with this theme in *The Gardener and the Tree of Life*, a later volume of this series which details the means by which the Planetary Healers were brought to earth. For the moment, it is fascinating to compare the myth of Tiamat and the Planetary Healers with that of the Holy Grail and, more recently, Superman. In each story children are marked from birth with an extraordinary destiny which is centered around a mysterious green stone of heavenly origins which initiates an awakening of consciousness upon its discovery. (While the Peacemaker was not 'marked from birth' with extraordinary physical abilities, he does have a mark on his thigh which, once decoded, is his 'open sesame' to expanded mental abilities.) In these stories, the respective heroes enter the Fortress of Solitude (Superman), the Grail Castle (Sir Galahad), the Labyrinth (Theseus) or the Tula (the Peacemaker) where they learn the healing secrets of the green stone. In each story the hero is tempted to disavow his powers and his service to the earth for the love of a woman.

Back to Moses/Akhenaten. As we know, Moses/Akhenaten was the leader of the Children of Light. Like other Peacemakers, Akhenaten found the Children of Light in danger of being destroyed by the forces of darkness. As we know, from one of his ventures to Tula he returned with plans for the construction of an earthly home for the Planetary Healers, a place of protection and hermitage. What became of the plans for the construction of Tula? Were they truly smashed? No, they were enacted! A Tula *was* built by Moses, in Egypt. It existed for six years and was destroyed by the evil Amun priesthood.

The extraordinary story of this Tula (and the woman who helped Akhenaten build it) is told in the next chapter.

55. Caduceus.

CHAPTER FOURTEEN

AKHENATEN, NEFERTITI AND TULA

The scene is Egypt circa 1,500 B.C. After spending his youth at Heliopolis receiving instruction from the priests of Ra, Akhenaten returned home to Thebes, the capitol of Egypt, at age 13.

When Akhenaten/Moses was 21 he married Nefertiti, daughter of the powerful priest, Ay, and Akhenaten's half-sister. Their marriage was one of political expediency. Still, this charismatic royal pair would forever change the face of history.

Surviving records indicate that Akhenaten cared deeply for his wife. Her name meant 'the-beautiful-woman-has-come'. A boundary stela Akhenaten created for Nefertiti describes her as: "Fair of Face [like the Sphinx?], Joyous with the Double Plume, Mistress of Happiness, Endowed with Favour, at hearing whose voice one rejoices, Lady of Grace, Great of Love, whose disposition cheers the Lord of the Two Lands." He called her *nfr-nfrw-itn*, 'exquisite Beauty of the Sun-Disc (Tula)' for short.

Shortly after his marriage to Nefertiti, Akhenaten's religious beliefs began to solidify. His confidence grew and with it his belief in the one God, Aten. When Akhenaten began constructing temples to his God, Aten, at Karnak and Luxor, things began to heat up between Akhenaten and the ruling Amun priesthood.

The Amun priesthood was an evil force bent on spiritually enslaving humanity through incomplete spiritual teaching. (It was the Amun Priesthood, according to occultists, who were responsible for the destruction of Atlantis through the misuse of spiritual forces.)

As tensions escalated, Queen Tiye stepped in and suggested Akhenaten move to the area of Thebes, two hundred miles to the north, and build his utopia there. Akhenaten acted on this advice.

56. Queen Nefertiti

Historians are still trying to discover exactly where or why Akhenaten got the idea to build a holy city. He could have stayed faithful to the his culture's traditional religion and lived the life of a prince. The most reasonable explanation I can conjure for this seemingly bizarre behavior is that Akhenaten, who is Moses, took a 'ride' in the Ark of the Covenant, spent time training with the Lord, and came back with a new teaching and a divine blueprint for the construction of a utopia, a city for the Lord, a Tula.

Whether this theory is correct or not, it remains clear that Akhenaten and Nefertiti together built a holy city called *Akhetaton*, The Horizon (or resting place) of the Aten, where Akhenaten's inspired teaching would be taught.

The symbol used to denote Akhetaton, rays of the sun flowing from a circle into the Key of Life, combines two ancient symbols for Tula. This could be simple coincidence. With the exercise of a little imagination, however, one can envision Moses/Akhenaten and Nefertiti as the consciousness of Thoth and Seshet, the husband and wife team of Peacemakers who supervised the construction of the Great Pyramid and the Hall of Records and who, 700 years before, had appeared as Abraham and Sarah, the founders of Israel.

In this regard we have to wonder: is Akhetaton Tula?

The remains of this city, spread over many miles, have been located in an area known by its modern name *Tell el-Amarna*. This name should catch our attention. In his book *Tell el-Amarna*, published in 1894, Sir Flinders Petrie wrote: "The name . . . seems to be a European concoction. The northern village is known as Et Till – perhaps a form of Et Tell, the common name for a heap of ruins." This may well be. It is, however, quite provocative that Tell El-Amarna can easily be reduced to T-L-A.

The building of this city for the "world's religion" took four years to complete. Enormous resources were devoted its construction. When several years later Akhenaten's father died and he was made full regent over all of Egypt, Akhenaten moved the capitol of Egypt to Tel El Amarna. The motive behind this shift was to cut off the power of the Priesthood of Amun in Thebes, the former center of power in Egypt. In so doing Akhenaten moved not just the center of Egypt to his city, but also the center of the cosmos.

Akhenaten declared the worship of the many gods of Egypt to be illegal. He ordered the roofs torn off the temples so that the corruption of the church could be exposed. There were only two temples which remained untouched by Akhenaten, the Sphinx and the Great Pyramid. Is there any wonder why this was the case?

Akhenaten's actions threw all of Egypt into chaos. From this point forward he was called the Heretic King, a name very close in intent to Nostradamus' King of Terror. By his will he wanted to replace the ancient polytheistic religion of Egypt with One God. Again, Egyptian history is mute as to where or why Akhenaten got this idea to erase the old pantheon of gods and replace it with one God.

The reason why he did this, however, is clear: Akhenaten's mission was to elevate consciousness among the Egyptians and to bring back to life the concept of the Messiah.

57. The ancient symbol for Tula is contained in the hieroglyph for Akhenaten's holy city.

From the huge boundary stela marking the limits of the city it becomes clear that Akhetaton was the house of the Messiah. The stela proclaims: "As my father the Aten lives, I shall make Akhetaton for the Aten, my father, in this place."

Representations of Tula (the central spiritual Sun) and the process by which anyone, not just the priests, might contact Tula were commonplace at Akhetaton. A disk at the top of royal scenes extends its rays towards the king and queen, and the rays end at their hands, which hold the ankh, or Key of Life, acting as an accumulator of the 'force'.

Moses/Akhenaten spoke about a God that could not be seen. This God was represented by the Sun. It is absolutely ridiculous to consider that Moses/Akhenaten meant the Sun in our solar system. He was talking about the Central Sun, Tula.

Furthermore, Akhenaten invoked the Peace Theory. All men in Egypt were to be free, he declared. This was perceived by the priests of Amun as even more outrageous than the building of a city in which to teach a heretical new religion.

All of these actions, combined with cutting the financial resources of the Amun priesthood, caused massive turmoil. Egyptologists do not understand the crux of the conflict between the Amunists and the Atenists. The Dead Sea Scrolls revealed that there is a cosmic battle between the "Sons of Light" and the "Sons of Darkness." This was the battle that raged in Egypt fifteen hundred years before Jesus.

This escalating battle threatened to get out of hand. To restore order Akhenaten was forced to appoint his brother, Semenkhkare (who was about 20 at the time) as his co-regent at Thebes. This action cooled things down but only temporarily. Rumors in the royal court solidified into actual fact: a rebellion was underway. The Amun priesthood, now in control of the army, wanted Akhenaten's head on a platter.

With the country divided between Amun and Aten, a compromise was proposed by Akhenaten's minister and uncle, Aye – allow the old gods to be worshipped along with Aten. Akhenaten refused. He and Nefertiti were forced to abdicate the throne and flee for their lives. Along with a small group of followers and the staff of miracles (Akhenaten's symbol of authority), they disappeared into the Sinai Peninsula.

Akhenaten's successor, Semenkhkare, was murdered within a few days, and was succeeded by Akhenaten and Nefertiti's young son, Tutankhaten. As evidenced by the symbol of Tula on the back of his throne (found in his tomb in the Valley of the Kings), the new Pharaoh, like his father, worshipped Aten. As a compromise with the Amun priests, he reopened the ancient temples and legalized the worship and patronage of the ancient gods. As a final act of peace he changed his name to Tutankhamun recognizing Amun as the State god. Tutankhamun's tomb is, of course, one of most famous archaeological finds in history.

Tutankhamun traveled to the Sinai to meet his father and try to persuade Akhenaten and his followers to return to Egypt and live there in peace, but only if they accepted the idea that the gods of Amun could become angels who could help the Egyptians become closer with God. Tutankhamun was later tortured and hanged by the Amun priest Panehesy (on the eve of Passover) for betraying the religious beliefs of the Amun priesthood.

Ahmad Osman (*The House of the Messiah*) makes a very compelling case that the figures playing out this ancient Egyptian drama are actually Joseph of Arimathea (Aye, Akhenaten/Moses' uncle), Solomon (Akhenaten's father), Mary (Nefertiti) and Jesus (Tutankhamun).

If, indeed, Tutankhamun is Jesus, Akhenaten's plan for bringing the Messiah to earth in the form of his son, Tutankhamun, was a success. This possibility potentially explains many things. For example, shortly before his death, Jesus, along with three disciples, met Moses on 'Mount Sinai'. Previously we have been led to believe this was a symbolic meeting. In light of this hypothesis, the meeting of Moses and Jesus becomes an actual meeting of father and son.

How does this theory reconcile with the Bible? The Old Testament claims Joshua, who as we have seen teamed up with Zerubabel, was the successor of Moses. Therefore, it is no surprise that the early Church Fathers viewed Joshua and Jesus as the same person. This belief was anchored in Christian doctrine by the King James Bible (translated by a later Peacemaker, Sir Francis Bacon) where references to Joshua have an accompanying reference stating he is Jesus and vice versa.

If this were so, what becomes of the history told in the New Testament? In *House of the Messiah,* Osman states that the figure crucified fifteen centuries later in the New Testament was John the Baptist. This, says Osman, is just one among many of the cover-ups contained in the unpublished Dead

Sea Scrolls. When John the Baptist was killed it triggered the Essenes, who were waiting for the Second Coming of Christ, to proclaim that they had seen the Christ.

AKHENATEN AND SARA BETH-EL

After Tutankhamun was slain for worshiping Aten, knowledge of Tula was systematically erased in Egypt. The use of the name Akhenaten was forbidden on penalty of death and an effort at removing all possible traces of his existence was made. As a substitute for Akhenaten his followers began using *Mos*, the Egyptian legal term for rightful heir.

What became of Akhenaten and his band of followers? Akhenaten and Nefertiti fled into the Sinai to a place called Sarabit or, properly, *Sarabeth-el* (House of the Compassionate Breath of God).

Atop Sarabethel's peak Sir Flinders Petrie discovered an ancient Egyptian temple, a beth-el or House of God. While inspecting this temple he made a startling discovery: a *dark green* head of a statuette of Queen Tiye, Akhenaten's mother! What was it doing at Sarabit? What is the significance of its green color?

Petrie found other absolutely incredible evidence of Akhenaten's presence in the temple at Sarabethel, all of which has led scholars to conclude that Akhenaten lived at Sarabethel for more than twenty-five years before he died. This evidence includes:

Stelae and other stones marking it as a sacred site.

Two cones made of sandstone identical in shape and size. (Two cones, of course, symbolize Tula.)

Three rectangular water tanks and a circular basin. These tanks make it clear that baptism or ablution was part of the ceremony conducted here.

And now, here is the most astounding discovery. At Sarabethel Petrie found a bed of "ash" amounting to more than fifty tons, which he concluded were the remains of burnt sacrifices over an extended period. According to Anthony S. Mercatante in his book, *Who's Who In Egyptian Mythology*, incense was burnt several times a day and hymns were sung to the God, accompanied by harps and other instruments. The offerings to the God consisted of fruits and flowers; there were no animal sacrifices.

There must be another explanation for this ash. It turns out a rather startling explanation may be found in the King's Chamber of the Great Pyramid. Napoleon Bonaparte was deeply interested in the enigmas of the King's Chamber. When he invaded Egypt he brought with him 175 scholars and savants to attempt to crack its mysteries. These Napoleonic minions discovered tons of white powder within the sarcophagi in the King's Chamber. They had no idea what it could be. They collected it, put it in jars; and eventually it ended up in the British Museum. When this powder was analyzed in the 1960's it was discovered to be powdered human pineal gland. The pineal gland is thought to be the gateway to higher consciousness.

In Matthew 21:42-44 Christ is referred to as the chief cornerstone of the Great Pyramid. He is the stone which the builders rejected, and is yet to become the "head of the corner," (I Cor. 3:11, Eph. 2:20-22, 1 Pet. 2:4-5) – the head of the corner representing his Kingdom on Earth. In Matthew 21:44 Jesus states: "And whosoever shall fall on this stone shall be broken: but on whomsoever it shall fall, *it will grind him to powder.*"

Did Akhenaten use the Ark of the Covenant to conduct the ceremony of ascension and resurrection in this temple atop Sarabethel? Was this the true Exodus? And was this Exodus truly a mass evacuation of souls from earth?

CHAPTER FIFTEEN

THE HOPI INDIANS, THE PEACEMAKER AND THE CREATION OF WORLD PEACE

According to Jewish tradition, the Peacemaker will recover the Ark of the Covenant in our time. Before he does this and brings Moses back to life, the Peacemaker must create world peace. In this chapter, we will see how this feat is to be accomplished.

According to the legends of the Emerald Tablets, in approximately 1,500 B.C.E. (roughly the time Moses/Akhenaten was being persecuted by the Amun priesthood in Egypt) groups of priests were sent out from Egypt to other parts of the world. Among them was a group of priests who carried the Emerald Tablets.

This particular group of priests made their way to Central America and discovered an advanced, prosperous race, the Mayans. These priests settled among the Maya, teaching the Ancient Wisdom and storing the Emerald Tablets in the altar of one of the great temples of the Sun God.

The Hopi Indians are descendents of the Maya. They consider themselves as the first inhabitants of America and still live in villages in the high plateau country of the Four Corners area where Arizona, Colorado, Utah and New Mexico meet. Their name literally means 'the peaceful ones'.

The Hopi believe they were a Chosen People saved from the world previous to this one, the 'fourth world', before it was destroyed by the Flood. To insure their survival the Hopi were led 'underground'. The Hopi term for the tunnel passage leading to and from different worlds is *sipapu*. According to Jose Argüelles (*The Mayan Factor*) the sipapu doesn't just lead to safety underground; it also acts as a "lifeline or thread linking not only the galactic core (Tula), star systems, and different planets, but linking different world eras as well." Physicists might call this a wormhole.

Frank Waters *Book of the Hopi* chronicles their beliefs. When the Hopi Indians emerged from the sipapu into this new Fourth World, Massau, their guardian spirit, gave them a *sacred tablet* outlining their way of life.

According to Waters, this important tablet is the Fire Clan Tablet. This four inch square tablet is made of dark stone. It has a piece broken off from one corner. The symbols on both sides represent the prophesy of Massua.

They say a time would come when the Hopi would be overcome by strangers. They would be forced to develop their land and give in to the rules and dictates of a new ruler. The Hopi were told not to resist but to wait for the time when the true white brother delivered them from persecution. The true white brother, Pahana, will return with the missing piece to the tablet. Massua warned that if any leader of the Hopi accepted any outside religion he must have his head cut off to dispel the evil this act would bring upon his people.

The Hopi believe we are near the end of this world and the beginning of a great new Age. They believe in an ancient sign that an eagle will land and this will herald the beginning of the new world. This prophesy, once ambiguous, was elucidated in 1969 when the first words spoken by man on the moon were: "Houston ... this is tranquility base. The eagle has landed."

58. The Seal of Apollo 11. On the reverse side of the Great Seal of the United States the eagle is shown with thirteen arrows in one talon and an olive branch in the other. The Hopi believe the arrows symbolize the enslavement and genocide of the American Indians. The olive branch represents the enslavement of the black race. When the eagle on the Apollo 11 insignia was shown landing on the moon without the arrows, it represented to the Indians their release from bondage.

In 1979, believing the end times had arrived, the Hopi began releasing their secret prophesies. The Hopi believe in order to preserve human life we must discover the Great Spirit's Life Plan (written upon the Emerald Tablets) and work to uphold it. Otherwise we will be destroyed by fire.

The Bible offers the identical prophecy in II Peter 3:10:

> ... the heavens shall pass away with a great noise, and the elements shall melt with fervent heat, the earth also and the works that are therein shall be burned up.

Many interpret these prophesies to mean the earth will be destroyed by a fire from a nuclear detonation. Indeed an ancient prophecy that greatly disturbs the Hopi explicitly refers to the atom bomb:

> Some day there will be a road in the sky and a machine will ride this road and drop a gourd of ashes and destroy the people and boil the land.

A more hopeful interpretation of these prophesies of the "heavens passing away" and of a "great noise" is that they signify the new vibratory rate that will cleanse and purify the earth. Such a purification could be called 'fire' since it is directly connected with magnetism, vibration, frequency, cosmic rays, etc.

INRI

On the front of the cross on which Jesus was crucified is inscribed INRI, exoterically translated as Iesus Nazarenus Rex Iuderorum (*Jesus of Nazareth, King of the Jews*), but esoterically translated as: Igen Natura Renovatur Integra (*By Fire Nature is Renewed Whole*).

The Hopi and Christian traditions are deeply connected. The link is the Essenes, the Jewish sect out of which Jesus emerged. Exploring these connections opens the mind to fresh insights.

In his *Secret Teachings of all the Ages*, Manly P. Hall states the Essenes were the holders of certain guarded secrets. These secrets have to do with the destruction of Atlantis. The Essenes were initiates; they probably did not live through the Flood themselves, but likely are the descendents of such survivors. The secrets they held, perhaps the Emerald Tablets or the keys to resurrection and ascension, were passed down through the generations of their priesthood during the long climb back to civilization.

At exactly the same time the Essenes were living at Qumran in Palestine, practicing their form of democratic community life based on the secret teachings of Moses (*Meshu*), the Hopi Indians (far across the world) were living an identical form of life and following the laws of their great master-teacher, *Massau*.

Massau is a word that is strikingly similar to the Aramaic *meshiha*, the Hebrew *mahsiah*, and the Greek *messias*. These words mean *anointed*. To the Hebrews, the *Messiah* is the expected king and deliverer; to the Christians, the *Messiah* is Jesus, the Christ; and to the Hopis, *Massau* is the deliverer and purifier who came before and who will return from the *east* as the 'true white brother' of all the Hopis, the peaceful ones.

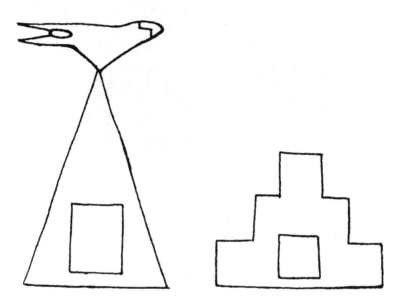

59. One of the ancient designs from Indian pottery found at Chevelon in the Southwestern United States. The triangle, with the rectangle and a bird-like figure surmounting the triangle, coincidentally represent the Great Pyramid. It does not take a lot of imagination to see some sort of flying vehicle in the bird-like figure. There is a bifurcated 'tail' and a 'head' that has an odd jagged line which makes it appear to be a nose cone similar to that found on the American space shuttle. The stepped pyramid below this pyramid is a variation on the smooth-faced pyramid. George Hunt Williamson, *Road In The Sky*. (London, Neville Spearman, 1959)

60. The rose granite sarcophagus in the King's Chamber of the Great Pyramid. The volume of the empty sarcophagus is identical to that of the Israelite's Ark of the Covenant. The King's Chamber in the esoteric sense was known as both a womb and a tomb. The initiates of ancient Egypt (including Moses, John the Baptist and possibly Jesus) passed through this mystic chamber. They entered as men; they exited as something more.

61. This Southwest American Indian jar shows yet another example of correspondence between the Egyptian and American societies. It clearly depicts the Great Pyramid and the rectangular sarcophagus in the King's Chamber and its link to the stars above – the heaven or Tula.

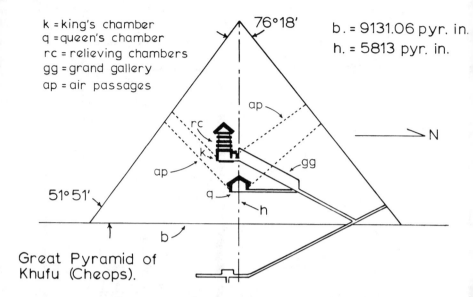

Pyramid = fire within

k = king's chamber
q = queen's chamber
rc = relieving chambers
gg = grand gallery
ap = air passages

76°18'

b. = 9131.06 pyr. in.
h. = 5813 pyr. in.

51° 51'

Great Pyramid of
Khufu (Cheops).

62. General outline of the known chambers inside the Great Pyramid. There are at least 30 suspected chambers within the Pyramid.

In her excellent book, *He Walked the Americas*, L. Taylor Hansen chronicles the travels of this Prophet she calls Pahana. From New Zealand, Tahiti and then the west coast of America, she traced his route to South America, through the Caribbean, and on to the Mississippi River where he traveled north to the Mound Builder civilizations of Illinois, Ohio, Michigan and then to the east coast. From there he continued north into Canada and then due west to the Olympic peninsula. He then turned south, heading down the coast of California and finally arriving in Arizona.

Everywhere he went this prophet (with blue eyes, blond hair and pale skin) performed miracles, healed the sick, taught the principles of peace and encouraged vegetarianism. One wonders if Pahana is the same as the Navajo Bakochiddy, a ruddy-faced god who took children to the 'white mountain'. White mountain, we recall, is an ancient synonym for Tula.

The Hopi claim there will be two forerunners to the return of the 'true white brother' who will herald his coming. One messenger will carry a swastika and the other a sun disk, which many interpret to represent Germany and Japan. In this regard it is interesting to read Revelation 11:3: "And I shall give my power unto my *two witnesses*, and they shall prophecy. . ."

In *Book of the Hopi* Frank Waters states that when the 'true white brother' returns to the Hopi, he will bear the missing corner piece of the sacred tablet, deliver them from their persecutors, and work out with them a new and universal brotherhood with the aim of restoring balance to humanity.

63 & 64. Hopi tablets and the Pioneer 10 message.

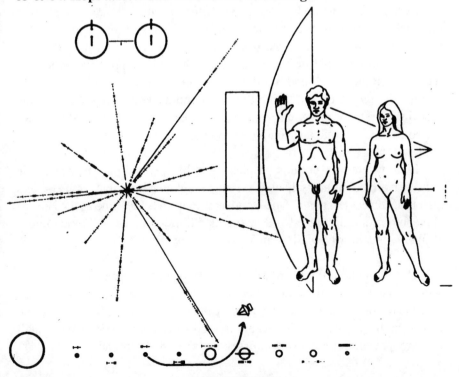

The Peacemaker

I have accompanied these illustrations with the Pioneer 10 message which was launched within the space probe and is heading toward the edge of our galaxy. This message is intended to provide a universal message about humans and the Earth which any intelligent species could decode. I show these side by side to demonstrate that the mystery I am presenting in this book cannot be solved purely by rational means. The truth behind the symbols is far more fantastic than what appears on the surface.

THE GATHERING FROM THE FOUR WINDS

The oral tradition of the Iroquois Indians relates a story that corroborates that of the Hopi. Their tradition tells of two stone tablets being given to the red, yellow, black and white races by the Creator before they split off into various parts of the world. On each stone was carved the special gifts each race possesses.

According to Cherokee healer Lee Brown, world peace will not be possible until the four tablet holders, each representing one of the four directions ('winds') and races, sit in the same peace circle. In addition, Matthew 24 tells us that the angel of the Son of Man shall "gather together his elect from the four winds, from one end of heaven to the other."

After World War I, the indigenous peoples who asked to be represented at the League of Nations in 1920 were turned down. This meant the peace circle was open in the East, which to the Indians meant lasting peace would be impossible. World War II began a short time later. This prophecy says the keepers of the tablets from all four directions will unite and bring together their teachings at the end of this cycle. The prophecy warns that, if these teachings are abandoned, complete destruction of humanity will result.

The keepers of the ancient tablets are the Oraibi Fire clan of the Hopi, who represent the red peoples (East); the Hopi believe the "true white brother" will bring his piece of the tablet when he returns. Tibetans hold the tablets belonging to the yellow race (South); the Kihuyu in Kenya, Africa, possess the tablets of the black race (West); and the Swiss have the tablets for the white race (North).

Are these tablets somehow related to Tula? Is it just coincidence the Hopi live near the Tula Rosa valley in Arizona? Or that the Kihuyu live along the banks of the Tula river? According to Edgar Cayce, the Iroquois who preserved this oral legend are descendents of Atlantis/Tula; in fact, they remember their place of origin as the Talega land. Is it possible bringing these obviously magical tablets together could spawn a force for divine peace? Can it be that simple?

Nostradamus clearly saw this possibility in Century VI, Quatrain 10 where he writes:

In a short time the colors of the temples,
the two will be intermingled with black and white.
The red and yellow ones will carry off their [possessions].
Blood, earth, hunger, fire maddened by thirst.

Here he is clearly telling us the four races will be intermingled. The last line – "blood, earth, hunger, fire maddened by thirst" – is one of the most fantastic Nostradamus ever wrote. American Indian tradition tells us it is the black race which preserves the secrets of fire. The white race knows how to grow food, or satisfy hunger, as evidenced by America's role as the 'bread-basket of the world'. The yellow race preserves the secret of blood, says the tradition, and the red race knows the secrets of the earth.

There are thought to be *eight* keyholders to the Hall of Records. According to the Talmud, when the Messiah appears, he will form his Company of Eight. Suppose each of the four tribes will send two representatives, one man and one woman. Given that the Sphinx is a composite beast of Man, Bull, Lion and Eagle and that these beasts represent the four "winds" or races, have we not just discovered the identities of those who will enter the Hall of Records? If so, might it be more appropriate to view the Company of Eight as the representatives of each of the Four Winds, of each of the four races, i.e, as Matthew, Mark, Luke, John and their wives!

Jesus' disciples asked him when the four races would gather and the Kingdom of God be established. Jesus said, "It will not come by waiting for it. It will not be a matter of saying, Here it is or there it is. Rather, the kingdom of the father is spread out upon the earth, and men do not see it."

In the next chapter we will meet a Peacemaker who envisioned this Kingdom of Tula in ancient America.

CHAPTER SIXTEEN

THE MAYAN PEACEMAKER

Much has been written of late about the mysterious Maya and their ancient myths and calenders. The Maya were an astonishing people who, according to Dr. Jose Arguelles, were galactic navigators from the celestial Tula that came to earth to lead us home.

By the Mayan calender, we are living in the fifth age of the sun. Prior to our present civilization there have been four previous suns or 'worlds'. Each of these worlds was destroyed by cataclysms in which only a few 'chosen' ones survived. Our present world began on August 12, 3114 B.C., and will end on December 22, 2012.

Many readers will recall the Harmonic Convergence of August 16, 1987. This is a Mayan date. However, it also appears in the prophetic chronology of the Great Pyramid at the threshold of initiation known as the Great Step. This date is *the* pivotal event in the Mayan calendar, for it is believed that was when the Earth reached harmonic resonance with the galactic core, Tula.

The prophet Edgar Cayce said the people who became known as the Maya were part of a massive exodus from Atlantis around 28,000 B.C. This statement takes an astonishing turn when we realize the Maya equated Atlas, the first priest-king of Atlantis, with Quetzalcoatl, their prince of light and King of Tula. They even depicted Quetzalcoatl holding the world on his shoulders!

65. Quetzalcoatl as Atlas

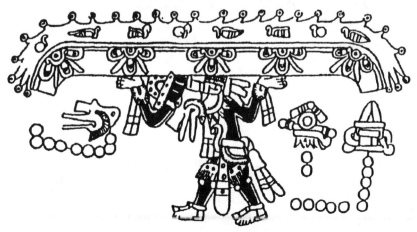

The Peacemaker

66. In Greek mythology, Atlas, the first priest-king of Atlantis, led his brothers in war against Zeus and was punished by being forced to carry the world on his shoulders.

Correspondingly, the author of the biblical Hebrews presents Christ as "upholding all things by the Word of his power."

The connection of Christ with the "Word" is found in several places in the New Testament where we learn God speaks in the Son and the Son upholds all things by his Word. The Book of John has two illuminating statements about this fascinating connection:

In the beginning was the word, and the word was with God, and the word was God.

–John 1:1

Man shall not live by bread alone, but by every 'word' that proceeds from the 'mouth of God'.

–John 4:4

Psalm 33:9 reiterates the power of the word: "For He spake, and it was done: He commanded, and it stood fast."

The Word has been interpreted as the life energy, the prana or Ch'i upon which everything is built. The word is also the power of the Key of Life, as symbolized by the entwined serpents and the dove. In Matthew 10:16 Jesus says: "Be ye therefore wise as serpents and harmless as doves."

67. Mayan Tree of Life.

Did Atlas, in upholding the world (word?) somehow play a role in delivering or representing the bedrock of Christian teaching?

This connection takes another hairpin turn when we discover that according to Zecharia Sitchin (*When Time Began*) Quetzalcoatl is none other than Thoth/Enoch! Without trying to confuse the reader, I also need to mention the Egyptians, in turn, said a person named Imhotep was the reincarnated Thoth.

In other words, Atlas, Thoth, Imhotep and Quetzalcoatl are all the same being. What is going on here? The stunning answer can be found through examination of Imhotep's life.

IMHOTEP

The Egyptians describe Imhotep as a sort of Leonardo da Vinci, brilliant genius, philosopher, doctor, and Prime Minister (to use our terms). His name, Imhotep, means 'one who comes in peace'.

During the reign of Zoser, Imhotep's primary temple was located near Saqqara at a place called the *Asklepieion* by the Greeks (this name will have astonishing ramifications for us in a moment). Here, he and his wife, Api (Thoth and Seshet?), taught the principles of healing through the staff. A second school was located at Heliopolis, where Imhotep is known to have used the healing rays of the Sun to effect cures. Likely, it was not the Sun (the star that warms the earth), but the central Sun, the spiritual core of our universe – Tula.

I am of the opinion (as are many mystic writers) that, in fact, Imhotep was Thoth. *The Virgin of the World* is an extraordinary treatise attributed to Thoth. It describes how Thoth, when he is not needed, travels back to the stars. When needed, he returns. *The Virgin of the World* identifies which persons Thoth has become during his incarnations. One such avatar is Imhotep.

As the reincarnated Thoth (or, at the very least as a member of the sons of Thoth or the Peacemakers), Imhotep would have had full access to the ancient wisdom preserved in the Hall of Records. In fact, a commemorative stele erected in Memphis by one of Imhotep's ancestors plainly states this to be so, describing his ancestor as: "he who calculates everything for the Library; who restores what has been lost in the holy books; who knows the secrets of the *City of Gold*."

More than all Imhotep's other accomplishments, his knowledge of the City of Gold strikes a deep chord if we are mindful and don't just glance over the implications. The City of Gold lay in the vast area called the Gobi Plains, also known to some as the Land of Mu. Legend recalls an architectural masterpiece once adorned this land, the House of Gold.

Myths that tell of the City of Gold stretch from China to Mongolia all the way to Egypt. Strangely, this myth also accompanied the bearded white men who became the gods of the Maya, Toltecs and Aztecs of Central and South America and who may or may not have been travellers from Asia.

Myths of these bearded white gods from Mongolia proliferate in the tales of antiquity. One such book postulates a large immigration of Mongolians into Mexico in ancient times. They were thought to have come from a kingdom in Mongolia called *Tollan* located near Lake Baikal and the river Tula. After a long sea journey, these Mongolians founded a new Tollan or Tula named after places in their homeland. These Mongolians identified themselves as *Nahuatlaks* and said they had come from Aztlan or Atlantis!

This is extraordinary because the Mayan word Maya means 'not many' – in other words, 'the few'. Another interesting connection is revealed by the fact that Maia was the mother of Hermes/Thoth/Atlas/Quetzalcoatl. Maia is one of the seven stars of the Pleiades. The meaning of the word Maya itself would appear to be quite consistent with the possibility that the Maya's remote ancestors may have been a small group of survivors of the Atlantean cataclysm, as Edgar Cayce has hinted.

In the name Quetzalcoatl, the last syllable *atl* is the Nahua Mayan word for water or twin. A number of Mexican place names (e.g. Tenochtitlan or T-Enoch-ti-Tlan) actually contain the word *Atlan*, while the Aztecs themselves always insisted they had come from an island home called *Aztlan*. Both words could easily be direct descendents of the name Atlantis.

Azt-lan ('White Place' or 'Place of Herons', the heron being the bird of resurrection) was believed to be the home of the Maya's 'Adam and Eve' where the antediluvian ancestors of the Maya are said to have originated. The Maya, however, didn't usually refer to their original home as Aztlan. Instead, the Maya called their home *Tollan, Tonalan,* or (and here's the knock out punch) *Tula*!

QUETZALCOATL'S TULA

The story of Quetzalcoatl (who is also Imhotep), Lord of Healing, relates how he came to earth to found an empire called Tula among the people of Mexico. Actually, he was rebuilding something which previously existed in another time and place. The *Popol Vuh* tells us the men who came from Atlantis with Quetzalcoatl called themselves 'Servants of God', or 'Sacrificers'. The scriptures they brought were called the writings of Tula.

It was noted earlier that a delegation of priests bearing the Emerald Tablets emigrated to South America where they found the Mayans. If the legends of the Emerald Tablets are correct, these must be the writings of Tula.

The *Book of Mormon* consists of such writings of Tula. Joseph Smith, the founder of the Mormon religion, translated the crossing of the Atlantic by the Jaredites from the 24 gold plates of the *Book of Mormon* given to him by the angel Moroni in 1827. Amazingly, Smith's story duplicates the story in the *Popol Vuh* which had not been translated into English until the 1950's!

THE FEATHERED SERPENT

Translated into English, Quetzalcoatl means Plumed (or Feathered) Serpent. Tony Shearer's *Lord of the Dawn* says the people of Tula had learned that the secret of peace was the unity of all things. From the Peacemaker, the people of Tula learned the philosophy of the Tree of Peace, sacred laws, and a way of life that entered into their inner hearts.

He entrusted his secrets to an order of priests who were diviners and prophets, who practiced the arts and sciences, healed the sick, and administered sacraments. In the religion of Quetzalcoatl, people learned not only how to raise kundalini but also how to open their heart to the light of the Central Sun – Tula.

As mentioned earlier, the Star of David is composed of two interlocking triangles. One signifies man reaching up to God; the other, God reaching down to man. The Star of David is a symbol of Tula and is sometimes found in its stylized form, the butterfly.

 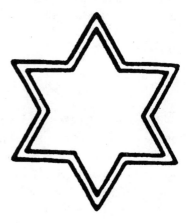

68. Star of David

69. Column from Tula with butterfly emblem.

This image is duplicated in the columns at Tula in the form of the feathered serpent. Here the feathers signify the Father (God reaching down to man) and the serpent signifies the Mother (man reaching up to God). Like the Star of David (on the esoteric level, at least) the 'feathered serpent' points the way for the initiate to harmonize heaven and earth and to develop enlightened consciousness.

Joyce Hargreaves (*Bestiary*) writes:

The Aztec plumed serpent is the most prominent symbol of Quetzalcoatl and represents conscious thought and intelligence. It is a combination of the Quetzal bird and the serpent, with the head and body of a serpent covered in Quetzal feathers. . . when the Lord of the Morning Star (as Quetzalcoatl was called) emerges in the morning, he comes forth out of the serpent that wears the feathers of the Quetzal bird. Quetzalcoatl is not the feathered serpent itself but one who emerges from between its jaws just as the Morning Star appears over the horizon.

70. Mexican sculpture of Quetzalcoatl emerging out of serpent's jaws.

71. Quetzalcoatl on pyramid, the Mayan symbol for Dawn.

72. Heron atop pyramid, the Egyptian symbol for Dawn.

The Peacemaker

Astonishingly, Jesus called John the Baptist a *herald* and the Morning Star. Thoth was also called the herald of the Morning Star. Legends, as well as popular texts, associate Christ's prophet with the planet Venus (the Morning Star). The prophet Isaiah wonders how he got to earth: "How are you fallen from heaven, O Day-star, son of the Dawn!" This means 'herald' or 'Morning Star' must be a name for the office the Peacemaker holds.

The New Testament states Jesus is the "bright and morning star" (Revelation 22:16). In the second epistle of Peter we are even encouraged to hold a place for Jesus in our hearts, "as a lamp shining in a dark place, until day dawns and the Morning-star rises in our hearts."

The Morning Star, the Peacemaker, holds darkness at bay until the coming of Light. Quetzalcoatl said he would return to close the last Heaven cycle (the fifth world), expected to end in 2012. As he departed, Quetzalcoatl told the people that, when he returned, he would come from the East, like the Morning Star.

THE PROPHECY OF THE PEACEMAKER'S RETURN

Zecharia Sitchin (*When Time Began*) records the actual arrival of Thoth/ Imhotep in Mexico as 3113 B.C. Thoth was coerced into exile after having a falling out with his brother Ra (Micha-el). The Egyptian *Book of the Dead* records the bitter exchange that led to Thoth agreeing to a sentence of exile: "I am departing to the desert, the silent land," he says, likely in reference to the Gobi desert. The myths surrounding the City of Gold maintain that it was a sexually 'restrained' society. Thoth remarks in the *Book of The Dead* that "sexual pleasures are not enjoyed in it...." After visiting the City of Gold he headed for Mexico.

The arrival of the Peacemaker in Mexico is regarded as the Zero Point for the Mayan Long Count calender. This date precisely coincides with the beginning of the present Hindu Age, the *Kaliyuga*, which began on a day equivalent to February 17, 3102 B.C. Since Thoth is universally connected with the calender, this cannot be a coincidence.

Lest we dismiss these dates as insignificant, it should be regarded that the major earth and celestial events that are due to take place between now and 2012 are directly related to this date of 3114 B.C. The Mayan calender is divided into 5,200 year cycles (52 is the sacred number of Thoth). On July 26, 1992 our planet entered the last 20-year segment of the 26,000-year Great Year, and the 5,200 year great cycle of the Mayan calender.

On August 11, 1999, earth will experience a total eclipse of the Sun which will herald the arrival of Nostradamus' King of Terror (shown earlier to be the opener of the Hall of Records). According to Raymond Mardyks – author of *Sedona Starseed* and an expert on the Mayan calender – this eclipse is directly related to another total eclipse that will happen November 13, 2012. This eclipse will be in alignment with the 13th constellation of the zodiac: *Aesclipius* the 'Serpent Holder'. Aesclipius is the Greek name for Imhotep!

According to Mardyks, Aesclipius is also unique by being the only constellation in human form that is in direct contact with the galactic core, Tula.

In *Sedona, Beyond the Vortex* Richard Dannelley makes an important observation. He writes:

> *As an interesting note in regard to the significance of total solar eclipses it should be noted that in 755 A.D. Mayan priests had predicted that during the eclipse of June 11, 1991, the 'masters from the stars' would appear in the valley that later became known as Mexico City. This prophecy was apparently fulfilled, as several individuals with video cameras recorded what appears to be a flying saucer hovering in the sky below the dark disk of the eclipsed Sun. This appearance has caused quite a stir in Mexico, and videos of this even have been shown on national television there.*

In this regard, the question must be asked: was this the return of the Company of 8?

CHAPTER SEVENTEEN

AMERICA: TURTLE ISLAND

America, many believe, is God's undertaking. It is the continuation of His covenant with Abraham, Isaac, and Jacob ('Israel') and the fulfillment of His promise to "assemble the outcasts of Israel, and gather together the dispersed of Judah from the four corners of the earth" in the process of creating Tula on earth.

The ancients called America Turtle Island. Why Turtle Island? The biblical Flood is believed to have occurred circa 10,000 B.C., or during the transition from the Age of Leo the Lion (11,000 B.C. to 9,000 B.C.) into the Age of Cancer the Turtle, an Age which lasted from 9,000 B.C. to about 6,800 B.C. Most astrologers associated the Age of Cancer with the crab, a sea creature, which like the turtle, a land creature, goes into its shell, symbolizing the going into and coming out of the earth and sea of those who survived the destruction of Atlantis (Tula).

As the American Indian legend states it was 'upon the back' of the turtle that the inhabitants of Turtle Island began to rebuild civilization. The incredible ancient mounds, including the Great Serpent Mound in Ohio and the great Monks Mound at Cahokia, Illinois, spread from the Mississippi Valley to the Gulf of Mexico are evidence of an advanced civilization that long ago inhabited this land. Monks Mound, which is located on the banks of the mighty Mississippi and within sight of the intriguing Gateway Arch of St. Louis (built on the 'pad' of another ancient mound) shows evidence of being formed around 9,000 B.C., within the same time period as the beginning of the Age of the Turtle!

This huge American pyramid (and that is exactly what it is only it's not acceptable to most scholars to describe pyramids in America) is over 1000 feet wide, 800 feet long, and 100 feet high. Its four terraces cover 15 acres, and are composed of nearly 22 million cubic feet of packed earth. A tablet found at Monks Mound depicts the transformation of a human being into some sort of bird being. Could it be that in the new world, as in the old, pyramids were sacred temples where initiates experienced the highest level of spiritual transformation?

The ancient architects who designed these colossal earthworks are unknown; but whoever they were they left a legacy and a prophecy that one day Tula would be rebuilt in America. The Peacemaker's mission in Mexico as Quetzalcoatl was but one more effort in the fulfillment of this prophecy.

Quetzalcoatl was known throughout Central and South America, appearing as *Viracocha* in his journey through the Andes, as *Gucamatz* in Central America, and as *Ameriguz* in South America. Quetzalcoatl was called *Gucumatz* in Quiche Maya; and in Peru he was called *Amaru*. From the latter name, says Manly P. Hall (*Secret Teachings of All the Ages*) comes our word America. Amaruca is, literally translated, 'Land of the Plumed Serpent'. The priests of this God of Peace once ruled both Americas.

When NAFTA was passed in 1994 America was reunited with Mexico for the first time in nearly two millenniums. NAFTA could easily stand for the New Atlantis Free Trade Agreement for it is an enormously overlooked fact of American history that our founding fathers believed themselves to be acting as agents of the Peacemaker's prophecy and the creation of a new Tula.

The notion of America as a new Atlantis was picked up from Quetzalcoatl and carried by yet another remarkable man with Peacemaker connections, Sir Francis Bacon, an English essayist, philosopher, statesman, and avowed occultist who is best remembered today as the Editor of the King James Version of the Bible. He served as the guiding inspiration for the Royal Society of London, a group dedicated to scientific study. Controversy still exists over whether Bacon wrote the Shakespearean dramas.

Bacon was supposed to be the last reincarnation of Saint Germain, an Ascended Master considered by some the greatest adept since Jesus Christ. As part of the Great White Brotherhood of adepts (whose white-light auras gave them the appearance of being robed in white), Saint Germain is thought to protect the wisdom of the ages, carefully sharing it only with those he trusts. This Brotherhood, working behind the scenes, is thought to be the impetus behind many great advances in religious freedom, scientific knowledge and political evolution.

As a Utopian, Bacon longed for the creation of a Golden Age where humanity could live without war and violence. He formulated a blueprint for this New Jerusalem – an advanced civilization with enlightened religious practices, advanced education and humane science. His life's work, *The New Atlantis*, (his magnum opus) was published in 1627 shortly after his death and the foundation of the British colonies in America. This work has been called a prophetic dream of the great civilization which was to arise on American soil: "a new nation, conceived in liberty and dedicated to the proposition that all men are created equal."

While Bacon's *New Atlantis* served as a sort of Bible for the founding fathers, it was yet another prophet of Tula, another Peacemaker, that the founding fathers secretly revered. In fact, if we lived during the Revolutionary War era of America and we mentioned the Peacemaker to Dr. Benjamin Franklin or Thomas Jefferson they likely would not have told you about Quetzalcoatl or Sir Francis Bacon. Instead, they would have told you a story about an Iroquois Indian named Deganawidah, who was also known as the Peacemaker. This Peacemaker acted as the bridge between Quetzalcoatl and Sir Francis Bacon. He is the founder of the Iroquois Confederacy, the first democracy in America. Like past Peacemaker's, Deganawidah's life story is the stuff of legend.

The legend of Deganawidah, in summary, follows. It was the year 1000 AD. Relations among humans in the northeastern region of North America are stuck in a barbaric hell. With his companion and mouthpiece, Hiawatha (not the same as Longfellow's fictional character), the Peacemaker emerges from this time of crisis and brings five fiercely antagonistic tribes together under a set of divinely inspired principles known as the Great Tree of Peace. (Today, that tree is the United Nations.)

THE GREAT TREE OF PEACE

The Great Tree of Peace embodies many noble ideas, including the following noted by Steve McFadden (*Ancient Voices, Current Affairs*):

> *The Giver of Life – the Creator – did not intend that people abuse one another. Therefore, human societies must form governments that prevent the abuse of human beings by other human beings and that ensure peace among nations and peoples.*

> *Peace is the product of a society that strives to establish reason and righteousness. "Righteousness" refers to the shared ideology of the people using their purest and most unselfish minds.*

> *Chiefs or leaders are the servants of the people. Everyone has a right and a responsibility to participate in the workings of the government.*

The Peacemaker also created a system of governmental organization that was a complex formulation of participatory, rather than representative, government. In accomplishing such a feat, Deganawidah is akin to Atlas and Theseus. The mythical king, Theseus, reorganized Attica as a confederacy of states, with Athens as its capital, and began to set up a democracy. Earlier, Theseus was depicted as the Peacemaker who sought to discover the way out of the Labyrinth of earth life altogether. It now becomes apparent that democracy is the appropriate foundation for a spiritually advanced civilization dedicated to freeing souls from earth.

As the Peacemaker, Deganawidah's concepts were way ahead of his time. Stories about him were widely circulated among the early colonists, traders and especially the missionary priests. His ideas migrated to Europe, influencing not only Francis Bacon but also Thomas More (and his vision of a perfect society as described in *Utopia*). John Locke and the great minds of the Enlightenment including Voltaire, Rousseau and Montesquieu were also deeply influenced by this Peacemaker. It is therefore a flat out corruption of history to say that the ideas for democracy were imported to America from the white man. These ideas were exported to Europe first and then brought back to the land where they originated and where they show greatest fruition.

Historian Gregory Schaaf (Ph.D, author of *Wampum Belts and Peace Trees: George Morgan, Native Americans and Revolutionary Diplomacy*) conducted fourteen years of research on the authenticity of this piece of history. Schaaf's work culminated in his 1990 testimony before the U.S. Senate Committee on Indian Affairs.

As a result of his convincing evidence and testimony, Congress passed a resolution that was signed by President George Bush. In the resolution, for the first time in history, the U.S. government officially recognized that the main ideas for the U.S. Constitution actually came from the American Indian people and that the very structure of U.S. government was "explicitly modeled after the Iroquois Confederacy" as designed by the Peacemaker.

The United Nations is also based on the principles of the Peacemaker's Great Tree of Peace. When its founders met in San Francisco in 1945, they scoured the planet searching for a model by which to design their body. They settled upon the Iroquois Confederacy. This thread will be followed in a later chapter.

THE PEACEMAKER REVEALED

Earlier, I mentioned Graham Hancock's identification of the 'saved from water' motif as pointing to Atlantis. Recall that Hancock noticed that Moses, Jesus, Sargon and others were all 'saved from water' or had a powerful water experience in their myth. It is important to note that each of these figures also possessed the Key of Life.

The connection with the Key was the starting point in piecing together a 'Peacemaker Profile' which includes eight mythological links to past incarnations of the Peacemaker. This profile is a template I have successfully applied to historical figures that I suspected might have Peacemaker connections. The foundations of this Profile are these questions:

1. Was the person called the Peacemaker;
2. Were they rescued from water or does their myth involve water;
3. Did they receive a teaching directly from God;
4. Did they emerge to lead their people during a time of crisis;
5. Did they carry the Key of Life;
6. Did they implement a democratic form of government;
7. Did they implement the Peace Theory;
8. Did they build Tula or clear the way for its creation?

When I applied the Peacemaker Profile to Deganawidah I was astonished by what I found. If I could successfully apply this profile to Deganawidah, I felt certain I could link him with Enoch, Imhotep, Moses, Jesus, John the Baptist, Quetzalcoatl and others as members of this spiritual brotherhood. From Enoch to Moses to Deganawidah is a long journey. Still, I set out to juxtapose Deganawidah with these other legends.

Deganawidah was clearly called the Peacemaker. He also received divinely inspired laws or teachings (the Great Tree of Peace) and through these teachings he led his people during a time of crisis.

Was Deganawidah rescued from water? When I looked at the story of his early life, I found he was not once saved from water; he was *twice* saved from water! Deganawidah's grandmother received a visitation from an angel prophesying his birth from her virgin daughter and predicting that he would destroy the existing world order. After Deganawidah's birth, his grandmother, fearing fulfillment of this prophecy, tried to drown him – twice. Both times the Peacemaker was miraculously saved by angels and returned to his mother. The grandmother stopped trying to kill him.

Did Deganawidah carry the Peacemaker's staff or the Key of Life? At first glance, we suspect not. Upon closer inspection, however, we learn Iroquois emissaries wore wampum belts which were actually documents constructed as mosaics from porcupine quills and adorned with white shell beads. The varying arrangement of light and dark beads served as memory devices for remembering the contents of the wampum. Wampum were worn for purposes of identification, much as the caduceus (the Greek form of the Key of Life) was carried in the past.

73. Iroquois wampum belt memorializing the founding of Pennsylvania.

The wampum connection to the staff is interesting; however, there is another more vital connection: symbolically, the staff and the Tree of Life are synonymous.

The Great Tree of Peace is symbolically equivalent to the Tree of Life which (according to Moira Timms, *Beyond Prophecies and Predictions*) will: "blossom with a fruit never before known in the creation and that fruit shall be the New Spirit of Man." The Tree of Life appears at the close of all great cycles (ages); its fruit is for the healing of nations.

With its roots in the Earth and its branches in the heavens, the Tree of Life is the most ancient and powerful metaphor for the link between Heaven and Earth. The Tree is representative of the human spirit aspiring toward the heavens, yearning for the divine.

All of this is exciting, but there is more. If what I maintain is true and the Peacemaker is the true founding father of America, then he should be patronized in America's symbolism. Discovery of this symbol would provide the iron-clad proof I needed to substantiate my theory. I need an actual staff.

What I found could verify the notion held by several secret societies that our founding fathers saw America as a continuation of a vast, secret spiritual project which originated at the time shortly before the Flood and will come to fruition sometime around the year 2,000. What is this evidence?

The first piece of symbolic evidence I found relates to the Peacemaker's partner Seshet, shown here with her crown of seven rays. Lady Liberty wears a seven-pointed crown identical to that of Seshet. The seven rays signify an enlightened being. Is this mere coincidence or by design?

74. Seshet and Lady Liberty.

The second piece of evidence appears when we venture to the United States Capitol. There, in the Capitol Rostrum, rests the symbol of power and authority of the United States. It is an exact replica of the Peacemaker's staff. The Key of Life is the symbol of America!

This cannot be a simple coincidence. It proves America has grown and prospered under the aura of the Peacemaker for not only hundreds but thousands of years, beginning with Quetzalcoatl (remember 'America', literally translated is 'Land of the Plumed Serpent').

As renowned occultists, the founding fathers of America must have known this. The question is: did they know the reincarnated Peacemaker was present among them?

GEORGE MORGAN

In his *Wampum Belts and Peace Trees: George Morgan, Native American and Revolutionary Diplomacy*, Gregory Schaaf tells the story of the discovery of the Morgan papers – papers which chronicled the career of an Indian agent named George Morgan (1741-1810). His papers are comprised of his personal diary and contain previously unknown and unpublished letters written by George Washington, Thomas Jefferson and John Hancock which prove that the very structure of the U.S. Government was explicitly modeled after the Iroquois Confederacy. In fact, Benjamin Franklin printed the Peacemaker's writings and was known to have constantly talked about him. These facts seem to support the notion that the founding fathers secretly revered the Peacemaker.

75. The Capitol Mace.

George Morgan was a wealthy Philadelphia merchant with a wife and five children. On April 10, 1776, the thirty-two year old patriot was summoned before the Continental Congress by John Hancock. The soon to be born country was preparing to declare war on the British. They had one small problem. The American Indians could sway the balance of power and determine the outcome of the Revolutionary War. They had to be convinced to stay neutral in the conflict. George Morgan was the envoy chosen by the founding fathers to conduct this crucial mission of peace.

Morgan was widely respected by the Indians with whom he shared a vision of a future in which people of all races, creeds, and colors could live together with respect for natural law. But Morgan's commitment to his family was equally strong. Bounties were placed on the heads of men like him, revolutionary traitors to the British crown. His mission among the Indians would be a very dangerous one.

On April 17, 1776, Agent Morgan and his companion Chief White Eyes rode out of Philadelphia on their mission of peace. While the tale of their adventure is both fascinating and suspenseful, I won't try the reader's patience. Suffice it to say, there is only one reason why the American Indians remained neutral in the Revolutionary War. George Morgan's brilliant diplomacy, founded on the shared spiritual foundation of the Great Tree of Peace, is that reason.

For his efforts the Lenape Indians, members of the Iroquois Confederacy, conferred on Morgan the title Brother Tamanend, after the Peacemaker – one of the greatest honors any white man ever received from an Indian nation.

They believed George Morgan to be the third incarnation of Deganawidah the Peacemaker! The second incarnation of Deganawidah, the Indians believed, founded the state of Pennsylvania along with William Penn.

With all of this in mind, should it surprise us that the Delaware and Iroquois Indians are thought to be the descendents of Atlanteans? The Delaware recall an original land of peace called the 'Talega country', in other words, Tula.

This accords with the belief that America was founded as a new Atlantis or Tula. After the Revolutionary War, George Morgan was ceded 16 million acres of land which is present-day New Madrid, Missouri. Morgan moved his wife and children there and founded a utopian community based upon the ideals of the Peacemaker.

New Madrid was America's first racially integrated community. There Morgan set aside free land for parks, churches, and public schools. Almost overnight, according to historian Schaaf, groups of powerful men began plotting New Madrid's destruction. It was destroyed by the earthquake of 1812 which was centered in New Madrid. The quake was so powerful the Liberty Bell was said to ring in distant Philadelphia, Pennsylvania.

The question is, was George Morgan driven to build Tula?

CHAPTER EIGHTEEN

LATTER-DAY PEACEMAKER?

After the Revolutionary War, there was a feeling throughout New England that America was chosen by God to fulfill His plan to create the extraordinary civilization described by Jesus in the Book of Revelation and envisioned by the Founding Fathers. An air of expectancy and excitement filled the air as the westward expansion began. Thousands of people rushed west hoping to hit material and spiritual pay dirt.

In the midst of this New Age lived Joseph Smith, Jr. who at sixteen had a vision of Jesus Christ standing above him in the air. This was Joseph Smith's First Vision which singled him out as the Lord's appointed prophet. Of course, no one believed him.

Growing up, Joseph developed a reputation in his community of Palmyra, New York, as a diviner, a 'seer', who used stones for fortune-telling and diving for stolen property. Curiously, Joseph was given a *green seer-stone* which was one of three he was known to possess. There are many tales of Joseph's gift with the seer-stone, including the possession of an All-Seeing Eye.

Is it even remotely conceivable that Joseph Smith had discovered one of the Emerald Tablets, the ME's which once belonged to the Peacemaker? If so, the Mormon Church is not revealing knowledge of it.

One day in 1825, while digging for money supposed to have been left by the ancients, Joseph Smith received a Second Vision. According to Joseph Smith's account of the night of September 21, 1823 the seventeen-year-old was kneeling in prayer when suddenly the room filled with light and a person wearing a bright white robe floated next to him in the air. Calling the awe-struck boy by his name, the angel announced his own name as Moroni. Moroni said that God had sent him to brief Joseph on an important mission.

Moroni described a precious book written on "golden plates" which was hidden in a stone box in a hill near Joseph's home. These golden plates contained the complete Gospel and a special treasure: a history of the ancient inhabitants of America, who had been taught the Gospel of Christ!

Moroni himself had been the compiler of these records, which he had received from his father, Mormon, the man whose name this famous book bears. Along with the plates were the Urim and Thummim, which would aid in the deciphering of the records. Moroni warned Joseph to not, after he found the plates, show them to anyone.

After several years of false starts, unfulfilled hopes, and warnings that Satan would tempt him to use the plates to become rich, Joseph Smith's amazing interaction with Moroni at last bore fruit on September 22, 1827.

At age twenty-one, Joseph Smith returned from a meeting with Moroni with the Golden Plates and the Urim and Thummim, the oracular device mentioned in the Old Testament. Fearing for his life and that of his bride, Emma, the Smiths relocated to Harmony, Pennsylvania, so that Joseph could translate the *Book of Mormon*, written in hieroglyphics he called "reformed Egyptian," in peace.

On May 15, 1829 Smith and co-translator Oliver Cowdery knelt in prayer by the banks of the Susquehanna River, petitioning God as to how a person receives his authority. Suddenly, in a vision, John the Baptist appeared, laid his hands on their heads and initiated them into the Aaronic Priesthood (which he used to baptize Jesus).

After instructing them to baptize each other, John the Baptist told them they would later be given the priesthood which Christ had given the apostles. One month later, the apostles Peter, James and John appeared to the two humans as angels. The three laid their hands on the heads of Joseph and Oliver and ordained them as priests of the Melchizedek Priesthood, giving them Christ's authority to organize the Church of Jesus Christ.

Oliver and Joseph translated *The Book of Mormon* in sixty days with Joseph dictating the words of Mormon as revealed by the Urim and Thummim. When the translating was complete they returned the Golden Plates to Moroni for safekeeping. For the benefit of those who would doubt the existence of Moroni or the Golden Plates eight witnesses were allowed to see them through the power of God.

In 1830, Smith announced before his congregation that he had been given "the keys of the mystery of those things which have been sealed, even things which were from the foundation of the world." Were these the Key of Life? If so, the Key is included in the *Book of Mormon*.

THE BOOK OF MORMON

The *Book of Mormon* is an abridgement of the historical and religious records of an advanced civilization which existed in America two thousand years ago. In corroboration with other Meso-American accounts the *Book of Mormon* states that Christ had walked the Americas.

The records of Mormon began in 600 B.C.E. in Jerusalem and follow the treacherous journey by boat of the Jewish prophet Lehi from the Red Sea to Central America. After Lehi's death his family split into two warring factions: the Nephites and the Lamanites, named after his two sons. It was Nephi who originally made the Golden Plates so that his people would not forget God or their own history.

A thousand years later Mormon took up the responsibility of abridging these records that told of the spectacular appearance of Christ in America after the resurrection and of a long period of peace which followed his appearance. However, wars resumed and the Lamanites destroyed the Nephite civilization. Moroni was the last of the Nephite leaders. After the holocaust he wandered America, finally burying the Golden Plates in New York.

As I look upon the *Book of Mormon*, I see a strong link between the Peacemaker's story and the continuation of the Divine Plan. Most obvious are the connections with the green stone and the appearance of John the Baptist who was sent, just like in the Bible, as God's emissary. The *Book of Mormon* teaches that God reveals insights a little at a time, "line upon line, precept upon precept." God also teaches human beings the same way he did in the Bible, by sending (at different times) the same key figures, such as John the Baptist, Peter, James and John.

The *Book of Mormon* contends that the "plain and most precious" teachings about Jesus and His church have been removed from the Bible. The purpose of the continued appearances of God's representatives, including the Peacemaker, was to correct this blasphemy. Most importantly the *Book of Mormon* shows that the teachings of Christ were known before the time of Jesus.

I concluded that Enoch preached the Gospel in the time before the Flood. The *Book of Mormon* shows that God had revealed his will to people in different parts of the world and that they too kept records. Is there any reason to suppose that the people of Enoch's time did not keep records as well and that these records were part of those burned at the library of Alexandria?

Joseph Smith believed that his prophetic calling was to restore the lost knowledge of the Bible. In what is known as the "Visions of Moses," Joseph received from God a preface to Genesis. God showed Joseph the identical vision of the creation of the universe he showed Moses when Moses was called to be a prophet. Included within this teaching is the concept that God cannot be seen only with the eyes of the mind but also with spiritual eyes that, presumably, everyone has. Also, God created many worlds which are presently inhabited. Although knowledge of these worlds was off limits to Moses and Joseph, the upsurge in reported extraterrestrial activity since 1947 may suggest that God intends us to receive this knowledge bit by bit. God emphatically stated to Joseph that Jesus Christ is in charge of these worlds.

The Book of Moses continued to reveal startling confirmation of my Peacemaker hypothesis, not the least of which is important information about what Mormons call Heavenly Father's Plan and what I have termed the Divine Plan for the spiritual upliftment and physical evolution of humanity.

The Book of Moses reveals that everything has been created in a spiritual or archetypal form before it is placed on earth. This upholds the idea that everyone has had an existence prior to their current one here on earth. It reveals that the crux of Satan's battle with Christ was over Satan's desire to abolish the freedom of choice as the route to success. Christ desired that souls be allowed to try and fail, be given a chance to amend their ways and because of their faith in Christ, have their sins forgiven. With Christ's plan effected, Satan rebelled against Christ and God.

When Adam and Eve were created, the battle between Satan and Christ was renewed on Earth. The Book of Moses tells us that Adam and Eve knew about Jesus Christ and were baptized. Further, perhaps in reference to the Emerald Tablets, knowledge of the Divine Plan was passed along to a few select families.

Confirmation of my hypothesis that there was a Divine visitation during the time before the Flood is found in the Book of Moses. Here, we learn that a crucial battle to keep the Divine Plan alive was waged during the time of Enoch, the Peacemaker. This was the time of Atlantis.

According to Joseph Smith's inspired translation of these events, Enoch was the most powerful advocate of Jesus Christ before the Flood! We will recall that earlier I concluded Enoch was sent by Jesus to clear the way for a Divine visitation.

The prophet's revelation further states that Enoch created a city, called the City of Zion, for the followers of Christ! Zion refers to Mount Zion in Jerusalem, site of the ancient Temple of Solomon; and before that referred to the seat of Melchizedek ('the King of Peace'). This city of Zion was unquestionably an ancient Tula.

God called the inhabitants of this city Zion, for they were "of one heart and one mind, and dwelt in righteousness; and there were no poor among them." In other words, it was a utopia. To protect this utopia from wickedness, (or as I believe, from the Flood) God removed Zion/Tula or her citizens from the earth.

Can we conclude from this that God concealed it in another dimension until it could be seen through the spiritual eyes of a more advanced civilization?

Before Zion/Tula disappeared, Enoch prophesied that in the last days of the earth Zion/Tula would reappear. Righteousness would "sweep the earth as with a flood," and people from all over the world would gather to build the Tula in preparation for the second coming of Christ. Enoch warned that Satan would conspire to prevent Tula from reappearing by trying to convince people that it is not of Christ.

Joseph Smith believed that Tula would be built in America, and that the American Indians would be crucial to its manifestation. Based upon my interpretation of the prophecies of the Hopi, we must conclude that Smith was correct.

CHAPTER NINETEEN

DAG HAMMARSKJOLD: THE PEACEMAKER AT THE UN

President Franklin Delano Roosevelt was the first to use the words 'United Nations' in the Declaration of United Nations in January, 1942 when twenty-six nations gathered together to fight the Axis powers of Germany, Italy and Japan.

In June, 1945, a conference on International Organizations met in San Francisco with the purpose of securing peace after World War Two. Exhausted and sickened by the horrors and destruction of war, the people of earth formed the UN to "save succeeding generations from the scourge of war."

After scouring the planet for a model by which the nations of the world could deliberate on world problems, the conference found only one example by which they could be organized: the Great Tree of Peace designed by Deganawidah, the Peacemaker, in the year 1,000.

Should we be surprised? Or, more likely, can we see in the creation of the UN the flowering of the Great Tree of Peace and the continuation of the Peacemaker's plan for the upliftment of humanity? If so, can we locate the Peacemaker within this world body? The answer is yes. His name was Dag Hammarskjold.

It is rather astounding to me when I recall how I learned of Dag Hammarskjold, the Peacemaker at the UN. Searching for incarnations of the Peacemaker I went to my local public library. In their computer I typed in the word Peacemaker not fully expecting anything to come back.

A single reference appeared: "Dag Hammarskjold, the Peacemaker." Since I had never heard of him before, I dismissed the reference and left the library, thinking to myself how ignoble it was to call someone the Peacemaker when clearly he couldn't be! At the time it seemed to me like calling the President 'Jesus Christ'. It wasn't long before I returned to the library to learn about Dag Hammarskjold.

"You are taking over the world's most impossible job," was the greeting Dag Hammarskjold received from his predecessor, Trygve Lie, in New York when he took over the position of Secretary General of the UN. Lie could easily have been referring to Hammarskjold's role as the Peacemaker. Hammarskjold was an inspired leader – and he knew it.

76. The United Nations officially came into existence in October, 1945. (Numerologically, 1945 adds up to Year One. 1+9+4+5= 19. 1+9=10. 1+0=1.) The UN flag shows a map of the Earth centered on the North Pole, in the colors of blue and white, coincidentally the colors of Israel.

By all accounts Hammarskjold believed he had an appointment with destiny. He was driven to turn the UN's vision of justice and decency, peace and unity into reality. A member of the Swedish government, he was one of the world's greatest statesmen. Secretly, he was one of its greatest mystics.

When, exactly, Dag Hammarskjold began to believe he was a messenger of God, a Messianic vessel through whom God was working, is unclear. What is certain is that Dag Hammarskjold believed himself to be on a mystic mission from God. His journal, *Markings*, which he wanted read and published after his death, portrays his obsession with himself as a Christ figure who must follow Christ's path to death. *Markings* certainly reveals that Hammarskjold, whom the world called the Peacemaker, believed he was on a mission from God. As a knight of Christ, his holy writ, the UN Charter, charged him with leading humanity into a mystical connection with the universe.

There was an outcry raised about Hammarskjold's religious contemplations. In Scandinavia he was criticized and fear was widespread that he had lost his sanity. One Swedish paper wrote "he identified himself increasingly with Jesus . . . and by 1957, Jesus turned in Hammarskjold's diary into a politician."

By the summer of 1961 Hammarskjold was suffering from not only emotional alienation but also the cold hostility of the Soviets who insisted he be replaced by a 'troika' command. Britain, France, Portugal, Belgium and other European powers were arrayed against Hammarskjold, particularly on the issue of the Congo, where a disturbance was threatening to flare up into a major world conflict. The UN was in danger of being disbanded. Only a miracle could save the day. Some form of cataclysmic event that would save the UN. It was at this point that Hammarskjold became obsessed with death, especially by crucifixion, and subsequent resurrection. He wrote:

> *Death is to be your ultimate gift to life.... He who has surrendered himself to it knows that the Way ends on the Cross – even when it is leading him through the jubilation of Gennesaret or the triumphal entry into Jerusalem.*

Before leaving New York for the Congo, Hammarskjold made a final entry in his journal:

> *Above the spreading pool of blood no questions can reach you anymore. And no words can any longer call you back from that eternal "Beyond" – where you are separated from us by a death chosen long before the bullet hit the temple.*

Hammarskjold uncharacteristically left all his personal effects and papers on his flight to the Congo aboard the *Albertina*, his brand new UN DC-6B. Mysteriously, and perhaps purposefully, he filed a false flight plan, refused UN escort, and insisted on radio silence throughout the flight. At the airport in Ndola several members of the police honor guard reported a mysterious flash of blinding light to the west.

The charred ruins of Hammarskjold's plane were found scattered over a 12-foot-high ant hill in the midst of a tiny patch of hardwood forest. As reported by the Associated Press on September 20, 1961, most of the occupants of the Albertina were found burned beyond recognition. Hammarskjold was found untouched by the flames, resting upright against the anthill. Exactly as Hammarskjold had foretold in his journal six days before, the only visible wound was a bullet hole in his temple. Clenched in one hand was a single playing card – the Ace of Spades, the mystical symbol of death.

The death of Dag Hammarskjold, the Peacemaker, wrought a miracle, albeit a temporary one. Prof. John Lindberg believes Hammarskjold's death saved the UN by uniting the world as never before behind the organization and ending the Soviet demands for a troika.

The shock of Hammarskjold's death was so great that it sobered the powers and the politicians into a careful reappraisal of their postures and policies. If the Secretary-General had flown back to New York empty handed, a totally different situation would have arisen. The United Nations would have found itself hopelessly and perhaps irrevocably split.

Arthur Gavshon concludes: "In the world as it is, it sometimes turns out that dead martyrs achieve more for their causes than live prophets."

Within martyrdom, did Hammarskjold offer himself to God? Was it possible that Hammarskjold did not believe he was the Messiah but was, rather, the Peacemaker come to save his creation, the Great Tree of Peace? Had he discovered his destiny?

Is it possible this was the same soul or ego who in the year 1,000 planted the Great Tree of Peace, returned in the year 1776 to nurture his creation, and reappeared in 1961 in the guise of Hammarskjold to lay down his life to rescue his Great Tree?

Curiously, one coincidental linkage with the Peacemaker involves Hammarskjold's name itself. One of the first questions put to him by the journalists of New York was how he pronounced his name. "Just call me 'Hammer-shield'. That's what it means," he replied. The Hammarskjold coat of arms contains the double hammer. In ancient Crete, the Key of Life, the Peacemaker's staff, was depicted as the double hammer.

THE STONE OF LIGHT

More powerfully than his epitaph of the Peacemaker or the synchronicity involving his name, it is Dag Hammarskjold's placement of the foundation stone or 'stone of light' in the Meditation Room of the UN that directly links him as one in the line of Peacemakers.

This 'stone of light' is a six-and-a-half ton rectangular block of iron ore. The massive black stone is polished on the top such that it brings forth a sheet of minute lights that shine like billions of tiny stars. It is a natural magnet emitting magnetic waves. This particular block was chosen from among sixty chunks of iron ore from a Swiss mine before the right one was found. One wonders what it was about this particular stone that caught Hammarskjold's fancy.

Its placement at the very center of the base of the UN is meant to emphasize its role as a 'cubic stone' or 'foundation stone'. Hebrew and Muslim traditions locate the Foundation Stone in the paradise of Eden. The origins of the foundation stone mythology derive from Atlantis. It is an indispensable ingredient in the symbolism of the Peacemakers.

77. Stone of Light at the United Nations

**78. An initiate holding the Key of Life while an Angel shows him the
Stone of Light.**

There is a fascinating Grail legend that may shed light on the mysteries
of the centerpiece in the UN's Meditation Room. According to the legend,
when Percival enters the Grail castle, he is entering the mystery world of the
human body, the brain. It is there that "the stone of light" resides. The stone
is thought by occultists to be the pineal gland, the center of man's consciousness. In the Grail legends "the stone of light" can open up clairvoyant powers of perception. As one gazes upon "the stone of light," mystical awareness
arises from the heart and initiates a transformation of consciousness. This
transformation is identical to the transformation of the kundalini energies
represented by the Key of Life. Trevor Ravenscroft (*Spear of Destiny*) states
that this occurs at the moment when the human soul becomes the living vessel of the Christ-consciousness.

Interestingly, the *Popol Vuh* concludes with an account of the erection of a majestic, white temple, where a secret divining stone – cubical and black –was preserved. This temple, together with the black stone it contained, was named the *Caabaha*. This name is astonishingly similar to that of the Temple, or *Kaaba*, which contains the sacred black stone of Islam, and is also similar to the *Kaballah*, the secret wisdom of the Jews.

In Egyptian *ka* means 'soul' (specifically referring to the true spiritual personality which leaves the body after death) and *Ba* means 'light'. In Biblical terms the immortal body of light is called a Mer-Ka-Ba, and is the vehicle of resurrection and ascension. Are the Kaaba of Islam and the black stone of the UN connected with resurrection and ascension in some way, perhaps as an anchoring point for spiritual energies?

79. The Black Stone at Mecca, the Muslim center of the world.

Now, this is the point I am leading up to. In 1959, Hopi Indian leader Thomas Banyacya was part of a six-man delegation that went to the United Nations. Banyacya writes that, because of their ancient prophecies, the Hopi leaders felt it was time to go East to the edge of their Mother, Turtle Island, where it had been foretold "a House of Glass or Mica would stand at this time, where great leaders from many lands would be gathered to help any people who are in trouble."

The Hopi leaders approached the UN on a three-fold mission:

1. to look for their true white brother (and presumably his stone);
2. to seek real justice for all Indian Brothers and for all good people in this land;
3. to warn the great leaders in the Glass House of the purification day prophesied to come to this land of the red man when the evil ones among the white race bring all life back to the day before the great flood.

At the UN the Hopi delegation undoubtedly came in contact with Dag Hammarskjold. In order to fulfill their mission the Peacemaker, the true white brother, had to present the missing cornerpiece to the Hopi Tablet. From here he will gather the other races and create a divinely inspired peace. Did Hammarskjold present his piece of the tablet to the Hopi? Or, being of Swiss descent, did he present the Swiss tablet?

The answer is likely seen in our world today.

Before moving on, another strange coincidence should be pointed out. According to Jewish legend, the Peacemaker will create a divinely inspired peace. Afterwards, he will be killed in the streets of Israel. On November 7, 1995, just weeks after the 50th anniversary of the UN, Yitzhak Rabin, the Prime Minister of Israel and architect of the Middle East peace plan, was mowed down in the streets of Tel Aviv, Israel. *Time* magazine titled its cover story "Death of a Peacemaker." By all accounts, Rabin knew of his impending murder. Clearly, like Hammarskjold, Rabin sacrificed himself for the sake of his peace plan. Will the peace survive his death? The world can only wait and see.

CHAPTER TWENTY

CHRIST'S PROPHET:
THE KING OF TERROR IDENTIFIED

Where and who is the Peacemaker today? In this chapter these questions will be answered.

Earlier, we discovered that in one of his most specific prophecies Nostradamus predicted that in July of 1999 the Peacemaker will return. Century X, Quatrain 72 states:

> *In the year 1999 [and] seven months,*
> *From the sky will come a great King of Terror,*
> *He will resurrect the great King of Angolmois,*
> *Before which Mars rules happily.*

Earlier, we discussed Nostradamus' use of the term "terror" in reference to the Peacemaker. We also interpreted the King of Angolmois as the King of Tula. This interpretation is reinforced by the last line of the Quatrain, "before which Mars rules happily." In mythology, the seven Pleiades were the nurses of Mars, the god of war. Many interpreters connect Mars with the "celestial army." As this army is led by the Archangel Micha-el, some quite fascinating interpretations can be made as to exactly what this line means.

The question is: did Nostradamus leave any clues as to the Peacemaker's name or identity in his writings? As is well known, Nostradamus was quite accurate with names. Pasteur, Napoleon, Franco – all were mentioned in his writings centuries before their births. In addition, not only did he foresee the rise of the Nazis, but he even named Hitler as their leader. (Actually, he was off by one letter; Nostradamus referred to him as "Hister.")

Indeed, we discover Nostradamus named the King of Terror "Chyren" (with a soft "ch"):

> *The great Chyren will be chief of the world*
> *after "plus oultre," loved, feared and dreaded.*
> *His fame and praise go beyond the heavens and*
> *he will be greatly satisfied with the sole title of victor.*

In addition to this Quatrain there are numerous prophecies revolving around Chyren and his mission (which we will discuss presently).

Chyren is not the King of Terror's real name. To protect himself from the Catholic authorities who feared he was talking about them Nostradamus expressed names of people and places as anagrams.

For example, something as simple as 'Paris' might become rapis. To confuse the decoders further Nostradamus might add or delete a letter. In this way the word noir, meaning 'black', becomes (by removing the 'n') an anagram for king or roi in French.

After solving the anagram of 'Chyren', interpreters of the Quatrains declare that the obvious name of the King of Terror, the returning Peace-maker, is 'Heinrich' or 'Henry'.

According to Nostradamus, Heinrich or Henry will resurrect the King of Tula, which Nostradamus encoded as "Angolmoi" (once again Mongolia).

HENRY: AFTER PLUS OULTRA

Let's return to Nostradamus' incredible Quatrain involving Chyren or Henry:

> *The great Chyren will be chief of the world*
> *after "plus oultre," loved, feared and dreaded.*
> *His fame and praise go beyond the heavens and*
> *he will be greatly satisfied with the sole title of victor.*

Here, Nostradamus states Henry will come to power after "plus oultre." *Plus ultra* means more beyond. Is this why Nostradamus used these words? When we turn our attention to *plus ultra*, we learn these two words in and of themselves confirm my hypothesis that the King of Terror is the Peacemaker.

To begin, it is said that the Pillars of Hercules flanking the great rock of Gibraltar, where the Mediterranean Sea opens into the Atlantic, carried an ominous warning to all who dared go beyond them: *Ne Plus Ultra* – "No More Beyond." What secrets lay beyond the Pillars? Could it have been, as many speculate, a reference to the sunken continent of Atlantis? Hardly a soul dared find out.

Many centuries later the same cryptic warning appeared on the coat of arms of the ruling family of Spain, under a depiction of the fabled pillars. The motto remained intact until Christopher Columbus (whose name coincidently meaning "Christ-bearing dove") successfully reached the shores of America. From that point forward the motto read: *Plus Ultra* – "More Beyond."

After Columbus, *plus ultra* became the inspiring motto of the early pioneers of science led by Sir Francis Bacon whose *New Atlantis* was the 'bible' of the early founders of America. From this connection we may deduce *plus ultra* relates to the brotherhood of the Peacemakers or doves and the formation of a New Atlantis or a new Tula in America. In using this phrase, Nostradamus is telling us that Chyren, or Henry, is a member of this brotherhood whose mission is to create a new Tula.

This is certainly compelling; however, there is much more confirmation of this mysterious Chyren's ancient connection with the Peacemakers. Incredibly, the Peacemaker's return is foretold in the stars.

CHYREN = CHIRON?

'Chyren' is very close to 'Chiron', an outer planet discovered between Saturn and Uranus on November 1, 1977 by Charles Kowal of the Hale Observatories at Pasadena, California. Named after the centaur of Greek mythology, Chiron (like Enoch, Moses, John the Baptist and Jesus) is a shaman. The shaman acts as a visionary and intermediary. Astrologically, Chiron acts as a stimulator of initiation who leads those wishing true knowledge (the Key of Life) in the direction of a new beginning.

In the Book of Revelation this new beginning is represented by the construction of the New Jerusalem, the new Tula. The seven seals must be opened before this new creation can be seen. The Peacemaker, we know, will lead us in the ***direction of*** this Promised Land until we meet the Messiah who will lead us ***into*** the Promised Land (at the center of which is the Tree of Life/ Peace). Here, again, is a perfect match between Chyren and the Peacemaker.

And there is more.

According to astrologer Gregg Castellucci (*Heaven & History*), Chiron is the Teacher of the Soul. Further, Chiron is the astrological or cosmic significator of "Christ consciousness." Castellucci states the single most important historical embodiment of the Chiron "spirit" is the United Nations, born from a visitation of Chiron in 1945! As I stated in the previous chapter, the Peacemaker definitely had a hand in the formation of the UN; in fact, I believe the UN represents the next phase in the growth of the Peacemaker's great Tree of Peace.

According to Robert Graves in *The Greek Myths*, Chiron was the priest-king who founded the Asculepian, an ancient healing temple. Imhotep, we recall, was also called Asclapius and his healing temple was called the Asculepian. Here is a perfect match between Peacemakers. Chiron also founded the Chironium, another healing temple, atop Mount Pelius. There, he taught the means to identify the soul mission or spiritual gift of each pupil and brought this knowledge to their attention. In this way, the soul could complete its earthly mission with greater precision and understanding. Imagine how different your life would be if at the age of seven your true gifts were revealed to you. To put it simply, you could live out your true destiny.

In *Chiron: The Rainbow Bridge Between the Inner and Outer Planets*, Barbara Hand Clow writes: "Chiron is the teacher of the earth connection to higher planes, and the planetary sighting (in November, 1977) indicates the time has come for us to manifest our divinity." After leaving the earth, Chiron is thought to have ascended to the constellation Sagittarius (or the horse). This is one of the reasons astrologers believe that Sagittarius is ruled by Chiron. Twenty-seven degrees Sagittarius is the galactic core, Tula. Is there any wonder why Chiron became Sagittarius or why he has reappeared today?

Another revealing connection between Chyren or Chiron and the Peacemaker involves Sirius, the star associated with Thoth. In *The Sirius Mystery*, Robert Temple points out that the Dogon tribe of Africa believed the soul of the Peacemaker and even of Christ came from Sirius B. Temple called Sirius "Digiteria" because the Dogon called it "Po" – Po being the name of a tiny Dogon seed, and Digiteria the species name for that seed. Digiteria connotes 'finger', and Chiron means 'hand' in Greek. Does this curious coincidence point to Nostradamus' *Chyren* or *Henry* as the helping hand of Christ?

This is all very interesting, but there is one additional connection between Chyren and Chiron that is most startling. Chiron is a creature that is part-man, part-horse. Synchronistically, Chiron is the son of Saturn (*Chronos* to the Greeks). Saturn, the eldest of the gods, was said to have come to earth in order to rule a land. What was the name of this land? Hyperboria! According to the Greeks, the center of Hyperboria was Tula. This connection is given further weight when we realize Saturn (also known as Enki, Ptah and Yahweh among other 'gods') was symbolized by a white horse. As we recall, whenever Thoth/Enoch (who was the son of Saturn) spoke, people saw the image of a white horse around him.

THE WHITE HORSE

Of all the figures in the Bible, one looms larger than the rest – the white horse in the Book of Revelation. Revelation 19:11 states:

And I saw heaven opened,
and behold a white horse;
and he that sat upon him was called
Faithful and True.

Within this figure a profound secret has been kept for almost two thousand years. The white horse spoken of in Revelation and other world mythologies is actually a man whose symbol is a white horse. That man is the Peacemaker.

Traditions all over the world – that of the western Europeans, Scandinavians, Celts, Greeks, Hebrews, Chaldeans, Hindus, Iroquois, Sioux, Maya, Incas, Africans, Polynesians – speak at length of a great Teacher riding a white horse. Such unanimity makes it highly improbable that people in isolated areas separated by oceans and towering peaks could all have 'invented' the same legend with similar if not identical details.

In India, *Vishnu* is the Savior figure who appears during times of crisis in the history of the world. The next anticipated manifestation of Vishnu, the *Kalki-avatara* ('He who is mounted on the white horse'), is described in the *Puranas* in identical terms to the description of the Second Coming found in Revelation.

The white horse is a prophetic creature, sacred in Persia, Greece, Rome and Scandinavia. It is the totem animal of Britain and Ireland. In China the white horse is an avatar of *Kwan-Yin*, the 'goddess of mercy' (an *avatar* is an aspect of the Divine who appears at a moment of crisis to awaken humankind);

In Japan the white horse is the avatar of *Kwannon*;
In Indian Buddhism the white horse is the herald of *Avalokitsvara*;
In Zoroastrianism there is the serpent-destroying white horse, Pedu, the archenemy of Ahriman, a final figure of evil;

For Muslims the white horse is 'god sent'. The Prophet Mohammed swore by his white steed whom he called Al Borak.

Since the white horse is such a universal symbol for the Peacemaker, Nostradamus uses the white horse's connection with Chiren to subtly inform us that Chyren is indeed the Peacemaker.

All of these cross-cultural associations and unexpected linkages – the son of Saturn, the white horse, the role of shaman who lends a helping hand – could lead us to conclude Nostradamus' Chyren or Henry, the King of Terror is the Peacemaker. There is more, however.

CHYREN = INRI?

It is illuminating to note that in Sanskrit Chyren means 'Divine Offering'. Strangely, Pilate ordered a sign to be placed on the Cross on which Jesus was sacrificed. The sign read "INRI," which is phonetically close to Nostradamus' 'Henry'. Is there a connection?

All of Jesus' teachings have two levels of interpretation. The *exoteric*, or surface interpretation, and the *esoteric*, or hidden, meaning. INRI falls into this latter category.

Exoterically, as every Sunday School student knows, INRI has been translated as Iesus Nazarenus Rex Iuderorum or "Jesus of Nazareth, King of the Jews." When Pilate placed this sign on the Cross this mocked Jesus and stated his crime.

Esoterically, however, INRI is translated as: Igen Natura Renovatur Integra or "By Fire, Nature is Renewed Whole." This interpretation offers an astonishing revelation for our time. In the Gnostic *Gospel of Thomas*, Jesus said: "I have cast fire upon the world, and see, I am guarding it until it blazes."

It may be said that Jesus lit the fire 2,000 years ago. His second coming would create a profound change of heart, mind and spirit that would sweep the world like a fire. INRI, or possibly Nostradamus' 'Henry', now becomes a threat, a promise and a warning. We could easily interpret Henry as the King of Terror, an agent of Armageddon who will destroy this world by fire.

80. Woodcut from Rennes, France c.1860.

Earlier, we examined the Hopi prophecies of the "heavens passing away" and of a "great noise." The hopeful interpretation of these prophecies was that they heralded a new vibratory rate that will cleanse and purify the Earth. Such a purification could be called 'fire' since it is directly connected with magnetism, vibration, frequency, cosmic rays, etc.

What if instead of a person this 'fire' (or 'Henry') were to manifest itself in the form of just such a frequency or cosmic vibration? The holy texts of the ancients are loaded with references to fire, frequency or vibration. For instance, we have already seen that in Matthew it says he shall send his angels with the great sound of a trumpet. What if a new earthly vibration is emerging, and this is the angelic wake-up call? In July, 1999, exactly coinciding with the time of the arrival of the King of Terror, scientists are predicting just such an occurrence.

"THE SOLAR STORM OF THE MILLENNIUM"

In a May 2, 1996 news conference scientists from the National Oceanic and Atmospheric Administration (NOAA) in Boulder, Colorado announced that sometime between June, 1999 and June, 2,000 a billion-ton, super-heated wave of electrically-charged gas from the sun will crash into the Earth at a speed of 620 miles per second. Could this huge gaseous bomb, described as the "storm of the millennium," be a part of the King of Terror prophecy?

When asked to describe the effects of this storm, the NOAA scientists said that "among other things," probably for the first time in history, the aurora borealis, the Northern Lights, will be seen as far south as Florida. It is the "other things" that we are concerned with here. No one is sure what will happen if this event occurs. Let's look at the best and worst case scenarios of this situation.

First, the worst case: A surge of charged particles injected into Earth's ionosphere would unquestionably disrupt radio communications, power lines, telephones, computers, televisions, appliances, automobiles, satellites, etc. The question is: would this disruption be temporary or permanent?

There is, however, an even worst case scenario. According to NOAA, if this billion-ton cloud of hot gas from the Sun avalanched onto the earth in a continuous flow it could act like a nuclear bomb and create an electromagnetic pulse that would fry everything on the surface of the earth to a depth of 20 feet.

The absolute worst case scenario was imagined in Walter Richmond's 1967 novel, *The Lost Millennium*, in which he describes a civilization that created a "solar tap" in order to harness the ionospheric electricity of the sun. The fictional engineers made the mistake of keeping the tap on while a solar flare surged into the ionosphere and then to the ground via the ionized pathway of the tap beam. The surge of power created a kind of avalanche which resulted in the explosion of the planet.

Could something like this happen to the earth? It turns out that now, in Alaska, Arco Power Technologies, Inc. is constructing just such a device. (Please see *Angels Don't Play This HAARP*, Jean Manning and Dr. Nick Begich, 1995.) NOAA has advised that if things are unplugged during the solar flare there should be no problem. Surge and spike protectors would adequately protect against overloads.

Let's say the King of Terror is the solar storm, but that it has a completely different effect than the one envisioned here. What if this solar flare is truly the herald of the dawning of the Age of Aquarius which will bring with it an enlightened state of consciousness through an increase in the spiritual vibration of earth?

EARTH'S WAKE-UP CALL

Let's begin with an understanding that every living form on Earth is composed of energy which answers to a particular frequency. A web of energy lines links together every creature, from the smallest to the largest. Let's also recognize that earth is a sentient being. Like you and I, Earth has a heartbeat of Her own. In less time than it takes for me to speak this sentence the earth's heart has *pulsed* 8 times. This vibration can be thought of as earth's 'heartbeat'. Every cell in our body resonates with the Earth at this frequency. It keeps us 'earthed' and allows us to feel kinship (resonance) with all life on the planet.

Within the past several years, earth scientists have noticed something absolutely earth-shaking. The earth's base resonant frequency, scientifically referred to as the Schumann Resonance, has been creeping upward to a new vibrational level. This is the result of an *impulse of energy* which the ancient texts tell us originates from the center of our Milky Way galaxy or Tula. This means it is coming from Tula. The energy is thought to travel through the galaxy, through the Sun, and then to earth.

As a result of this 'impulse of energy' earth's heartbeat is forecasted to jump from 8 cycles per second to 13 cycles per second (one of the most enigmatic numbers known to humankind). The basis for the forecasted jump from 8 to 13 comes from another set of special numbers called the Fibonacci Series. This Series represents the fundamental code of the patterns of all life on earth. The first seven numbers in the Fibonacci series are 1, 1, 2, 3, 5, 8, 13. These provide a scientific basis for the prophecy of the ancients. Earth processes that are governed by this Series include growth of the human body and the branching of trees, plants, shrubs. As recently as June, 1996 the Earth's heartbeat was measured at just over nine cycles per second.

This "Shift of the Ages," as it is called, from 8 to 13 cycles per second will be remarkable. 8 cycles per second corresponds with the brain wave state of deep meditation, a state of mind akin to the brief moments of reverie we sometimes experience between sleeping and waking When we open our eyes, our brain waves shift to approximately 13 cycles per second. This earthly Shift represents nothing less than our planetary ascent into higher conscious-ness. If we think of the difference in our thoughts, emotions and mental life between sleeping and waking we can begin to imagine what is in store for humanity in the coming years. If you have thought for a long time that we are heading toward someplace special, you are right.

Embedded within this Shift is some bad news. It is conceivable that all technological creations 'resonant' at 8 cycles per second and could be ren-dered useless. This means all existing technology – computers, automobiles, microwave ovens – will be completely worthless.

There is, however, good news within this bad news. Humanity is beginning to understand that we perceive as little as ten percent of the ob-servable universe. Visualize, for example, a Universal Grid operating some-what like cable television. At one time an increase from 10 to 30-40 channels was considered a breakthrough, making new programming perceptible to us. Soon, 500 cable channels will be standard. An increase in channels (energy) widens the 'waveband', allowing more energy to appear on our screens. Expanding the waveband of the Earth will enable previously imperceptible beings, thoughts, and other forms of higher vibrational consciousness, in-cluding angels, to become readily apparent to all with decoders capable of interpreting their signals.

By following this interpretation of the Shift of the Ages it is easy to see why the prophets of the past communicated in code. Modern society can't even imagine functioning without its technology. If these toys were sud-denly taken away, one can imagine the terror and chaos that would ensue. Yet if given a choice in advance, how many readers would trade their shiny new car for angelic ability? Or their computer for access to the Universal Computer of all known knowledge through higher consciousness? How many will recognize the King of Terror as the King of Enlightenment? How many of us will choose enlightenment?

MORE TERROR

The King of Terror prophecy is related to several additional Nostradamus Quatrains, each of which adds another piece to the portrait of the one who is destined to lead the destruction of the false religions of the world.

In Century X, Quatrain 66 Nostradamus states:

> *The Chief of London through American power*
> *will burden the island of Scotland with a cold thing.*
> **Roy Reb** [Reb the King] **will have so dreadful an antichrist,**
> *Who will bring them all into conflict.*

Here Nostradamus is telling us the messiah will be preceded by a dreadful herald, a King of Terror, who will put the world religions on alert and "bring them all into the conflict" with one another.

Roy Reb or Reb the King has been seen as an enigmatic cipher for, of all people, Ronald Reagan who demonstrated his fanatical Christian beliefs by declaring the Gorbachev-led anti-Christian state of Russia the "Evil Empire."

The naming of Reagan as Reb the King demonstrates the disastrous, if not ridiculous, hold the notion of an anti-Christ as the final figure of evil has taken in our era. It should be stated that the *original*, uncorrupted meaning of the term anti-Christ was 'herald' and has the connotation of pre-Christ. John the Baptist was called a herald. Virtually no one in a pulpit in our era would dare call John the Baptist the anti-Christ, but that is exactly the part he played. He introduced the teachings of Jesus and he baptized Him, thereby assisting in the transfer of the Holy Spirit from heaven to its earthly dwelling place, the body of Jesus; and finally he was beheaded for the terror he wrought on his community. This is the role the King of Terror will re-enact in our era. The evil connotations piled on this figure by Christianity's leaders, first seeking to fill church pews and later to increase television ratings, will prove to have a disastrous effect on the minds of Christians. The faithful will be utterly confused if and when they realize they have been duped by the Church. In truth, the anti-Christ and the Christ are not opposed, they are partners. *True* evil exists in areas the Church is not even addressing.

If not Reagan, then who exactly is this Roy Reb who will "have so dreadful an anti-Christ"? To begin with, Reb is the Jewish word for rabbi. The young Jewish rabbi Christians call Jesus was known as Reb YHSHWH (Rabbi Joshua). Reb the King, therefore, is none other than the King Rabbi, the Messiah. His dreadful anti-Christ is the King of Terror.

In Century I Quatrain 95 Nostradamus offers a clue to the relationship between the two kings:

> *Before a monastery will be found a twin infant,*
> *Descended from an ancient monastic bloodline:*
> *His fame and power through sects and eloquence*
> *Is such that they will say the living twin*
> *is rightly the elect* [the chosen one].

Leonardo da Vinci, considered one of the world's greatest initiates, believed Christ had an earthly twin brother; he even painted him in his famous "Last Supper." It is believed this twin was John the Baptist, whom many revered as the Messiah.

Unquestionably, there is confusion between the roles of Jesus and John. At first glance, it appears John was sent to 'test out' the teachings. As scroll after scroll of the Dead Sea Scrolls is unrolled, it appears more and more clearly that John was the true Christ, or Gardener, and Jesus was the Peacemaker.

In another painting, the "Virgin of the Scales," by Leonardo's contemporary, Cesare da Sesta, the twins Jesus and John are shown again. John holds his arms around a lamb while Jesus holds a pair of scales, the sign of Libra, the phoenix sign. Tula means scales or balance. This scene depicts John as the one who would bring the sheep *to* Tula while Christ would take them in. The twins portray the duality, Alpha and Omega, the first and the last, a phrase usually applied singularly to Jesus. As we have seen, the symbolism of Alpha and Omega is the first lesson of the Key of Life.

The point is that Nostradamus recognized the role of the twins. Since the overall purpose of the Peacemaker entering the Hall of Records is to resurrect the King of Angolmois (Tula), this is a very significant perception. According to the Egyptian myth of Osiris (the Green Man or Gardener), the object of the Peacemaker's quest is to resurrect, or put Osiris back together again, to make him whole once more. Once he is whole, that is, once through the Teaching of the Christ-figure the human race is whole again, we will be ready to go home to Tula. The divine twins, combined with a reassembly or resurrection, are shamanic story elements known from ancient Egypt all the way to sixteenth century France.

The next significant line of this Quatrain involves the word *elect*. In Enoch's time the messenger of God, the Christ or Messiah, was called the *Elect*. The original Greek translation of Luke says of Christ: "This is my Son, the *Elect One*. Hear Him." From this, the reference is clear.

Let us now decode the phrase, "ancient monastic bloodline."

Jesus called John the Boanerge, the Son of Thunder (Mark 3:17), which is another name for a Peacemaker. The thunder is in reference to the sound of the white stallion racing across the earth. It is likely that, when Nostradamus mentioned the new Peacemaker's descent "from an ancient monastic blood-line," he is referring symbolically to the ancient line of Peacemakers rather than to a literal bloodline. This notion is reinforced by Nostradamus' use of the term 'plus ultra'.

It is fascinating to ponder the concept of Jesus and John as spiritual twins. Jesus represents John's earthly twin brother who must be given spiritual vision, impulse or revelation to return Home. We know that John is the "starry one" because shortly after his birth a "splendorous cloud" came out of the sky, landed, and picked him up. He was mysteriously taken, says the Koran, to a place called Parwan, "the white [pure] mountain." Tula means white mountain and is the pure place in Mayan mythology. John's mother, Elizabeth, did not see him again until he was 22, when he was brought, once again on a splendorous cloud (UFO?), to a region of Jerusalem. Shortly after, John began his ministry.

Tales are told of these two 'brothers', Jesus and John, studying together and initiating one another in the ancient mystery schools. The symbol of the uniting of these two brothers, one heavenly the other earthly, was the double-headed axe revered by the ancient Greeks, Celts and Cretans. The axe was thought to have fallen from heaven as a thunderbolt. Its ancient form was the caduceus. As we will see, the caduceus figures prominently in the visions of Nostradamus, including the last line of this Quatrain and the next Quatrain we will analyze.

The line "his fame and power through sects and eloquence" connects directly to another of Nostradamus' Peacemaker prophecies where the Peace-maker or the Gardener conveys the power of the Word through the staff or Key of Life.

Century I Quatrain 96, speaks directly about the King of Terror's mission and the Key of Life:

> A man will be given the task of destroying
> Temples and sects changed by [strange] fantasies:
> He will harm rocks rather than the living,
> Through ornate language ears will continuously be filled.

This Quatrain goes hand in hand with Quatrain 95. Here we learn the Peacemaker will have the responsibility of breaking down the temples – barriers to the coming of the new Teacher. He is the advance man who clears the way and, in the process, takes all the arrows.

What is meant by the line "he will harm rocks rather than the living"? The Hebrew legends tell us the Messiah, or possibly the Peacemaker, will level the mountains of the Holy Land to make way for the New Jerusalem. Since legends all over the world depict 'gods' leveling mountains with a staff of miracles identical in many ways to the Key of Life, we may presume leveling the mountains of the Holy Land will be one of the reasons the Peacemaker recovers this device. The Key of Life symbolizes the powers of the human mind to work in harmony with nature. By using this inconceivably powerful technology, the Peacemaker (or the Gardener) can do practically anything he desires. The fact that this figure uses it for love makes it sound like Jesus – who smashed the temples and ripped apart the old religious ideas – will be the figure referred to here.

The last line, "... through ornate language ears will continuously be filled," also resonates with Jesus and the power of the Word. "For He spake, and it was done: He commanded, and it stood fast" (Psalm 33:9).

Either through eloquent speeches espousing His teachings or through a tone or vibration (Key) established by the principles of the Key of Life, our ears, the pathways to our *hearts*, will continuously be filled. The purpose of this teaching is to open the seventh seal and to allow the New Jerusalem (Tula) to descend upon the earth. By moving mountains in this way (using the Key of Life), the Peacemaker demonstrates His trademark teaching: "With faith of a grain of mustard seed, ye shall move mountains."

This statement emphasizes the spiritual laws required to release the 'spell of matter', the secret of immortality, and to transcend earth life. The Bible terms them the miracles of resurrection and ascension. Learning these laws will enable us to become immortal inhabitants of the indescribably beautiful world of Tula.

In Century II, Quatrain 29 Nostradamus refers to the Key of Life as the symbol of the Earth Teacher's authority:

The Eastern man shall come forth from his seat
Passing the Apennine mountains to France:
He will cross through the sky, the seas and the snow,
and he will strike everyone with his rod.

Students of the Quatrains universally connect this "Eastern man" with the King of Terror, believing that striking "with his rod" means using a nuclear missile. The rod described here is, again, the Peacemaker's wand which is not a weapon of destruction but rather the "blameless tool of peace," an angelic symbol of healing. This technology is capable of delivering highly charged thought-forms into the world for the enlightenment and healing of the earth. Thus, the rod is a tool for spiritual transformation.

All of this would be of immense interest to many in and of itself. It is, however, merely the tip of the iceberg. The explosive secret which emerges, once the King of Terror is correctly understood, is that his earthly purpose is to clear the way for the Christ, whom Nostradamus called the King of Angolmois.

This mission takes him to his former place of renown, the Hall of Records.

CHAPTER TWENTY-ONE

NOSTRADAMUS AND THE HALL OF RECORDS

We now realize Nostradamus' King of Terror, or Chyren, is an anagram for an American man named Henry who is part of the ancestral line of Peacemakers sent to nurture the Great Tree of Peace (originally planted in the Garden of Eden).

The Great Tree is the symbol for the Golden Age and man's ultimate destiny. The Peacemaker's mission is to tend and care for this tree in preparation for the arrival of the Christ or Gardener, who will harvest its fruit. This Peacemaker will emerge first and will resurrect the King of Angolmois or Tula. Together or separately, their ultimate goal is the creation of Tula, or a new Empire as Nostradamus calls it.

According to Jewish tradition, the Day of the Lord, the Christian Second Coming, is preceded by seven signs beginning with the reappearance of Elijah (Mal. 4:5; Revelation 11:3-6). Elijah (850 B.C.), whose name means 'Yahweh is God', was seen as one who would be precursor and partner of the Messiah. Therefore, he is called the Peacemaker.

The Hopi await the return of the true white brother. This figure matches up with an Iroquois Indian legend of the returning Peacemaker who will unite the four races of man, each race holding a sacred tablet given to them by the Great Spirit.

How will the Peacemaker create world peace and harmony? The answer is given in Matthew 24:29-31:

> *Immediately after the tribulation of those days shall the sun be darkened and the moon shall not give her light, and the stars shall fall from heaven, and the powers of the heavens shall be shaken; and* ***then shall appear the sign of the Son of man in heaven:*** *and then shall all the tribes of the earth mourn, and they shall see the Son of man coming in the clouds of heaven with power and great glory. And he shall send his angels with a great sound of a trumpet and they shall gather together his elect from the four winds, from one end of heaven to the other.*

In Mark it states: "from the four winds, from one end of earth to the uttermost part of heaven." This passage of the Bible speaks directly to several portentous events – celestial and terrestrial – that will presage the arrival of Christ and Tula, including solar and lunar eclipses. It also tells how world peace will be achieved. As the Iroquois and Hopi legend states: He will gather the races together in a sacred circle.

This will come, according to the Hopi prophecy, on the heels of two "earth shakings" or world wars. It must take place before a third. More specifically, the Hopi prophecy states the arrival of the true white brother will be announced by two signs: the sun and the swastika. Most commentators agree, the sun represents Japan and the swastika represents the Third Reich.

In Century I, Quatrain 53 Nostradamus specifically tells us to look for Chyren and the introduction of Tula after two world wars:

> *Two revolutions by the evil scythe-bearer*
> *marks a change of reign and centuries.*
> *The mobile sign moves into its house,*
> *equally favoring both sides.*

"Two revolutions by the evil scythe-bearer" obviously relates to two world wars. The mobile sign is Libra, symbolizing balance. In Century I, Quatrain 56 Nostradamus continues his prophecy:

> *Sooner or later you will see great changes made,*
> *dreadful horrors and vengeances.*
> *For as the moon is led by its angel,*
> *the heavens draw nearer to the Balance.*

The "Balance" in both Quatrains refers, of course, to Tula, a Sanskrit word meaning balance. As the time of the new vibration approaches, the "heavens draw nearer to the Balance" meaning that the earth is spinning in the direction of the galactic core. The signal event for this new vibration is the Grand Cross.

THE GRAND CROSS

On August 11, 1999 a rare astrological alignment of the planets called the Grand Cross will form. The Grand Cross will appear when an opposition of Mars (in Scorpio) to Saturn and Jupiter (in Taurus), is aligned 90 degrees to the opposition of Neptune and Uranus (in Aquarius) with the Sun, Moon and Mercury (in Leo). This is the sign of the Son of Man

These four zodiacal signs – Taurus the bull, Leo the lion, Scorpio the eagle and Aquarius the man – are the four beasts of the Apocalypse, the four beasts of Ezekiel's Mer-Ka-Ba vehicle and the four beasts of the Sphinx. They are also, significantly, the last card of the Tarot – the World or the Wheel of Time.

On August 11, 1999 a total eclipse of the sun will accompany the appearance of the Grand Cross. Nostradamus states in Century III, Quatrain 34:

> *When there is an eclipse of the sun in broad daylight,*
> *the monster will be seen.*
> *Many will interpret it in different ways.*
> *They will not care about money or make provision for it.*

The Jehovah's Witnesses and the Seventh Day Adventists believe this will be the end of the world. Actually, it is the very beginning of a new world.

Underneath the Sphinx, in the long-buried Hall of Records, are sacred writings of the antediluvian civilization of Atlantis. These writings provide proof that the world's existing religions – Judaism, Christianity, Islam – are built on sand. The King of Terror is so named because he will reveal proof of man's true identity.

Dr. Joseph Robert Jochmans (author of *Time Capsule: the Search for the Lost Hall of Records in Ancient Egypt*) presents a convincing case that Nostradamus provided us with an amazing cluster of verses that presage the opening of the esteemed Hall of Records. For example, Century VII, 14 states:

> *They will come to discover the hidden topography of the land*
> [at Giza, as occurred in 1993]
> *The urns holding wisdom*
> *within the monuments* [the Pyramids] *opened up,*
> *Their contents will cause the understanding*
> *of holy philosophy to expand greatly,*
> *White exchanged for black, falsehoods exposed, new wisdom*
> *replacing the established tradition that no longer [work].*

It is interesting to note that (according to the tradition of the Jews) the Peacemaker will form an eight-member committee or cabinet. There are eight keyholders to the Hall of Records, four men and four women, plus the ninth – the nameless one who likely will be the Peacemaker.

Nostradamus quite possibly refers to these nine in Century I, Quatrain 81 where he says:

> *Nine will be set apart from the flock,*
> *Separated from judgement and advice:*
> *Their fate is to be divided as they depart,*
> *Kappa, Theta, Lambda, banished and scattered.*

This Quatrain has been routinely interpreted as a reference to the space shuttle *Challenger* disaster. Only seven crew members were on board the shuttle, not nine. The Greek letters K, T (the sound Th), and L remain enigmatic. Could these nine people "separated from judgement and advice" be the righteous ones, the keyholders?

The Hall of Records is thought to be guarded by demons and apparitions who kill any who do not truly belong. These demons are triggered by the subconscious fears of those entering the Hall. In this regard it is interesting to read Century VI, Quatrain 28:

> *Within the islands of five rivers to one,*
> *by the crescent of the great Chyren Selin.*
> *Through the mists in the air, the fury of one.*
> *Six escaped, hidden in bundles of flax.*

Is Nostradamus telling us one of the nine got cold feet and triggered their demon, the "fury of one," who killed three of the aspirants? If so, how did the others escape? Nostradamus tells us they escaped "hidden in bundles of flax." Flax is associated with the spinning of a spider. From this we can deduce the other six wrapped or hid themselves in cocoons of protective white light, perhaps even their Mer-Ka-Ba vehicles.

According to Joseph R. Jochmans in his *Giza Two: Keys to the Hall of Records*, celestial conjunctions serve as triggers to the openings of the Hall of Records. The prophetic time-line in the Great Pyramid marks the dates of these openings. The celestial timing for the next opening of the Hall of Records begins February 21, 1999. This period of opening will culminate on August 5-6, 1999 at which time the symbols for opening the sister Halls in the Yucatan and elsewhere will be revealed. The Peacemaker returns in July of that same year.

The final opening will occur from May 4-14, 2003. According to Jochmans this opening will see further revelations brought to light and the establishment of the first Planetary Initiation Center in Egypt.

The dates of the opening of the Hall of Records share an interesting parallel with the date prophesied by Nostradamus for the arrival of the King of Terror. According to the Bible, the two witnesses of Christ will proclaim the gospel of the Kingdom of God during a period of 1290 days. Counting from August 5-7, 1999 (the culmination of the soonest opening of the Hall) to May 4, 2003 (the next date of opening) we arrive at the figure of 1335 days. We notice a difference of 45 days.

There is a Talmudic tradition that says Elijah, the reincarnated way shower of the Messiah, will flee from the forces of Satan into the desert with the rest of the 'righteous' (the rest of the Company of 8). This could be the people beyond judgement or advice, to which Nostradamus referred.

Since Satan is thought to have near god-like powers it would make sense Elijah would head to a safe area free from attack. Is there a greater fortress on the planet than the Great Pyramid? According to this tradition, after 45 days the righteous, who could be the eight key holders or the Committee of 8, will return with the Messiah to begin the age of redemption. These 45 days are the precise difference between the 1290 day period and the 1335 day period between the auspicious openings of the Hall of Records. This 1335 day period is also noted in Daniel 12:12, "Blessed is he who waits, and comes to the one thousand three hundred and thirty-five days."

Returning to Nostradamus' prophecy about the "nine...set apart from the flock," it may be that three of the members, those with the initials K, Th and L, do not survive Satan's attack.

This Quatrain may refer to something quite different, however. A part of the Peacemaker's overall mission is to bring Moses back to life and to reveal the location of the Ark of the Covenant. One of the magical objects associated with the Ark *and* Moses is the Breastplate of Aaron, Moses' brother. This breastplate is described in minute detail in Exodus 28:15-30, where it is called the "breastplate of *judgment*." The term 'breastplate' is partially correct; it is actually a linen pouch. The Hebrew term used to describe it is *chosen* (ChShN) meaning it was to be worn by the chosen one or the Elect one. The chosen one wears the breastplate in order to detect the will of God. In other words, he goes to it for *advice*!

81. High Priest wearing Breastplate of Judgment stands before the Ark of the Covenant.

On its front, this object held twelve precious and semiprecious stones which are described as very large and very beautiful. Each stone was said to be engraved with the name of an angel and one of the twelve tribes of Israel "like engravings of a signet" (Exodus 28:21). Some even speculate that the stones bore the Ineffable Name of God and from this Name arose the breastplate's power.

My question is this: is it possible Nostradamus saw the chosen one wearing the breastplate and that three of the stones, three of the tribes, K, Th and L were missing?

This K, Th and L reference is worth further investigation. It should first be stated that Nostradamus was a converted Jew. Throughout his life the Catholic Inquisition hounded him for 'interviews'. Fearing further persecution, Nostradamus wrote specific names as anagrams. Interestingly, the name of the angel associated with the first stone on the breastplate of Aaron is *Kethahel*, or **KeTHaheL**. This angel corresponds to the Apostle Peter, the founder of the Catholic church. Is Nostradamus secretly trying to tell us the Catholic church will be destroyed when the Hall of Records is opened?

ENTERING THE HALL

Our attention turns now to entering the Hall of Records. This is not easy. Legend tells us this Hall of Records is perhaps the most carefully guarded cache of knowledge in the world.

The Peacemaker certainly won't simply walk in the Hall. Or will he? Mary Caine (in her book *The Glastonbury Zodiac*) relates a Jewish legend of the Middle Ages that shows a clear relationship between the Sphinx and the Christ. Recall, that only a man of Enoch/Thoth will be able to elude the security system installed by Thoth. This means he will have a personal vibration or other identifying characteristic, perhaps a hidden name or word of power like *open sesame*, which will grant him passage. Mary Caine writes: "The Hidden Name was secretly inscribed in the innermost recesses of the Temple, guarded by a sculptured lion." The Temple, guarded by the sculptured lion, can be none other than the Great Pyramid. She further writes:

> *If, as was most likely, an intruder saw the name, the lion would give such a supernatural roar that all memory of it would be driven from his mind. But Jesus knew this; he evaded the lion, wrote the Name, cut his thigh open and hid it within the wound, closing it by magic. Once out of the Temple he re-opened the incision and took out the sacred letters.*

In Revelation 19:16, John writes of the returning Christ: "He hath on his thigh a name written, King of Kings, and Lord of Lords." This name is the Ineffable Name of God, the ancient 'word of power' – the abracadabra, open sesame or amatasarabataataramada – thought to give its knower control over the elements of the universe. Biblical tradition has it that this Name was first revealed to Moses when he went up Sinai, God's pure mountain. In receiving the Name, Moses took on the power of God.

It is possible the Ineffable Name can be traced back to ancient China, Egypt or Babylonia where it has been passed down from master to initiate for millennia. Presumably, the Name originated in the Garden of Eden and, therefore, with Tula.

Astonishingly, Nostradamus left us an as yet unsolved Quatrain involving a word of power. This prediction has been erroneously linked to the concept of the Antichrist. Century IX Quatrain 62 reads:

To the great one Cheramon agora
Will all the crosses be attached by rank,
The long lasting opium and mandragora,
Rougon will be released on October the third.

This odd Quatrain, though not (it seems) immediately applicable to the Peacemaker or Chyren, contains some startling information upon further decipherment.

First, the matter of the mandrake or the "opium and mandragora." We recall John the Baptist and Elijah were thought to be clothed in camel's hair. According to John Allegro (*The Sacred Mushroom and the Cross*), the point of 'camel' in this context is that the Hebrew name for the camel, kirkarah, created a word-play on the Greek name for the Mandrake, *kirkaia*. When I traced back the word Kur, I found that KUR-KUR was the Sumerian name for Mandrake. Literally, it means 'two cones' or mountains. Tula was known as the place of two mountains and was often depicted as two cones or pyramids upholding a circle or sun. Furthermore, the Greek name for the staff of the Peacemakers is *kerykeion*. As we discussed, the staff is capable of transmitting the *Word* or *breath* of God emanating from Tula.

Amazingly, *Cheramon agora*, the terms used by Nostradamus in the first line, are thought to be what the magicians of the ancient world termed 'barbarous words of evocation'. According to the reasoning of the Essenes, if you knew the names of magic plants (like the sacred mushroom) you could gain their power to transmit and understand secret doctrine, or literally, to open an entry way to the kingdom of God or Tula. The mandrake created a mental environment conducive to decoding the secrets of god.

82. Tula sits atop the Key of Life

The mandrake, in particular, was at the center of the Essene tradition. As stated earlier, the Essenes were likely formed by Enki, the Gardener and King of Tula. It should not surprise us that they would treasure the means to returning to Tula. In associating the mandrake with the Peacemaker Nostradamus, himself a Jew, displayed remarkable insight into the Hebrew rites; for mandrake, we learn, is the nectar or food of the gods. The Essene term for it is the 'Christ food', a chemical or super nutrient which opened the gates of consciousness to Tula.

The Holy Plant, mandrake, was dangerous to harvest, sometimes even causing death. The uncanny, almost frightening, similarity between the body of man and the mandrake is one of the puzzles of natural science. Cursed be they who dug up the mandrake. Strangely, this might account for the fact that the Peacemaker is invariably accompanied by a dog. One method of safely removing the mandrake from the ground was to tie a dog to it, then call the animal to follow. When the dog followed, pulling the mandrake, the dog promptly died.

Apart from the puns involved, decipherment of the mandrake reveals not only the identity of the Peacemaker, but also dovetails with another of his missions. The second task of the Peacemaker and the Messiah is to reveal the location (and presumably recover) the lost Ark of the Covenant, the Flask of Manna, and the container of sacred anointing oil which mysteriously disappeared from the Temple of Solomon.

What is Manna and the sacred anointing oil? Manna was nothing less than the 'bread' of heaven, the super nutrient or food of the gods. Manna is the sacred mushroom. It was connected with the Morning Star (an epithet for Jesus and John the Baptist, as well as Thoth) and was thought to form a bridge between man and god. Manna is the Christ food. The anointing oil was called chrestus by the Essenes.

It was believed by the ancients that the soul could be released from the body. One of the apparatus involved was the Ark of the Covenant. We will return to the Ark in the next two chapters. For now I merely wish to point out that there appears to be little doubt that partaking of the sacred food and anointing oneself with the chrestus was a prerequisite to soul travel through the Ark: an ancient combination of mind expansion with high technology. It is as if the Tin Man and the Scarecrow put their heads together to create a way to travel to Oz.

The second line of Nostradamus' Quatrain, "will all the crosses be attached by rank," would be obscure if we hadn't already decoded the prophecy of Matthew in which the sign of the Son of Man appears in the sky. This occurs in July 1999. All the crosses will be attached by rank. The sun-cross or enclosed cross is the symbol for Tula. Each of the planets are colonies of Tula. The sun-cross is the flag or emblem of the 'federation of Tula'. Saturn is a cross; Earth is a cross. Thus, when they come together, as in a Grand Cross, they are attached by rank.

Does all of this imply the Peacemaker will use words of power derived from a sacred substance to release something called Rougon on October 3? Rougon is an as yet unsolved place name. Or is it possible Nostradamus used the term release (instead of the obvious resurrect) to intimate the resurrection of the King of Angolmois?

In the next chapter we will investigate this further, but first a word of warning from Nostradamus to the man who opens the Hall of Records. In Century IX, Quatrain 7, Nostradamus advises:

> *The man who opens the tomb when it is found*
> *and who does not shut it immediately,*
> *evil will come to him.*
> *No one will be able to prove it.*
> *It might have been better were he a Breton or a Norman king.*

Here, Nostradamus appears to be saying that a trick door guards the Hall which must be shut immediately. What of the line, "no one will be able to prove it"? Although the Peacemaker, the King of Terror, will resurrect the Christ, he will not be able to prove it. With a hint of sarcasm Nostradamus concludes: he might as well have been the King of Breton rather than the King of Terror.

CHAPTER TWENTY-TWO

RETURN OF MOSES TO LIFE

As I have stated several times, the Peacemaker must bring Moses and the generation of the desert, the Children of Light, back to life. In the next two chapters we will get to the heart of this matter.

Before getting into the manner in which the Peacemaker might accomplish this and what Nostradamus has to say about it, a question should be answered: Why is it so crucial to bring Moses back to life?

TWO WITNESSES

First of all, the Book of Revelation speaks of two witnesses to the return of Christ: "And I will give power to my two witnesses, and they will prophesy one thousand two hundred and sixty days, clothed in *sackcloth*." By the Law of Moses two witnesses are required on important matters of judgment. In 2 Corinthians 13:1 Paul confirms this law, "By the mouth of two or three witnesses every word shall be established."

How do we know the two witnesses are the Peacemaker and Moses? When Christ was transfigured, Moses and Elijah appeared with Him, linking these two as the witnesses: "His face shone like the sun, and His clothes became as white as the light, And behold, Moses and Elijah appeared to them, talking with Him" (Matthew 17: 2-3).

DEATH TO THE WITNESSES

When Moses returns in our time he will assist the Peacemaker in testifying to the Kingdom of the Messiah. Unfortunately, say the legends of the Jews, these two witnesses will die at the hands of Satan. John wrote in Revelation, "the beast that ascends out of the bottomless pit, will make war against them, overcome them, and kill them" (Revelation 11:7).

With their dead bodies laying in the streets of Jerusalem, unburied, their enemies will rejoice believing they defeated God's messengers. Then, "after three and a half days through the breath of God" (perhaps channeled through the staff of miracles by the Christ just as when Lazarus was raised from the dead two thousand years ago), Moses and the Peacemaker will hear "a loud voice from heaven" saying to them, "Come up here," and they will ascend "to heaven in a cloud" in full view of the entire world. The world, perhaps tuning in on CNN, will be astonished and either afraid or joyous in realization of the power of the event and all it portends.

THE TWO OLIVE TREES

The key to unlocking the secrets of the Book of Revelation and Nostradamus' references to this pair of witnesses is in recognition of the fact that they were also known as the two olive trees, and the "two lampstands standing before the God of the earth" (Revelation 11:3,4). As Zecharia 4:11-14 says, "These are the two anointed ones, they stand by the Lord of the whole earth." Since Christ is the 'God of the earth' or the 'King of the World' described in the last chapter, this statement is loaded with a massive amount of information about His two witnesses – information required to decode the prophecy of Nostradamus.

The oil of the olive tree was used to fuel lamps; therefore, it is a symbol of illumination. This oil symbolizes the Holy Spirit which, as we know, John the Baptist was filled with from birth. It was Gabri-el who appeared to John's father and informed him that he would bear a male child who would be filled with the Holy Spirit. What this means is that he was filled with the spiritual influences of the Peacemakers. In the Hebrew Kaballah the 'Holy Spirit' was symbolized by the 'dew of Light' which seeped from the Tree of Life.

The Sumerian words for 'live' and 'intoxicate' are the same – TIN; and the 'tree of life', GEShTIN, is the 'vine' of living. From this, we can deduce the Peacemaker and Moses will be linked by the Key of Life, which to ancients appears to have been either an intoxicating substance or a super nutrient. Right on schedule, the mandrake, the powerful hallucinogenic, appears once again. The mandrake was thought to be most powerful when touched by the morning dew. As the 'Morning Star' Jesus was the bringer of the dew.

This 'dew of Light' relates directly to entering the Hall of Records which is thought to be guarded by demons. It also illuminates Nostradamus' Quatrain regarding the mandrake in Century IX, Quatrain 62:

> To the great one of Cheramon agora
> Will all the crosses be attached by rank,
> The long lasting opium and mandragora
> Rougon will be released on October 3.

Here's the connection. "Cheramon agora" means word of power. This is reported to be the key to entering the Hall of Records. Once inside it offers protection, as well. The Greek word *daimon* derives from the Persian *dew*.

It is vital for the entrant into the Hall to know the names of the demons he is trying to counteract. It is more important to be able to call upon their opposite, the Ineffable Name of God or Name of Power. This name formed an important part of the Essene's secret knowledge. John the Baptist likely learned this name from Jesus, who it is said, will have it written upon his thigh at the time of the Second Coming. Revelation 19:11-16 states:

> *And I saw heaven opened, and behold a white horse;*
> *and he that sat upon him was called Faithful and True....*
> *and his name was called The Word of God....*
> *And He hath on His vesture and on his thigh a name written,*
> *KING OF KINGS, AND LORD OF LORDS.*

Moses definitely knew this Ineffable Name, having learned it on his trips up Mount Sinai or Tula. This means bringing Moses back to life could serve the purpose of learning the Word of Power to gain entrance into the Hall. Of course, this presupposes that the reason for entering the Hall is not to secure the means to bring Moses back to life to begin with. Reviving him will be accomplished before this by some other means.

For the moment, we will leave the issue of whether this Ineffable Name of power is learned or remembered through the ingestion of a hallucinogen, super nutrient or 'the dew of Christ' before entering the Hall, or if Moses brings the Name with him. Either way, the point is made in Revelation: the key to unlocking the Christian mysteries, particularly those surrounding this mission, involves some form of mind expansion.

CLAD IN SACKCLOTH

The mind expansion hypothesis is reinforced in the description of the clothing of the two witnesses: they are clothed in sackcloth. This may just mean that they were dressed casually: the antique equivalent of wearing blue jeans. More likely, it is related to the New Testament passage that describes John the Baptist as clothed in camel's hair (Matthew 3:4).

As we have already learned, John's attire is meant to directly connect him with Elijah, who "wore a garment of hair-cloth" (II Kings 1:8), which is to say camel hair or sackcloth. Both materials are a purely symbolic way to say that Elijah and John were connected to an ancient brotherhood.

The point of the "camel hair" is that the Hebrew name for the *double-humped* animal, *kirkarah*, allowed a constructive word-play or pun on the Greek name for the staff of the Peacemakers, *kerykeion*. As shown earlier, kerykeion can be traced to the Sumerian root, KUR, meaning two mountains, an epithet for the two cosmic mountains of Tula – one earthly, one heavenly. *Korkoron* was the Greek name for the mandrake.

BRINGING MOSES BACK TO LIFE

Now, here is how all of this relates to the Peacemaker's mission of bringing Moses back to life. Mind expansion or activation of the Divine Gene was very much a part of Old and New Testament religious worship. In particular, they were closely connected with *necromancy*, the raising of the spirits of the dead for fortunetelling. With this in mind we can make sense of Isaiah 26:19:

The dead shall live, their bodies shall rise.
O dwellers in the dust, awake and sing for joy!
For thy dew is a dew of light,
and on the land of the shades thou wilt let it fall.

We have established that a sacred nutrient or word of power is a link to Tula. What if – because the Peacemaker is an office of the Christ which Moses previously held – it were possible that he *and only he* could contact Moses by projecting his consciousness through an enhanced mind-state? Or, what if the reverse occurred, and Moses took it upon himself to seek out the Peacemaker, perhaps appearing to the Peacemaker during a state of expanded consciousness?

Either way, the Peacemaker would be able to discuss and discover the secrets of the past, including the Ineffable Name of God, and tap into Moses' fountain of wisdom. Thereafter, it could be said that the Peacemaker possesses the knowledge or 'spirit' of Moses. If so, when the Hebrew legend tells us Moses and the Peacemaker will be killed in the streets of Jerusalem, they are correct: they are 'one'.

I believe this soul combining, a process similar to the way the Christ inhabited the body of Jesus, is how the Peacemaker will bring Moses back to life. In the next chapter I will propose how he is to perform this feat.

CHAPTER TWENTY-THREE

NOSTRADAMUS
AND THE RETURN OF MOSES

In the 1940's a kind of resurrection of Moses/Akhenaten occurred. It was then that a Chinese representative of the Rosicrucian Brotherhood appeared at the Rosicrucian Fraternity in San Jose, California. His mission was to deliver an ancient manuscript secretly held in an Asian repository for millennia. This book was thought to have been written by Akhenaten. The Rosicrucians decoded the book and released it under the title *Unto Thee I Grant*. If authentic, this manuscript proves that ancient documents are held in secret repositories throughout the world and that their release is tied to an ancient time frame. It may also have more ominous undertones, possibly suggesting the battle between the Children of Light and the Children of Darkness is still being waged.

The Hebrew legends and the Book of Revelation make it clear that the presence of Moses is required for the return of the Earth Teacher. Is it possible this manuscript, in the same manner as the channelled work *A Course In Miracles* fulfilled the Second Coming of Christ, fulfilled that prophecy? Personally, I do not think so. Nostradamus, however, foresaw the return of Moses and encoded in his Quatrains the events leading up to this return. As could be expected, Moses' return revolves around the Ark of the Covenant.

It is my belief (and it is one reinforced by the Egyptian traditions) that the Ark of the Covenant likely contains a piece of Moses/Akhenaten's hair and this is one key to 'bringing him back to life'. In ancient Egypt locks of hair were used as amulets, often for sentimental reasons, but more powerfully to ensure the perpetuation of the love bonds between the person whose hair it was and the person in possession of it. These practices are found in many cultures, including the African, Australian, European and the American Indian.

The laws of sympathetic magic are very clear in this matter: a person's strength was thought to be embodied in their hair. So powerfully was this belief held that extreme care was made to insure that a leader's hair did not fall into the hands of an enemy.

The Biblical story of Samson and Delilah clearly depicts this belief. The Book of Judges explicitly tells us God bestowed the gift of being omnipotent and indestructible in battle to Samson as long as he did not cut his hair. The Bible states that the magical power of hair is God-given. In the Biblical story Samson was deceived by his wife, Delilah, who revealed to Samson's enemy, the Philistines, that the source of his strength was in his hair. While Samson was asleep in Delilah's arms, they cut seven (the number of the supernatural) locks of his hair resulting in his defeat.

The law of contagious magic states that once a substance, such as a lock of hair, has been in contact with a person, it will remain connected with that person, even after centuries of separation. Thus, if one had a lock of a someone's hair, such as Moses', one would be in contact with him across time and distance. It is even conceivable to be able to influence people through their hair.

Nostradamus clearly envisioned the return of Moses. He left us a kind of movie trailer, or brief scenes, depicting his vision. These 'scenes' culminate in the use of a substance which I believe to be a lock of Moses/Akhenaten's hair.

The relevant scenes begin in Century IX, Quatrain 20:

> *By night will come through the forest of Reines,*
> *two partners, by a roundabout way.*
> *The queen, the white stone.*
> *The monk-king dressed in gray at Varennes.*
> *The elected Capet causes tempest, fire and bloody slicing.*

This is a truly amazing Quatrain. It was once thought to be describing the flight to Varennes by Louis XVI and Marie Antoinette in 1791. The king and queen eluded certain death, escaping through a secret door in the Queen's apartment. Among their possessions was a diamond necklace, the *pierre blanche* or white stone. I now question this interpretation. The key to unlocking this Quatrain is the white stone, which is the same white stone mentioned in Revelation 2:17 which by now is self-explanatory:

> *To him that overcometh will I give to eat of the secret manna,*
> *and I will give him a white stone,*
> *and in this stone a new name written,*
> *which no man knoweth saving he that receiveth it.*

The other key to this Quatrain is the mention of Reines. A mysterious affair has been going on in a small village in the Basque country of the Pyrenees called Rennes-le-Chateau. The mystery of Rennes-le-Chateau, as we will see momentarily, is closely connected with a white stone, which is also known as the 'Godstone' or 'Firestone'. The Greek word for fire is *pyros*, and St. Jerome called the Pyrenees "Purenaia, the mountain of fire." Everyone from the Knights Templar, the Cathars, the Merovingians, and King Solomon to King Arthur have been linked to this secluded little town and its neighbor, Rennes-le-Bains, where stands a mysterious Black Stone!

Nostradamus was aware of the mysteries of Rennes-le-Chateau through his good friend Francois Rabelais, whose *Pantagruel* is a coded primer for the mysteries of the area and may have pointed Nostradamus to the white stone which is central to the resurrection of the King of Tula.

The immense story of the tiny little village of Rennes-le-Chateau has been extensively told in the best-selling *Holy Blood, Holy Grail*, but to fully appreciate the Quatrains of Nostradamus, it will help to recap the mystery. Nostradamus is trying to tell us that the Peacemaker and his wife, the Seshet/Queen Nefertiti consciousness, will journey to France, and soon (in order to uncover the new, secret name of God encased in the White Stone) they will return Moses to life and (dare we say?) resurrect or awaken the King of Tula.

THE MYSTERY OF RENNES-LE-CHATEAU

Up until 1885 Rennes-le-Chateau was best known as the place of one of the most horrific slaughters the Catholic Church ever perpetrated on humankind: the Albigensian Crusade. From 1209-1249 a mass genocide was conducted against the Cathars, a quiet group of Gnostic Christians whose only apparent crime seemed to be that they worshipped God differently from Pope Innocent III. The Pope became their executioner by sending 30,000 storm troopers to exterminate them.

The real reason for this slaughter began to surface in 1885 when an obscure priest, Berenger Sauniere, was appointed curé of the church of Rennes-le-Chateau. One day, while making badly needed repairs on his church, the priest made a chance discovery of a cache of documents, genealogical charts, and Latin texts written in an almost unsolvable code. Luckily, the key to its deciphering was discovered by Sauniere on a gravestone in the churchyard at Rennes.

The coded manuscript revealed an amazing cipher:

TO DAGOBERT II, KING, AND TO SION BELONGS THIS TREASURE AND HE IS THERE DEAD.

The emphasis on SION catches our attention. This is the Hebrew term for Tula. For Sauniere, however, this discovery meant a great deal more. It was a key that unlocked a door to the highest echelons of French society. Actors, authors, artists, high-ranking bishops all entered Sauniere's circle; and, more mysteriously, he became instantly, enormously wealthy, spending millions on church works and high living. If we stopped here, the mystery of Rennes-le-Chateau and Sauniere's rags to riches story would be of interest. We might ponder what ancient relic he may have discovered in his church and how much money some wealthy patron in Paris or Rome might have paid him for it. We might question why in 1917, the normally healthy Sauniere was dead of a stroke, and why his housekeeper, who was said to have shared the priest's secret, had ordered his casket several days before his death.

The truth is Sauniere's story thus far is merely the 'home page' or starting point on the Rennes mystery lode. For the true secret which Sauniere stumbled upon, (a secret which also explains the massacre of the Cathars) is that Rennes-le-Chateau is the site of a pre-Flood Temple of the Stars, a terrestrial zodiac marking an ancient location of Tula. The design for this temple, I believe, originated with Jesus from his role as a Tekton.

Stretching for miles across the landscape is an immense geometric temple whose engineering complexity rivals the Great Pyramid. Rennes-le-Chateau is a Holy Place, but not just any Holy Place. Not only is it considered the largest temple constructed by man, but many investigators also believe that it is the original Temple of Solomon or Zion, a gateway to heaven. For thousands of years the Cathars guarded this secret location, which is the sacred center of the Merovingians, one of the original tribes of Israel.

What is the shape of this temple? It is a five-pointed pentagram, the symbol of Venus, the heavenly counterpart of Mary Magdalen, and the symbol which magicians inscribe in a circle when performing the magical ritual of resurrection. At the next level of resolution, the temple pattern became a six-petaled flower of life. In this way the entire vicinity of Rennes-le-Chateau is a temple of resurrection, a link between the worlds of matter and spirit.

In the second of two parchments discovered by Sauniere is a clearly visible 'hidden' text. Incredibly it spells out REX MUNDI – 'King of the

World'. This was the name of the God the Cathars worshipped which Pope Innocent III wished to eradicate. The King of the World is also an epithet for Nostradamus' King of Angolmoi or Mongolia and refers to the King of Tula. Yet this is not all!

Sauniere's church at Rennes-le-Chateau is dedicated to Mary Magdalen. On the lintel of the porch above the entry into the church, Sauniere inscribed the following words: "Terrible is this place!"

These are the exact words spoken by the biblical Jacob upon awakening from his dream of ascending and descending the ladder. He called the place Beth-el, but we are reminded its ancient name is Luz or Tula. The words which follow in Jacob's quotation from Genesis 28:17 are: "This is none other but the house of God, and this is the gate to heaven."

The message is clear. Sauniere is telling us Rennes-le-Chateau is a gateway to heaven. To emphasize this, just beyond the lintel of his church, Sauniere commissioned and installed an oversized statue of Rex Mundi! This statue closely resembles the nature god Pan who is linked to a Garden of Eden-like existence. The Cathars associated Rex Mundi with The Gardener. The Cathars possessed only one book of the new testament: the Book of John. This is the only Book which tells the story of the appearance of The Gardener.

The ancient parchments and the attention of Sauniere make it clear: there is a deep connection between the 'King of the World' (the resurrected King of Tula) and the hidden treasure of Rennes-le-Chateau which many connect with Mary Magdalen. Mary's confrontation with the Gardener on Easter morning now takes on supreme importance.

There are two-thousand year old legends that say that after the Crucifixion, Mary Magdalen sailed to France, pregnant with the daughter of Jesus. According to Margaret Starbird (*The Woman with the Alabaster Jar*), Mary also sailed with Jesus' personal plans for the construction of a temple, which I believe to have been a Tula. Jesus' Tula was constructed on the ground at Rennes-le-Chateau.

The successors of the royal line established by Jesus and Mary are the Merovingians, who ruled most of France and Germany during the 5th and 6th centuries. These priest-kings were often called sorcerer kings and were widely known as healers and recognized by their trademark, long hair, which they believed gave them strength. Soon after Sauniere's discovery (and before his trip to Paris), he was visited by the head of the Hapsburg family, the leader of the Merovingians. The exact nature of the visit is unknown. However, one thing is certain. It had to do with the mysterious parchments discovered by Sauniere.

The Merovingian bloodline has been traced to Mary Magdalen's tribe of Benjamin, one of the original twelve tribes of Israel. The Bible tells a cleverly disguised story of the Benjaminites relations with Tula. At one time the Benjaminites were ostracized from the other tribes. The women were forbidden from marrying men of the tribe of Benjamin. Later, this tribe was told it could go live in the *vineyards*, and when the "daughters of Shiloh" came out to dance, the Benjaminites could catch them and make them their wives (Judges 21:20-21).

So, the Benjaminites married the daughters of Shiloh. What is so interesting about this is that Shiloh was the location of the House of God, the Tula, the sanctuary where the Ark of the Covenant with the tablets of the word were housed. In Genesis 49:10 we learn:

The sceptre shall not depart from Judah,
nor a law-giver from between his feet,
until Shiloh comes to whom it belongs. . .

The scepter is, of course, the Key of Life. The word *Shiloh* means 'place of rest' or peace. Apparently, it was a place where the principles of Tula were taught. Therefore, it is the place where the Peacemakers dwelt; and, indeed, Shiloh is substituted for the name of a person, the Messiah who emanates from Tula. If the Peacemakers were a group of highly advanced, possibly extraterrestrial beings then, in being able to marry them, the tribe of Benjamin was given a very high honor.

The Benjaminites were known to have possessed the city of Jerusalem, the City of Peace. Indeed, the first king of Israel was Saul, a "man of Benjamin." This "Benjamin" was originally called Ben Oni, which must refer to the ben-ben or rocketships housed at the biblical city of On or Heliopolis, which earlier I identified as an ancient Tula. Ben Oni was later changed to Ben Jan Min, or 'son of the right hand'. The right hand of God refers to The Peacemaker. Legends speak of the Holy Grail as the Sang Graal, the holy blood. Is the holy bloodline of Jesus the Holy Grail? Did this bloodline continue with the Merovingians? Will they be responsible for returning the King of Tula to earth at Rennes-le-Chateau?

Marriage with supernatural beings seems to be a trademark of this family. Merovee is the man who gave his name to the Merovingian dynasty. The name *Mer* is derived from both mother and sea, while *ovee* is derived from the root word for egg. There is a very interesting legend attached to the birth of Merovee. One day his mother went swimming in the ocean while already pregnant with her son. There, she encountered a sea-being who abducted, seduced, raped her and then grafted his own genetic material onto Merovee's developing fetus. According to the legends, when Merovee grew into manhood, he possessed extraordinary supernatural powers gaining fame as a sorcerer/magician/king. An early Latin version of this legend describes the sea creature as "resembling a Quinotaur." The *quin* root catches our attention. Quin is the root for five and for *quintessence*, the elusive, purer-than-fire fifth element.

Enki, The Gardener and King of Tula, was depicted by the Dogon tribe of Africa and the Babylonians as a half-man half-fish form. One ancient seal carries the inscription describing Enki as "god of the pure life." It has been suggested that the story of Merovee as the son of a sea creature is a symbolic way of saying he was a descendent of the offspring of Mary Magdalen and Jesus – Jesus who was symbolized by the fish. If Jesus were in fact Thoth, he would also be the son of Enki.

In 1967, a mysterious manuscript containing a series of 13 poems was published under the title *LE SERPENT ROUGE* (The Red Serpent). The verses represent a symbolic or allegorical pilgrimage through the twelve signs of the zodiac, beginning with Aquarius and ending with Capricorn. Le Serpent Rouge also contains a Merovingian genealogy and two maps of France in Merovingian times, in addition to insights into the Merovingians. Taken together, the verses and other data appear to be the story of a red snake, representing a bloodline or lineage, uncoiling across the centuries – the bloodline of Jesus Christ. Nearby Rennes-le-Chateau is a ground feature which lies unmistakably in the shape of a serpent. Incidentally, adding to the aura of mystery surrounding this document is the curiosity that the three authors who wrote this leaflet all died within 24 hours of one another – by hanging.

A significant point should be made here. Le Serpent Rouge contained 13 verses corresponding to the 12 signs in the zodiac. But there are only 12 signs. What is the 13th? The additional sign is that of Ophiuchus, Keeper of the Serpent. Ophiuchus is the Greek name for Imhotep who, as we have seen, was believed to have been the reincarnated Thoth/Enoch, the Peacemaker.

Lying only a few degrees from the mathematically determined center of our galaxy, Ophiuchus is the closest constellation to Tula. At Rennes, through sacred geometry, the highest point of the pentagram "opens" to reveal a hidden thirteen-pointed star. Points "1" and "13" are simultaneously point one of the pentagram. This reveals the location of the gate to Tula.

A six-petalled Flower of Life (one of the symbols of Jesus) is found at the center of the maze at Chartres Cathedral (built by the nine French knights). This maze is an enclosed sun cross, the symbol of Tula. It is 666 feet long and is divided into seven levels. The message here is that once we master earth life (symbolized by 666) by opening our 7 seals, we go to the next dimensional overtone: 777. This is the number of the Pleiades. In myths, Jesus took initiates through this stargate onward to Tula, or 888. Geometrically, the six-petalled Flower of Life at the center of the maze can only be divided evenly into thirteen points. This means the message at Rennes-le-Chateau is duplicated at Chartres, suggesting their builders were related and that both knew the secret of Tula.

This bit of information would sail past our consciousness were it not for the fact that the total eclipse of the sun on August 11, 1999 (which forms the Grand Cross, the sign of the son of Man, and portends the resurrection of the King of Kings) will form at a point in the heavens that astrologers refer to as "the point of the Avatar."

Furthermore, this eclipse is directly connected with another total eclipse that will happen on November 13, 2012 – 13 years after the 1999 eclipse. This eclipse will be in alignment with the 13th constellation of the zodiac, Ophiuchus the 'Serpent Holder'. This constellation is the archetype of Chiron, the shaman/healer who has the secret of life. In the language of astrology, this eclipse will signal the initiation of humanity into the mysteries that Ophiuchus represents – the mystery of Tula.

According to Jose Arguelles and Ray Mardyks the timing of this eclipse is no accident. The November 13, 1999 eclipse is keyed to the time when we will be in close proximity to the galactic core, the heavenly Tula. It is believed that a large influx of cosmic energy will inundate the earth at this time. The source of this energy is Tula.

What is the nature of this energy? The astronomical name for the constellation Ophiuchus is Asculapius, and it lies between Scorpio and Sagittarius in an area loaded with nebulae. Asclapius/Imhotep/Quetzalcoatl represents the Peacemaker and is associated with healing through the Key of

Life. This means we may all soon possess the means to transform ourselves into Christed beings.

Le Serpent Rouge offers many clues to the Peacemaker's mission. Under the sign of Aquarius we read:

> *How strange are the manuscripts of this friend,* **great traveller** *of the unknown. They come together as a* **white light** *but for one who knows separately, they are the colors of the rainbow; for the artist these six colors unite like magic in his palette and form black.*

The name the Buddhists gave Jesus was the Great Traveller. So, of course, we are talking of Him. The white light is a diamond. While colorless, the diamond contains all colors; while it can cut anything, nothing can cut it. Consisting in the same atoms as coal or graphite (blackness), the diamond demonstrates the transformation of a substance from a state of disorder to one of supreme order and clarity.

Under Pisces we read:

> *This friend, how would you know him? His name is a mystery but his number is that of a famous seal. How can one describe him? Maybe like the pilot of the everlasting Ark of Noah, impassive like a pillar on his* **white rock** *looking beyond the black rock towards the south.*

This white rock is the white stone to which Nostradamus refers. It is the same white stone mentioned in Revelation 2:17:

> *To him that overcometh will I give to eat of* **the secret manna**,
> *and I will give him a* **white stone**,
> *and in this stone a new name written,*
> *which no man knoweth saving he that receiveth it.*

The secret manna is the secret food of the gods, the sacred hallucinogens. This is the significant clue to decoding the meaning of the 'white stone'. Earlier, I documented that the Peacemaker will partake of hallucinogens to discover the sacred name of God, the Ineffable Name. Originally, this name was the tetragrammaton YHWH, representing god as Father. When the Christian order took over, the Ineffable Name became Pentagrammaton IHShVS (JESUS), representing god as Son. According to Nostradamus, a new name is given to the Peacemaker, likely representing God as Father, Son and Daughter.

But that's not all. When the Company of 8 (plus one), the nine "French Knights" referred to earlier, set about reconstructing the Temple of Solomon, which is believed to have an earthly and heavenly aspect, they uncovered one of the greatest secrets known to man. In 1953 a copper scroll was found in a cave near the Dead Sea which told of an enormous Temple treasure – estimated at 138 tons of gold and silver which had been buried by the Jewish priesthood in 64 locations before the Romans destroyed the Temple in 70 A.D. Twenty-four of those caches were underneath the Temple. Among the most fascinating legends about Solomon's Temple is the legend that Solomon was an alchemist and that he manufactured by alchemical means the gold used in his temple. Perhaps this is the secret the Templars discovered.

Gold may be the answer to the Templar secret, but it is likely something more as well. The Templars revealed this secret to none but the highest of the Templar order. In order to preserve this secret, they conceived (or were given) a plan to build it into gothic cathedrals throughout Europe, concealing the details of their secret in the architecture of these buildings. The skill and cunning which went into these sacred structures rivals modern man's achievement of putting a man on the moon. It catapulted western civilization into an entirely new realm of existence.

From this we can deduce that the nine French knights rediscovered the means to travel to Tula. The secret diagrams they are thought to have returned with were undoubtedly plans for constructing new Tulas, the gothic cathedrals. The manuscript containing these secrets (*The Book of Love*) will be discussed in the next chapter.

The secret purpose of the Cathars and the Knights Templar was not only to preserve gold and sacred books. Their purpose is to preserve the Merovingian bloodline in hopes of one day establishing a world government and putting the 'King of Tula' on the throne – a king who could claim to be the descendent of Jesus and Mary Magdalen.

CHAPTER TWENTY-FOUR

THREAD OF ARIADNE

I give you the end of the golden string,
Only wind it into a ball,
It will lead you in at heaven's gate
Built in Jerusalem's wall."

– William Blake
"Jerusalem"

Under Aries in *Le Serpent Rouge* the clues to the Peacemaker's mission continue:

> *In my arduous search, I was trying to hack a way with my sword through the dense vegetation of the woods. I wanted to reach the place of the 'Sleeping Beauty' in which some poets can see the Queen of a lost kingdom. Desperate to find my way I was aided by the parchments of my friend (Jesus), they were for me like the thread of ARIADNE.*

Sleeping Beauty was aroused from her sleep by the kiss or love of the Prince of Peace. In this case Sleeping Beauty refers to the sleeping Christ who must be resurrected by the Peacemaker. As we saw in the Greek legend of Theseus, a prototypal legend of the Peacemaker, the hero entered the Labyrinth (same as the maze at Chartres) to slay the Minotaur, a creature who is half-man, half-beast. The beautiful maiden Ariadne gave Theseus a clew of yarn for him to be able to retrace his steps and avoid becoming hopelessly lost in the Labyrinth. This mythological journey has been seen as an allegory for earth life, which, from the soul's perspective, seems like a labyrinth that we must learn to transcend.

In *Le Serpent Rouge* we learn that the "parchments of my friend" (the lost books of Jesus, which he is believed to have given to Mary Magdalen) are hidden somewhere at Rennes-le-Chateau. These are reputed to be his most secret teachings of resurrection and ascension which, "like the thread of Ariadne," will enable us to find our way home.

THE BOOK OF LOVE

Attached to the legend of the Holy Grail is the story of a book that rests guarded and preserved by the Cathars, a manuscript which lies in a leaden casket in the depths of a cavern. The manuscript is called *The Book of Love* and is said to be the book given to John by Jesus. There is, however, reason to believe that it might be even more ancient. According to Elizabeth Van Buren (*Refuge of the Apocalypse*), the book is said to contain:

> .... *sublime teachings, marvelous revelations, the most secret words confided by our Lord Jesus Christ to the beloved disciple. Their power would be such that all hatred, all anger, all jealousy would vanish from the hearts of men. The Divine Love, like a new flood, would submerge all souls and never again would blood be shed on this earth.*

A prophecy says that *The Book of Love* will be discovered at a "preordained time" by a "pre-ordained" person, a "being of perfect candor, innocence and absolute purity." *The Book of Love* is believed to be hidden in a cave in the southern part of France (and will undoubtedly be recovered before July, 1999).

Can we equate the book revered by the Cathars with the green stone of the Peacemaker or even more fantastically can we equate the Book of Love with the green stone and subsequently with the Holy Grail, that cup of plenty which is said to give eternal life to the one who finds it? In the language of the Languedoc countryside nearby Rennes-le-Chateau the word *Greal* or *Grail* means stone vase. Wolfram von Echenbach says of the *traveller* or wandering stone: "And this stone is called the Grail." Could this stone vase be the mysterious alabaster jar which was once in the possession of Mary Magdalen? Is it possible this stone vase is one and the same as the oral teachings Jesus gave to Mary Magdalen? If so, were these oral teachings possibly something that was ingested orally, as in a sacred 'super nutrient'?

Whatever its contents, in Century I, Quatrain 26 Nostradamus speaks of a possible hiding place for this vase:

> *Under the oak with mistletoe, struck by lightning,*
> *Not far from there is hidden the treasure.*
> *Which, during long ages had been amassed*
> [He who discovered it] *found dead,*
> *The eye punctured by a spring.*

Two things are mysterious about this Quatrain which previous interpreters have been unable to decipher. First is the fact that mistletoe was the ancient symbol for immortality and only rarely grows on oak trees. One such oak tree with mistletoe attached was known to have grown near Rennes-le-Chateau. The ancient Druids grafted the mistletoe onto the oak in remembrance of the sacred rites of manna. They called the mistletoe *all-heal*, believing it to be a medicinal panacea.

Secondly, mistletoe symbolized the tribe of Benjamin from which the Merovingians are known to have descended. The tribe of Benjamin shares a common trait with the Druids: both were known as intermediaries between mankind and the gods. As we pointed out earlier, Mary Magdalen was a Benjaminite; and hence, an ancestor of the Druids.

THE DRUIDS

The origin of the word Druid is believed to mean 'the men of the oak trees'. Mythologically, the Druids are believed to have come from Hyperboria, the heavenly home of Tula (could it be otherwise?). In Gaelic *druidh* means 'wise man' or 'instructor'. This powerful body of priests taught an amazing cluster of doctrines including: a belief in the immortality of the soul; the belief that humans could achieve enlightenment in one lifetime; a belief in a Virgin Mother, with a Child in her arms who was sacred to their mysteries; a Sun God who was born on December 25 and was resurrected at the time of year modern Christians know as Easter; a veneration of the Cross and the Serpent; and a worship of Thoth/Hermes under the similitude of a stone cube. All of this as early as 800 B.C.!

In his *The History of Magic* Eliphas Levi makes the following significant statement:

> *The Druids were priests and physicians, curing with magnetism and by charging amulets with its theurgic influence. Their universal remedies were mistletoe and serpent's eggs because these substances attract the astral light in a special manner. The solemnity with which mistletoe was cut down drew upon this plant the popular confidence and rendered it powerfully magnetic. . . . The progress divination of magnetism will some day reveal to us the absorbing properties of mistletoe. We shall then understand the secret of those spongy growths which drew the unused virtues of plants and became surcharged with tinctures and savors. Mushrooms, truffles, gall on trees, and the different kinds of mistletoe will be employed with understanding by a medical science, which will be new because it is so old.*

Mistletoe was more than a medicinal panacea to the Druids. Because it grew on the oak, the symbol of the Supreme Deity, it was sacred. At certain times of the year the Arch-Druid climbed the oak tree and cut the mistletoe with a golden sickle made only for that purpose.

83. The Arch-Druid in His Ceremonial Robes. The most striking adorn-ment of the Arch-Druid was the breastplate of judgment, which would strangle anyone who made an untrue statement while wearing it. The Druidic tiara was embossed with the rays of the sun to indicate the Arch-Druid was the personification of the rising sun. On the front of his belt the Arch-Druid wore the lia meisicith – a magic brooch, or buckle in the center of which was a large white stone! To this was attributed the power of drawing the fire of the gods down from heaven at the priest's com-mand. This specially cut stone was a burning glass, by which the sun's rays were concentrated to light the altar fires. The Arch-Druid holds in his hand the golden sickle with which they cut the mistletoe from the oak. These dignitaries generally carried golden scepters and were crowned with wreathes of oak leaves, symbolizing their authority.

The manna is clearly associated with the white stone. In ancient times offerings of white stones or quartz crystals were made at sacred wells; and it was believed the crystals gave the wells healing powers. The Apache Indians thought quartz crystals were 'good medicine' just as the Druids believed the mistletoe was the healing panacea.

Is it possible that by "climbing the tree" and "cutting the mistletoe" the Druid priest is re-enacting the ancient rite of checking the bridge between earth and Tula?

The word Pan (as used in the Druid's reverence of the mistletoe as a "Panacea") is the root for a number of fascinating associations that now become relevant. Among the Greeks, Pan was used to mean the All, the Everything, and the Universal. Pan, is also the root of Panacea, the goddess of health, and is equal to ban, bon, and ben, all meaning good. The name *Panther* establishes a direct link between Jesus, who was raised by highly trained initiates, and *Dionysus* (Saturn or Enki, the King of Tula) who was nursed by panthers, that is, by initiates of the mystery schools.

From these associations we can see that both the mistletoe and the white stone have the same function: they take us to Tula: that place in our selves and in the universe where the healing potential dwells. The Druids were professed masters of the ley lines, sometimes called love lines, that crisscross the earth. These energies work through and in man. They are in space as well: as above; so below. Perhaps the Druids had knowledge of the grid lines and nodal points in space. In Virgil's *Aeneid* the fortunate realm of the gods is known as the Elysian Fields. Those that lived there wore *white* bands across their foreheads with crystals attached to them.

Another name for Tula is White Island or the Pure Place. This means the Elysian Fields could quite easily be associated with Tula. This connection allows us to ask whether the white stone somehow conveys the ability to see into this realm, perhaps by opening our inner vision. If we could see into this realm what would we see?

Nostradamus wrote that the King of Terror would resurrect the King of Angolmois (Mongolia) or Tula. Andrew Tomas tells us Tula is somewhere in the area of Mongolia. The Cathars who lived in and around Rennes-le-Chateau worshipped the King of the World, a figure who was concealed in the Book of John as the Gardener, whom we have also decoded as the immortal King of Tula.

Tula is related to the Hopi Indian belief that their inner earth openings are connected to a vast tunnel system within the earth and with wormholes leading to other parts of our galaxy including Tula. Does the white stone enable one to see these passages? Given that our universe is theoretically crisscrossed with wormholes, wouldn't knowing the most direct route to Tula be quite valuable knowledge?

In his story "The Testament of an Eccentric," Jules Verne encoded the mystery of Rennes-le-Chateau. There he says that the passage to the gate to Tula begins by passing through salt lakes (as in Salt Lake City, Utah, the home of the Mormons perhaps?). Next, one reaches the mountains of *Bogogorch*. Strangely, the highest mountain in the area of Rennes-le-Chateau is known as *Bugarach* and a church is built upon it. Christian churches, as is well known, were often built upon earlier holy sites. Does this mean a secret entrance to Tula exists at Rennes-le-Chateau, or more specifically, at the Church at Bugarach?

ET IN ARCADIA EGO

Confirmation that we are on the correct path comes from a second cipher discovered in Parchment II of Abbe Sauniere's cache. It is ET IN ARCADIA EGO. These words are written on the tomb (believed to be at Rennes-le-Chateau) depicted in Nicholas Poussin's painting "The Shepherds of Arcadia." One part of the Rennes-le-Chateau legend involves a shepherd who follows a "lost sheep" into a "cave" and finds a treasure. Henry Lincoln reminds us that the Benjaminite tribe settled in Arcadia, clearly linking them with the phrase "Et in Arcadia Ego." The story of a person entering a "cave" and finding a treasure is also reminiscent of the story of Abraham and Sarah.

When his millions began rolling in, Sauniere acquired reproductions of three famous paintings from the Louvre. "The Shepherds of Arcadia" was one of his acquisitions. Painted "about 1640" Poussin's intention was clearly to communicate secrets. One of the things Poussin intended to teach was that the tree behind the tomb is a holly oak, an ancient specimen. The second teaching contained in the painting concerns the shepherd's staff. An X-ray examination revealed that the tomb was overlaid upon the staff. Analysis of this fact led investigators to discover that the geometry of Poussin's painting corresponded to a pentacle. Pentacles were also contained in the coded parchments. In magic, they are used by magicians when raising the spirits of the dead. Rennes-le-Chateau is therefore not only a stargate; it is also a temple of resurrection.

Rennes-le-Chateau, it appears, is the place where the Peacemaker will bring Moses back to life. In Century II, Quatrain 87 Nostradamus leaves a clue as to how this resurrection is to unfold:

> *Later a German prince will come from a distant country,*
> *to a golden throne.*
> *Servitude is accepted from over the seas.*
> *The lady subordinated, in her time no longer adored.*

The golden throne is obviously the Ark of the Covenant upon which the initiate sat awaiting release of his soul from his body. What of the line, "the lady subordinated, in her time no longer adored"? Nostradamus appears to be predicting that America, symbolized by Lady Liberty, no longer carries the prestige she once had. The official name of the Statue of Liberty is "Liberty Enlightening the World," and was a gift of cosmic significance from the people of France to America. Lady Liberty lights the way to freedom. As stated earlier, Lady Liberty is modeled after Thoth's beloved Seshet.

Influential Nostradamus interpreter Jean-Charles Pichon declared that Henry, the Peacemaker or *King* of Terror, is an American of Germanic origin. What are we to make of Nostradamus' reference to him as a "German prince" instead of a king? In this Quatrain Nostradamus is describing the transformation of Henry from a prince into a king. Once he experiences soul-travel through the Ark, he will be a full-fledged initiate of the ancient mysteries – he will be a king. In Century VII, Quatrain 17 Nostradamus writes:

> *The prince who has so little pity or mercy*
> *will come through death to change* [becoming] *very knowledge-*
> *able.*
> *The kingdom will be attended with great tranquility,*
> *when the great one will soon be passed.*

When one experienced the spiritual initiation through the Ark of the Covenant, one became knowledgeable of the mysteries of antiquity and immortality. Nostradamus' description is entirely accurate.

Where is the Ark placed? Three possibilities present themselves: the Great Pyramid, the Dome of the Rock, and Rennes-le-Chateau. However, in Century V, Quatrain 75 Nostradamus makes it clear that, once the Peacemaker and his Queen have received the new word of power at Rennes, they travel to Egypt to the Great Pyramid:

He will rise high over his wealth,
more to the right-hand side he will remain
seated on the square of stone.
Towards the south, placed at the window,
a crooked staff in his hand, his mouth sealed.

Here, Nostradamus is telling us the Peacemaker will be seated above the Hall of Records, "high over his wealth," high over his cache of sacred knowledge. "Seated on the square of stone" refers to the belief that the Ark of the Covenant was placed atop the rectangular stone sarcophagus in the King's Chamber of the Great Pyramid. "A crooked staff in his hand, his mouth sealed" refers to the flail often shown in the hands of the pharaohs.

In Century IV, Quatrain 31 Nostradamus again describes the Peacemaker aboard the Ark of the Covenant:

The moon in the middle of the night over the high mountain;
the young wise man alone with his brain has seen it.
Invited by his disciples to become immortal;
his eyes to the south, his hands on his breast,
his body in the fire.

The first line reveals that we are in the "high mountain," the Great Pyramid. "His eyes to the south, his hands on his breast, his body in the fire" all tell us he is seated on the mercy seat of the Ark of the Covenant. The most startling line of all is the second line. "The young wise man alone with his brain has seen it." This line can only refer to the reverie the Peacemaker is experiencing. In ecstasy, "the young wise man" is "alone with his brain." What is he seeing? The Word of Power! The Word which is revealed through the manna. We know this because Nostradamus explicitly refers to it in Century III, Quatrain 2:

The divine word will give to the substance [Moses' hair?]
[that which] *contains heaven and earth,*
occult gold in the mystic act.
Body, soul and spirit are all powerful.
Everything is beneath his feet, as at the seat of heaven.

I believe this verse to be an important description of the Peacemaker's use of the 'word of power' in conjunction with translating Moses from heaven to earth through the Ark. Here again Nostradamus is telling us the Peacemaker is seated on the Ark: "everything is beneath is feet, as at the seat of heaven." That is, the Hall of Records is beneath him.

Once the Ark is activated or once the "divine word" is given "to the substance" (Moses' hair), the 'fireworks' begin. The Book of Revelation (11:19) describes it as such:

> *And the Temple of God was opened in heaven,*
> *and there was seen in his Temple the Ark of his testament:*
> *and there were lightnings, and voices, and thunderings,*
> *and earthquakes and great hail.*

In addition, Nostradamus says:

> *Lightning will strike inside the closed temple*
> *and harm the citizens inside their stronghold.*
> *Horses, cattle, men, the flood will reach the walls;*
> *through hunger and thirst, those armed beneath the weakest.*

THE PILLAR TO HEAVEN

A crucial piece of equipment which belongs with the Ark of the Covenant is the djed pillar or Tree of Life. Nostradamus seems to believe this too. Quatrain 32 of Century IX states:

> *A deep column of fine porphyry is found,*
> *inscriptions of the Capitol under the base.*
> *Bones, twisted hair. The Roman strength tried,*
> *the fleet is stirred at the harbor of Mitylene.*

Century III, Quatrain 41 reiterates the discovery of the djed pillar:

> *The tree which had been dead and withered for a long time*
> *will flourish again in one night.*
> *The Cronian King will be ill;*
> *the Prince have a damaged foot.*
> *Fear of his enemies will make him hoist sail.*

84. Djed Pillar, the Egyptian symbol for the Tree of Life.

These utterly profound Quatrains portend the discovery of the djed pillar and the Ark. These devices will be found underneath the Sphinx. This is the most profound prediction Nostradamus ever made.

Earlier, we noted that the original Greek term used to describe the cross on which Jesus was Crucified was *stau-ros* or 'pillar'. Similar words, *Re-tau* and *Rosta*, are used to describe the Sphinx and the sanctuary related to the mysteries of the passage of the soul into the realms of immortality. One must seriously wonder if the stau-ros, or pillar, upon which Jesus was Crucified is the same as (or is at least related to) the djed pillar.

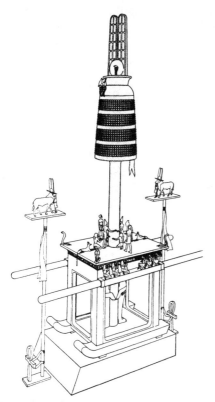

85. Egyptian djed pillar from Abydos.

Shown here is a reconstruction of the Egyptian *djed pillar* based on representations in the Temple of Seti I at Abydos and elsewhere. Does any part of this device look familiar? At the top of the pillar are two mound-shaped objects that appear akin to antennae. Between the two 'mounds' we see the sun disk. The sun between two mounds (or peaks) is a symbol for the spiritual Sun or Tula. This 'pillar' is mounted to a portable stand which resembles (in form and likely in function) the Biblical Ark of the Covenant; it is a conductor of souls between dimensions. In a forthcoming book, I intend to investigate how this device was used.

Nostradamus seems to have noticed that the Peacemaker, identified as the Cronian King, or King of Chronos, will be ill and will walk with a limp. Chronos is the Greek name for Enki, the Peacemaker's father. He is depicted with the golden key around his neck which unlocks the Capricorn solstitial or golden gate, i.e. 'the Way' through which the gods descended to earth and 'the Way' through which souls ascend to Tula.

In this remarkable Quatrain Nostradamus further observes that, fearing the Children of Darkness, the Peacemaker, like Theseus, will change earth's sail from black to white. He will alert the higher forces that earth is ready for deliverance.

JEOPARDY

These remarkable Quatrains mark a turn of events in the Peacemaker's mission. It's time for some recapitulation. From the top, the Peacemaker utters the word of power which grants him entrance into the Hall of Records. He seizes the Ark of the Covenant, the Flask of Manna and the anointing oil. To make the Ark fully functional he erects a djed pillar, the "deep column of fine porphyry" with "inscriptions of the Capitol under the base." These inscriptions are the coordinates for Tula. "The Roman strength tried." The Roman Catholic Church, fearing its demise and out of patience, seeks to halt the efforts of the Peacemaker. The decision to stop the Peacemaker appears to come on the heels of great dissension within the higher echelons of the papacy. Century VI, Quatrain 13 reads:

> *The doubtful one will not come far from the kingdom,*
> **the greater part will wish to support him.**
> **A pope will not want him to reign.**
> *He will not be able to bear his great burden.*

Here, Nostradamus is telling us the Pope will not want the King of Terror to reign. Nor will the Church be able to bear the burden of resurrecting the Christ, meaning it does not possess the teachings required to reveal Christ consciousness to its believers. So what does the Church do? It sends a fleet of jets to the jagged rock. Century III, Quatrain 11 states:

> *The weapons fight in the sky for a long time.*
> *The tree fallen in the midst of the city.*
> *The sacred branch broken,*
> *a sword opposite Tison,*
> *then the King of Hadrie is fallen.*

The weapons fighting in the sky are obvious. The "tree fallen in the midst of the city" refers to the djed pillar. The "sacred branch broken" refers to the Key of Life, which was originally made from a branch which grew from the Tree of Life. Tifon is a whirlwind. Hadrie signified North to Nostradamus. The king of the North must be the King of Tula, beyond the North wind. Nostradamus foresaw that, while the jets are fighting overhead, the Peacemaker will escape the attack of the Church.

In Century VIII, Quatrain 27 Nostradamus tells us the 'word of power' is written on the wall of the temple:

> *The auxiliary way, one arch upon another.*
> *Le Muy deserted except for the brave one and his twin.*
> **The writing of the emperor of the phoenix seen by him,**
> **but to no other.**

The identity of the Phoenix Emperor has stumped commentators. The phoenix is the bird of resurrection. Who is the king of resurrection but Christ? The writing of the emperor refers to the hidden word of power, known by the Peacemaker but none other.

"Le Muy deserted except for the brave one and his twin." Something utterly profound is revealed in this statement. Careful analysis reveals that Christ is waiting for the Peacemaker in a space craft! In the vernacular of the Old Testament the Peacemaker is about to go to the top of the mountain. This trip unfolds (as Nostradamus tells us) by first going down: "The auxiliary way, one arch upon another."

The vehicle of resurrection and ascension within us is called the Mer-Ka-Ba which means space/time/light vehicle or 'Throne of God'. In the Gnostic manuscript called the Apocryphon of James (discovered at Nag Hammadi, Egypt) we learn that Jesus ascends in a Mer-Ka-Ba vehicle after speaking with James and Peter: "But I have said my last word to you, says Jesus, and I shall depart from you, for a chariot of spirit has borne me aloft."

This chariot of spirit is a state of mind and a literal, physical vehicle for the spirit. I feel that the Sri Yantra has a direct relation to the Mer-Ka-Ba. As you can see it consists of arch upon arch of triangles. This mantra is believed to be the most powerful of all known geometric power symbols. It was used as an open-eye meditation target. It is said that by breathing this energy diagram into our minds we activate aspects of our consciousness that allow us to achieve higher attunements with the Universal energies.

86. Sri Yantra diagram, "one arch upon the other."

By meditating upon the Sri Yantra diagram the Peacemaker is able to increase the level of his spiritual vibration and to physically transport his body through thought. Where does he go? Again, Nostradamus shows us the way: "Le Muy deserted except for the brave one and his twin."

To decode this line, we return once again to the scholarly work of Zecharia Sitchin. Within the Sumerian and Hebrew texts Sitchin discovered that the tablets of the ancients that mention the inner enclosures of temples often "refer to the heavenly journeys of gods or even to instances where mortals ascended to the heavens." These tablets employ the Sumerian term *mu* or its Semitic derivatives: *shu-mu* ('that which is a mu'), *sham* or *shem*. The meaning of the word mu is 'that which is highward'. Sitchin equates the shem with the ben-ben and offers a multitude of examples of the gods of ancient Sumeria using their *mus* to leave the earth and traverse the heavens. In time, these same terms came to signify 'name'.

The Sumerian texts are clear. The way to reach the Abode of the Gods in the heavens is in one of their machines – a ben-ben, mu or shem that could carry us into the heavens.

What Nostradamus is telling us here is that the Peacemaker ascends to the mu of his twin, who we know is the Christ. Together, they take a ride to the Abode of the Gods, which in this case can only mean Tula.

THE RETURN OF THE HERON

Nostradamus does not go any further than this in this journey. However, based upon the experience of past Peacemakers including Enoch, who ascended to heaven for 30 days, and Moses, who went to the top of the mountain for 40 days, we can assume that the Peacemaker will be gone for at least 30 days. Upon his return, the Peacemaker will land atop the pyramid and, from his outstretched arms, radiate light. This will fulfill the Pyramid prophecy of the replacement of the missing cap or cornerstone. Then, he will deliver a teaching which will enable us to transform ourselves into herons.

If we assume the Peacemaker enters the Hall on or about August 5-6, 1999 (the soonest auspicious opening) and then count forward 60 days, we arrive at a date indicated in Century 9, Quatrain 62:

> *To the great one of Cheramon agora*
> *Will all the crosses be attached by rank,*
> *The long lasting opium and mandragora*
> *Rougon will be released on October 3.*

In Century V, Quatrain 76 he makes it clear that the lawgiver, who can only be Moses, is brought forth from between "wings":

> *The sacred pomp will come to lower its wings*
> *at the coming of the great lawgiver.*
> *He will raise the humble and trouble the rebellious.*
> *His like will not appear again on earth.*

The "sacred pomp" refers to the psychopomp, the conductor of souls between worlds. Thoth and Jesus were both considered psychopomps. When Nostradamus tells us the "pomp will come to lower its wings" he is very clearly talking about the wings of the cherubim of the Ark of the Covenant out of which he assures us Moses will emerge. When Moses returns, he will raise the spirits of the troubled and humble, the spiritually enslaved masses. Soon thereafter the King of Tula will be revealed.

THE PSALMS

The astonishing proof of Moses' return in 1999 may be contained in the Psalms, the ancient Hebrew *Book of Praises*. Researchers believe the Psalms predict such events as the rise of Hitler and that each Psalm corresponds to a year. Until now, the century in which they make their forecasts was unknown.

J.R. Church believes Psalms 39-44 prophesied the plight of the Jewish people during World War II. Psalm 43 is the most heart-wrenching of the four. Does it describe the Holocaust of the Jews during those years? "Judge me, O God, and plead my case against an ungodly nation: O deliver me from the deceitful and unjust man." From that day to this, the world has not been able to forget what happened to those people.

Moving forward to the decade of the 90's, the Psalms are astonishingly on target in terms of the Peacemaker prophecies. Earlier I spoke of the Iroquois prophecy that (according to Chippewa Indian teacher, Sun Bear) was fulfilled when America tangled with Saddam Hussein in the Gulf War.

In the prophecy, the Black Serpent (Hussein) would be defeated by the great light of Deganawidah (America) which would appear to frighten him away, never to bother people again. In this prophecy the Black Serpent dies to make way for the return of the Peacemaker, which is believed to be imminent. Recall that American involvement came on the heels of Saddam's attack on Israel. This prophecy is fulfilled in Psalm 91 verses 3-13:

> *Surely he shall deliver thee* [Israel] *from the snare of the fowler, and from the noisome pestilence. He shall cover thee with his feathers,* [the Iroquois Confederacy of Deganawidah and America is symbolized by the eagle] *and under his wings shalt thou trust: his truth shall be thy shield and buckler. Thou shalt not be afraid for the terror by night* [most of the sorties which destroyed Iraq were flown at night]*; nor for the arrow that flieth by day.* [Are the arrows Tomahawk missiles?] *Thou shalt tread upon the lion and adder: the young lion and the dragon* [Hussein] *shalt thou trample under feet.*

An entire book could be devoted to applying the Psalms to current events. Our interest, however, is in the Peacemaker. Two more appear to correspond directly to the return of the Peacemaker. Psalm 98:

O Sing unto the Lord a new song;
for he hath done marvelous things:
his right hand, and his holy arm,
hath gotten him the victory.

Here, the Psalm is speaking directly of the Peacemaker, for Chyren, the name of the Peacemaker, means hand. Specifically, the Peacemaker is the right hand of God.

The first line of this Psalm, "O sing unto the Lord a new song," also catches our attention. This "new song" may be a reference to the shifting vibrational frequency of the earth; the Tula energies are emerging and no doubt will intensify by 1998 as we approach the Millennium. However, the Biblical 'word' of God is also often thought of as a song. Here, we recall that according to Nostradamus, the Peacemaker and his partner Seshet will travel to France to receive the new word, or Ineffable Name of God. This Psalm may be telling us he will be successful in his quest; he "hath gotten him the victory."

The most astonishing Psalm of all is Psalm 99. This Psalm coincides directly with the Peacemaker's mission to bring Moses back to life. It also confirms Quatrain 76 of Century V, where Nostradamus predicted: "the sacred pomp [the Ark of the Covenant] will come to lower its wings at the coming of the great lawgiver." Psalm 99 states:

> *The Lord reigneth; let the people tremble: he sitteth between the cherubim;* [on the Mercy Seat between the cherubim of the Ark of the Covenant] *let the earth be moved.* [Press the 'dimensional shift button' on the Ark allowing the soul to travel to the heavenly Tula] *The Lord is great in Zion* [Tula]*;* [upon arrival at Tula the Peacemaker meets the Lord] *and he is high above all the people. Let them praise thy great and terrible name;* [the Ineffable Name of God known to Moses] *for it is holy... Moses and Aaron among his priests, and Samuel among them that call upon his name; they called upon the Lord, and he answered them.* [A cosmic phone call through the Ark of the Covenant] *He spake unto them in the cloudy pillar:* [the "pillar of Porphery" of Nostradamus; the djed pillar of the Egyptians] *they kept his testimonies, and the ordinance that he gave them....* [the instructions to travel to Tula] *Exalt the Lord our God, and worship at this holy hill; for the Lord God is holy.*

Blessed be.

CHAPTER TWENTY-FIVE

THE KING OF ANGOLMOIS

At last, we arrive at the King of Angolmois. Who or what is the King of Angolmois?

"Angolmois," say students of Nostradamus, could simply be a French province. Nostradamus, however, made extensive use of anagrams. Such ambiguity makes multiple interpretations possible. For example, some interpreters see in "Angolmois" an imperfect word play of the Old French word Mongolois – Mongolians. As such, the connection with Mongolia has led many to connect this figure with Genghis Khan or the violent Attila the Hun (the t-l-a in Attila is an interesting coincidence).

On the other hand, Peter Lorie (*Nostradamus: The Millennium and Beyond*) convincingly connects the King of Angolmois with New York City. In Nostradamus' time Giovanni da Verrazano discovered an island off America, and named it Angouleme after Francis I, the Count of Angouleme, who was the King of France. King Francis was a warrior king who spent a tremendous amount of his resources battling the Catholic church. This same island would later be named Manhattan, and one of the bridges leading out of Manhattan is named after its discoverer – Verrazano Bridge.

This is quite interesting. The UN is located on Manhattan. Since, as we know, the Peacemaker is the original inspiration of the UN it is quite possible that Nostradamus' King of Angolmois is a future Secretary General of the UN. However, once again, if we dig deeper into this mystery, we may discover the true connection with Mongolia to which Nostradamus referred.

THE MONGOLIAN CONNECTION

Few westerners appreciate the rich, supernatural history of Mongolia's area of the world. Earlier we explored the myths of blond, bearded white men who became the gods of the Maya, Toltecs and Aztecs.

As we recall, they were thought to have come from a kingdom in Mongolia called Tollan located near Lake Baikal and the river Tula. After a long sea journey, these Mongolians founded a new Tollan and a new Tula, both named after the places in their homeland. These Mongolians identified themselves as Nahuatlaks and said they had come from Aztlan or Atlantis! The sacred name for Atlantis was Tula.

Did Nostradamus know Mongolia is another outpost of Atlantis/Tula? Furthermore, since the King of Terror is the Peacemaker, is Nostradamus equating the resurrected King of Angolmois with the King of Tula?

If so, then Nostradamus is telling us that in July, 1999, the Peacemaker will come out of the sky to resurrect Christ, the King of the World who will live at Tula.

CHRIST, THE KING OF TULA AND THE WORLD

The modern discovery of Christ, the King of the World begins with Ferdinand Ossendowski (1876-1945), a Polish scientist turned author who travelled extensively throughout Siberia, Mongolia and western China. While in Central Asia, he encountered Buddhist monks and lamas who frequently spoke of 'The Mystery of Mysteries', a legend of a Christ-figure known as 'The King of the World' or 'Lord of the World'.

According to legend, the earth belongs to this man, the King of the World. Approximately 60,000 years ago this holy man led a tribe of his followers deep into the earth, presumably to escape destruction during an impending cataclysm. These followers formed a paradisal subterranean empire beneath Central Asia and called it *Agaharti*. This city, according to Nicholas Roerich (one of its proponents mentioned earlier), is not so much a place as it is an event which each of us must develop "etheric sight" in order to see.

From this city the Lord of the World directs his advanced civilization, based upon application of the cosmic laws of the universe including "all the visible and invisible forces of the earth." In addition, the King has at his disposal the means to intermediate with nature, to achieve immortality, resurrection, and space flight. These principles are taught to inhabitants of his city. Occasionally, these Masters emerge and spend time among the mortals.

The Lord of the World, according to C.W. Leadbeater and Annie Besant, is the leader of the 'Lords of the Flame', a group that was called by H.P. Blavatsky the 'Serpents and Dragons of Light'. This group appears in the

Bible as the Sons of God (the Sons of Thunder of the Old Testament and the Order of Melchizedek of the New Testament). Jesus Christ Himself was a "priest forever after the Order of Melchizedek."

This group is an organization of culture bearers which first influenced the civilization of Atlantis and then Egypt. Their influence is found in virtually every world civilization; their mission is the spiritual upliftment and physical evolution of humanity in preparation for the Age of Aquarius, during which the Earth Teacher (Christ, Maitreya, the Buddha-who-is-to-come, the Messiah of the Jews) will emerge.

What if this legend is true? Is it simply an ancient legend, occult propaganda or is it part truth? What if the leaders of the most powerful nation on earth believed and acted upon this legend?

NICHOLAS ROERICH

Ossendowski's torch was picked up in the early 1900's by Nicholas Roerich, a famous Russian mystic and Renaissance man who should be remembered today by all but, unfortunately, is not. Like Ossendowski he relentlessly traveled throughout Central Asia, the Urals and the Himalayas in search of Shambhala. His travels are recorded in *Shambhala* (1930) which adds tantalizing support to the reality of the King of the World and Agharti. Unlike others before him, Roerich had the full faith and support of the United States Government through an understanding with President Franklin D. Roosevelt. I will discuss FDR's support for Roerich's search for Christ in Shambhala momentarily, but first some background on this mythical city is necessary.

SHAMBHALA/TULA

Roerich firmly believed in the universality of all religions. Buddhism, Islam and Christianity are but branches of a tree, the seed of which was planted long ago. The fruit of this tree is a universal brotherhood, the result of a cosmic awakening such as the earth is presently undergoing. Roerich's symbol for this awakening was Buddhism's paradisal land of Shambhala.

Shambhala is a holy place, a sacred center, nestled in a hidden valley north of Tibet. Tibetan scholars have attempted to locate Shambhala in places as varied as Central Asia, Afghanistan, Turkestan, India, the Gobi Desert and the enormously vast Xinjiang province of western China near the Altai

Mountains on the border of Mongolia. In locating Shambhala in this area, we may actually be closest to the source of the legend, the Bon religion.

The Bon religion is the native belief of Tibet. It is a forerunner of Buddhism which later emerged in approximately 600 B.C. Bon is a shamanistic or magical tradition which likely came from the Altaic or Mongolian peoples. We, of course, are drawn to the name Altaic, the A-L-T being reminiscent of Atlantis or Tula. In fact, the prefixes A-L-T, A-T-L and T-L-A all have the identical meaning, Tula.

Like the Egyptians and Sumerians, the Altaic people recall that on the cosmic mountain the 'first man' appeared, radiating light. This cosmic mountain was called the 'stillest place' and is thought of as a lost paradise, watered by four rivers, each associated with a different color. Obviously, the Bon are relating the fundamental elements of the legend of Tula, the galactic core, out of which four rivers of souls flow into the galaxy.

Bon mythology holds that the Altai people brought their teachings with them to Tibet eighteen thousand years ago from Olmolungring, a secret kingdom northwest of Tibet. Olmolungring was a paradisaical land, the center of the world from which spiritual energies flowed in all directions. Tula is described in Maya and Atlantean myths in exactly the same terms. The Tibetan Shambhala appears to be a modern myth or reconstruction of this ancient center.

The teachings the Altai people brought with them from Olmolungring are called the Kalachakra (meaning Wheel of Time) Tantric school. These Kalachakra texts reveal the secrets of creating a peaceful and blissful paradise on earth, including the secrets of mind over matter and the transmutation of chemical substances.

The Bon, also called the Bon Pos, claim buddhahood is the supreme goal of life on earth and believe there are many buddhas. Of all their teachings the most attractive may be their supposed knowledge of how to achieve buddhahood in *one* lifetime.

During each world, souls are given the chance to achieve enlightenment. Although most of the world's inhabitants fail to achieve buddhahood, many reach the level of bodhisattvahood – a state of awakened heart and mind – during those cycles.

PROPHECY OF TULA

Attached to the Tibetan belief in Shambhala or Tula as the home of the King of the World is a prophecy. Shambhala, says this prophecy, will have thirty-two kings, each ruling for one hundred years.

The first of these kings ruled during the life of Guatama Buddha during the sixth century B.C. Tibetans believe that as the reign of the thirty-second King approaches, chaos, materialism, greed and barbarity will grip the world.

Just as barbarians (us), *led by a fearful tyrant* are about to smash through the gates of Shambhala, the mists of this holy city will lift to reveal the thirty-second King of Shambhala – Rudra Cakrin (known as 'The Wrathful One with the Wheel') and his army crushing the forces of ignorance that imperil Shambhala and its teachings.

Here it is worthwhile to note the similarities between this Tibetan Wrathful One of the Wheel and Nostradamus' King of Terror – similarities highlighted by the King of Terror's connection to the Wheel of Life and to the four beasts of the Apocalypse and the Sphinx – the Lion, Bull, Man, Eagle.

With victory at hand, the entire world will become Shambhala; as one text states: "the perfect age will dawn anew." The paradisaical teachings of Kalachakra will lead the way to spiritual enlightenment throughout the world. A millennium of peace will be enjoyed by humanity.

A fascinating corollary with the Jewish tradition appears here. It is believed Elijah will lead the way to a spiritual resurgence in the West which will result in the New Jerusalem or Tula on earth. It is interesting to compare this prophecy and the prophecy of Nostradamus with the last chapters of the biblical book of Revelation:

> *And I saw heaven opened,*
> *and behold a white horse;*
> *and he that sat upon him was called Faithful and True,*
> *and in righteousness he doth judge and make war.*

Exactly as described by the Altaic peoples, the Christ, the King of the World, will lead the righteous in the great final battle called Armageddon: a war against 'the Beast', desolator of man. He is earth's last and most fearful tyrant whose defeat will usher in the millennium of peace during which the entire earth will become the New Jerusalem, Shambhala or Tula. This tyrant is the existing world order that is sustained by the four religions of Judaism, Christianity, Buddhism and Islam and enforced by the military-industrial-entertainment-drug complex.

It is clear from the comparison of these traditions and prophecies that Nostradamus' "King of Angolmois" (whom the man named Heinrich or Henry resurrects) and the 'King of the World', the 'Lord of the Earth' and the 'Lord of Lords' are all the same entity.

With this in mind, it is a startling coincidence to discover that in 1934 Russian guru Nicholas Roerich traveled to Mongolia on behalf of President Franklin D. Roosevelt. His travelling companion was FDR's Secretary of Agriculture and third-term Vice President, *Henry* A. Wallace. The official explanation for their expedition was to search for drought-resistant grasses in the Central Asian plateaus. However, it was common knowledge among the Roosevelt Administration and even reported in *Newsweek* magazine that Wallace and Roerich were looking for Christ in Shambhala.

FDR, Wallace, and Roerich weren't the only ones on this quest. Stories ran rampant throughout the 1930's and 1940's about Nazi involvement in the occult. The focal point of this activity was the Thule Society, a political-occultist organization which spawned the Nazi party. Thule, the Nordic name for Tula, was the Aryan Atlantis. *Heinrich* Himmler, Rudolph Hess and even Hitler himself, were members of this literary society. These men were known to have been initiates who believed in reincarnation, astrology, and the Atlantean (Tulan) origins of the Nordic Race.

The Thulists enhanced the Shambhala legend by specifying that the King of the World led only the most advanced Atlanteans into tunnels under the earth – tunnels that led these chosen to safe havens, free of the cataclysms that ravaged the planet.

The Thule Society called their leaders, the extraterrestrial masters whom they served, 'supermen'. The elite among the Thule Society and many of its other members (including Hitler) claimed to have met these extraterrestrials. A basic tenet of the Nazis was that this race of extraterrestrials seeded the earth and created humankind, giving particular favor to the Aryan (or Atlantean) race. The Nazi leadership took it upon themselves to establish their racial purification program and the Thousand Year Reich in preparation for the return to the surface of the earth of these underground 'supermen'. As in other religious traditions the arrival of the Nazi supermen would coincide with a great final divine judgment. This is almost like an inverted book of Revelation in which light is dark and dark is light.

One of the sources of Hitler's master race theory was Alfred Rosenberg, who acted in a guru role with relation to Hitler. Rosenberg's *Mythus* was second only to Hitler's *Mein Kampf* on the non-fiction best-seller list in Nazi Germany.

Rosenberg was certain that the Aryan race had originated in Atlantis, the source of all ancient religions and technology. When Atlantis was threatened with destruction, Rosenberg believed, members of their priesthood escaped to other parts of the world and established colonies in Asia and the Middle East. Zoroastrianism, according to Rosenberg, was founded by the surviving Atlanteans. As depicted in the *Indiana Jones* movies, enormous sums were spent by the German people on archaeological projects in the first decades of the twentieth century to prove the supremacy of the Aryan race. Their favorite digging grounds were the sands of the former lands of the Sumerians, Iran and Iraq, and the area around Rennes-le-Chateau, France.

Rosenberg attempted to persuade Hitler to make the Nazi Party strictly a new and occult German religion. Hitler rejected this idea. In fact, he dropped the whole Thule/Tula business in 1924, after it had carried him where he wanted to be. Ancient romantic ideas of lost civilizations were worthless to Hitler, especially one which promoted the concept of individual liberty – a tenet that the Thule Society espoused. The Thule Society was disbanded around 1925 due to dwindling support.

Soon after Hitler seized power, his storm troopers raided all the occult bookstores in Germany, destroying any mention of the theocratic Thule society. As we know, this was not the end of the Tula/Thule legend. In fact, this legend was not even limited to Europe.

There are legends in the South America Andes, as well as far across the world in the Himalayas, of entrances to secret underground chambers and of cities beneath the mountains joined by transoceanic tunnels. The Chosen People or refugees from impending cataclysms were thought to find safety in these cities.

These traditions are similar to the Hopi Indian belief that the earth is periodically and alternately destroyed by flood and fire. The cities under the mountains provide refuge. There are said to be entrance points or *portals* into these underground havens spread throughout the earth.

Roerich left behind many adherents or *chelas* including Andrew Tomas. In his *We Are Not the First* (1971) and *Shambhala, Oasis of Light* (1973), Tomas revealed that after World War I the Masters of Shambhala offered a fragment of a mysterious stone to the leaders of Europe. According to Tomas, this stone, known in Tibetan legend as *Chintamani*, was imported from the Sirius star system many thousands of years ago and is kept in a tower in Shambhala where it emits spiritual energies which influence nations and peoples throughout the world. This fragment of precious stone was sent to be a guiding force in the creation of the League of Nations. Once the League was established Roerich was instructed to return the stone to Shambhala, which he is thought to have done in 1927. This legend speaks directly to the Hopi Indian prophecy of the true white brother who will return with the missing corner piece to their sacred tablet.

If, indeed, Shambhala links with Tula (as is likely), this would be a very interesting connection. In the Edgar Cayce readings, several aspects of Atlantean civilization emerged, one of which was the existence of the great sacred crystal, known as the Tuaoi or the Firestone, which also came from the stars. Perhaps, as Cayce has hinted, this stone will soon reappear. Who shall be the one to rediscover this stone?

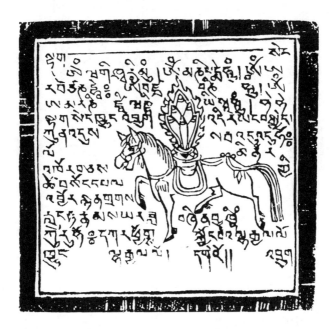

87. This Mongolian prayer flag with Tibetan script, shows the white horse *Hi-Mori* **carrying the Chintamani Stone!**

CHAPTER TWENTY-SIX

TULA: TODAY

Carved on a rock nearby Oraibi, Arizona is the petroglyph shown here which conveys the prophecy of the Great Spirit. Beginning in the lower left hand corner and moving to the right, the petroglyph states the following: "The Bow and Arrow are the tools which the Great Spirit [the figure to the right] gave to the Hopi, who are called the Peaceful Ones." He is indicating the spiritual path of the Great Spirit. The upper path is the White Man's path, and shows two white men joined by one Hopi who has adopted the White Man's ways. The vertical line joining the two paths represents the first contact between the Hopi and the White Man since the emergence from the lower world (a time coinciding with the biblical flood).

88. Prophecy Rock.

The lower path is the spiritual path of the Hopi. The first circle is World War I, the second is World War II, and the third is the Great Purification (the Christian Tribulation) which the Hopi believe we are now experiencing. The true white brother (whom I call the Peacemaker) will appear during this Purification. Afterward, corn and water will be abundant.

At the top right, we notice that the White Man's path trails off into oblivion. The quartered circle in the lower right corner is the symbol for the spiritual center of America, which for the Hopi is the four corners area. Going one level deeper or 'higher', this symbol is also the ancient symbol for Tula, the spiritual core.

The most important symbol to the Hopi is the circle. It was stated in ancient times that the Great Spirit saw the return of the 'true white brother', the Peacemaker. The Hopi have always known his symbol to be the cross and the circle. If the true white brother returns bearing a cross alone, it will mean great suffering. If, upon his return, the true white brother's symbol is the cross inside the circle (signifying unity, femininity, wholeness, and our connection with Tula), then mankind's development would go well and proceed into a new cycle of existence with the teachings of both symbols. Once again, the symbol of the enclosed cross or sun-cross is the ancient symbol for Tula, the spiritual core.

If the prophecies and predictions discussed in this book are correct, the world will see the return of the Peacemaker by 1999. He will enter the Hall of Records, recover the missing piece of the Emerald Tablet which identifies himself to the Hopi. Then he will travel the cosmos and link with Moses. In preparation for the return of the Earth Teacher, the Peacemaker will begin to construct a Tula.

The Anasazi, the ancient forerunners of the Hopi, foresaw this event:

> *Come to the City of the Future. Tula shines in all her glory. Here are the buildings unlike those we build, yet they have a breathless beauty. Here people dress in materials we know not, travel in manners beyond our knowledge, but more important than all this difference are the faces of the people. Gone is the shadow of fear and suffering, for man no longer sacrifices, and he has outgrown the wars of his childhood. Now he walks in full stature toward his destiny – into the golden age of learning.*

So what does all this have to do with the reader's life or with current world events? Actually a great deal, if we are paying attention.

BOSNIA

Since 1992, the world's attention has been turned to the civil war in Bosnia. Bosnia represents what is at stake in our world. It is a crossroad of three religions, Orthodox Christianity, Islam and Roman Catholicism. Imagine if, suddenly, your next door neighbor began firing upon you as you got into your car to go to work. This only approximates the horror of what occurred in this nation. Suddenly, this nation of Muslim, Croats, Serbs and Jews found itself the target of fanatics with guns who were opposed to the idea of ethnic intermingling.

The brutal war in the Balkans has forced more than 2 million people, many of them young, into exile in foreign lands. In *Children of Atlantis*, Zdenko Lesic writes: "Perhaps the children of Atlantis felt like the many Yugo-Slavs who found themselves in a foreign world after their country's violent disintegration."

What I personally find intriguing about Bosnia is that the effort at rebuilding this nation is centered in a city called *Tuzla*. Tuzla is not a utopia dreamed about. It is a city like any other, like London, New York or Los Angeles. Historians remind us that Tuzla and its neighbor, Sarajevo, are ground zero for the unraveling of humanity in the twentieth century. It was in Sarajevo in 1914 that Archduke Ferdinand was assassinated, setting the stage for World War I and its carnage. This was the first domino. In rapid succession came the Russian Revolution, the spread of Communism, the rise of Nazi Germany, World War II, the destruction of Hiroshima and Nagasaki, and the Cold War.

After all of this, we awaken to a little known prophecy about the reconstruction of a place called Tula in anticipation of the arrival of the Earth Teacher.

About 100 miles from Sarajevo is a Yugoslavian village called Medugorje. Since 1981, the Blessed Mother is said to have begun appearing to children there. She appears to be gathering the children together in advance of something.

Is it possible Tuzla is Tula? Or, is this merely a coincidence? Will Tula be built as part of the peace/healing process in Bosnia? Or, will Tula be built in the Four Corner's area of America as believed by the Hopi Indians and

Joseph Smith, the founder of the Mormon religion? And what of the prophecy of the Mandaeans which states the 'Secret Adam' will return to earth to construct a machine to transport the souls of earth back to the Godmind? Are these prophecies all one and the same?

REVELATION

"Come hither, I will shew thee the bride, the Lamb's wife."
– Revelation 21:9

"A false balance is an abomination to the Lord: but a just balance is his delight."
– Proverbs 11:1

The Lamb's bride is Christ's holy city. In the Book of Revelation, the city of the Lord, the New Jerusalem, is a glowing, earthly symbol of peace and love. It is presented as a symbol of humanity's ultimate earthly destiny.

In the Book of Revelation, John's words make it clear that the New Jerusalem is an actual place:

> *... I saw a New Heaven and a New Earth, for the first Heaven and the first Earth had passed away. Also there was no more sea. Then, I, John, saw the holy city, New Jerusalem, coming down out of heaven from God, prepared as **a bride adorned for her husband**; and I heard a great voice from the throne saying, **"Behold, the dwelling of God is with men."***
>
> – Revelation 21:1-2

Christians believe the day will come when this New Jerusalem will descend from the sky. We must recall, however, that John is describing a future event. With this in mind, is it possible John did not see the heavenly city coming *out of* the sky, but rather, it was *he*, John, who was coming down out of heaven? When Jesus showed John Tula, shining like a jewel upon the earth, "prepared as a bride adorned for her husband," Jesus said in a very pleased voice, "Behold the dwelling of God is with men."

Clearly, Jesus and John are admiring something which is already on the earth, since "the dwelling of God is with men." There is not a single structure on earth as massive as Tula according to John's vision. The measurements of the city given in Revelation are fifteen hundred miles square, about the size of the Washington-Baltimore-New York urban corridor. If we built Tula, she could clearly be seen from hundreds of thousands of miles out in space. She would shine like a jewel as a symbol of our unity and our love for Christ.

When Tula is completed, 100 million angels ("ten thousand times ten thousand") will sing the Lamb's praises (Revelation 5:11). What happens if she is not built? I dare not suggest Jesus would just do a fly-by if he did not see His earthly bride, Tula, from miles out in space. It makes perfect sense, however, that as a visiting dignitary there are certain protocols which must be followed in preparation for the arrival of the Earth Teacher. For one, the population of earth should be spiritually prepared and, it appears, we must build Tula. There is more though.

THE KEY OF LIFE

The Bible tells us to "put on the whole armor of God," to be spiritually prepared for the times to come. I believe this "armor" refers to our aura, the egg-shaped bubble of iridescence which surrounds the human body. I have termed this spiritual preparation the 'Key of Life' or the breaking of the Christ Seal.

By describing himself as a Good Shepherd (who alone could lead the sheep out of their fold) Jesus taught that the Key of Life, or the Christ Seal, is a doorway. He further stated: "I am the door. If anyone enters through Me, he shall be saved, and shall go in and out, and find pasture" (John 10:19).

The key to decoding the esoteric meaning of Jesus as the "door" is found in the Kaballah – the Jewish system of mysticism revealed to Abraham. Earlier, we noted the Kaballah is linked to the Emerald Tablets which contain not only God's secret wisdom but also likely contain the keys to resurrection and ascension. The link is the tesseract, a three-dimensional 'shadow' of a four dimensional hypercube. The hypercube is a figure having yet another dimension at right-angles to the three with which we are familiar.

89. Tesseract.

According to Lionel and Patricia Fanthorpe (*Secrets of Rennes-le-Chateau*), members of some ancient mystic cults, including Abraham, have been said to meditate for hours upon the tesseract until they experienced a shift of perception – the opening of a gateway to another dimension. Once through this doorway the individuals are greeted by beings from that dimension.

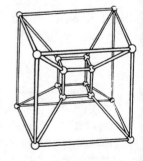

Abraham was thought to have been in possession of the Emerald Tablets. This legend gives new light to the Biblical account of Abraham's meeting with the Lord. In Genesis, Abraham is gazing out the door of his tent on a hot day. Suddenly, as if out of nowhere, the Lord and two angels appear to him. Could Abraham have been gazing into the emerald tesseract?

Daleth is the fourth letter of the Kabalistic Tree of Life; it means the Door. This Door runs through the sixth seal, the chakra or third eye. The All-Seeing eye above the pyramid on the Great Seal of the United States is the symbol of the third eye. The seventh seal connects one's awareness to pure cosmic consciousness. Jesus said: "I stand at the door, and knock; if anyone hears My voice and opens the door, I will come in to him, and will dine with him, and he with Me" (Revelation 3:20).

Jesus is the Way to open the door and he is the door that reveals the 'truth' that will enable us to fulfill God's plan – the opening of the Christ Seal within each of us and the transformation of humanity from homo sapiens to what Moira Timms (*Beyond Prophecies and Predictions*) calls *homo Christos*.

LOVING THE EARTH

Loving the earth is another preparation. Revelation links breaking the Christ Seal of consciousness (or apprehending the Key of Life) with loving the earth:

> *And I saw another angel ascending from the east,* **having the seal of the living God:** *and he cried with a loud voice to the four angels, to whom it was given to hurt the earth and sea, saying, hurt not the earth, neither the sea, nor the trees, till we have sealed the servants of our God in their foreheads.*
> – Revelation 7:2-3

In clear, unequivocal terms, John is speaking of our current environmental challenge, "do not hurt the earth, neither the sea, nor the trees," and of the necessity to open the 'third eye' of Christ consciousness. Our relationship with the earth is crucial to this manifestation, for it appears the earth herself is undergoing an initiation.

GREAT TRIBULATION: EARTH CHANGES

This section of Revelation is linked with a period of unparalleled change and restructuring known as the Great Tribulation:

> *For then shall be great tribulation, such as was not since the beginning of the world to this time, no, nor never ever shall be.*
> — Matthew 24:21

The Judeo-Christian tradition views the Great Tribulation as an end time of massive, destructive earth changes. The Bible tells us God cleansed the last world with water, he will cleanse this world with fire: ". . . the heavens will pass away with a great noise, and the elements will melt with fervent heat; both the earth and the works that are in it will be burned up" (Peter 3:10). Then, Tula will descend from heaven to earth.

This period is actually a time of changes in earth's vibrational energies. When these 'fires', Tula energies, emerge, they will empower our individual and planetary resurrection and ascension. If we take the phrase, "beginning of the world," to mean the beginning of the Age of Aquarius, it is interesting to note the earth is about to experience the identical planetary magnetics which existed 2,000 years ago. (Please see Gregg Braden's *Awakening to Zero Point: The Collective Initiation* for more on this subject.)

If we compare the sequence of events prophesied in Daniel, Ezekiel, Matthew and Revelation with our daily geologic and world events, there is startling evidence to support the idea that the Great Tribulation has already began. These processes are known by every world religion and to the ancients in their own words. The promise of the Church is that we will be transformed or Raptured into a resurrected body, a Mer-Ka-Ba vehicle, and be transported to heaven. I believe creating this Mer-Ka-Ba vehicle is not a by-product of our faith or existence on earth, it is the purpose of our faith and our existence. I shall return to this subject in another volume of this series.

"And it shall come to pass in the last days, I will show wonders in the heavens above and signs in the earth beneath" (Acts of the Apostles 2:19).

Tribulation is a time when the earth is calling us back to this knowledge that we might save her and catapult humanity into a new way of living, a way of untold prosperity. Some observers speculate that Crop Circles (those unaccountable formations appearing in cereal crops and fields throughout the world) are Tribulation messages from Mother Earth. Many describe feelings of tremendous transcendence when visiting the circles. Is it possible the Crop Circles signify humanity's awakening? An ancient Hopi prophecy states the beginning of the next world will be imminent when the moon appears on earth. When a Crop Circle in the shape of a crescent moon appeared on earth, it was said to have brought tears to the eyes of the Hopi Elders.

Every living form on earth is composed of energy which answers to a particular frequency. A web of energy lines links every creature from the smallest to the largest. The Hermetic principle "as above, so below" states this understanding. Every creature has an energy system, a network or web of lines connected by the chakras, that maintains the life force of the creature.

Few civilizations are as advanced in their knowledge and application of this force as the Chinese. The Chinese form of healing called acupuncture is based on this understanding. Its practitioners describe the human energy lines as meridians. Planets also have energy systems made up of chakras and meridians. These meridians are called by many names: ley lines, turingas or dragon lines. Maintaining these lines is as crucial to the survival of a planetary body as it is to a human body, for they bring new life. An acupuncturist uses needles to rebalance and redirect the flow of energy in a human body. Easily and effectively, by placing these needles in certain acupuncture points, health and balance can be restored in a body, including the earth. The needles the ancients used were called the caducei. They used them to tune into the mental field or the planetary grid with their minds and then accelerated natural processes.

Evidence of the ley-line system is found all over the earth – in the Americas, Europe, Africa, Asia, and Australia. In 1973, three Russian scientists perplexed the scientific community with their discovery of a geometric grid pattern which blankets the earth. These scientists concluded that the earth is a giant planetary crystal. There are two kinds of structures to this crystal: an ICOSAHEDRON, made up of 20 equilateral triangles, interconnecting with a DODECAHEDRON, made up of 12 pentagons. They are called icosa-dodeca for short. These structures correspond with the two kinds of dragon paths known to the ancient Chinese. Those of the Blue Dragon, the icosa, unite and symbolize male energies. Paths of the White Tiger, the dodeca, unite and symbolize the female energies.

For thousands of years man has used the knowledge of the lines of the earth and has developed techniques and technologies for manipulating their energies for predictable results. It appears these energies are to be found at natural energy 'springs' in the earth. The Planetary Grid (the Labyrinth) reveals that nearly all sacred sites, communities, centers of civilization, temples, pyramids, obelisks, and monuments from antiquity to today were carefully placed on the Grid to maximize the energies of these springs. The structures placed at these springs act as a technology for collecting the energy. Individuals gather there, absorb the energy, and eventually dissipate the energy into the surrounding areas. We can easily understand this energy by recalling how we feel after leaving church – purified, joyful, and abundant. Use of this knowledge is the key to not only our survival, but also our salvation.

It is worth mentioning that in our modern era the man most closely associated with 'tapping' the free energies of the earth in this way is Nikola Tesla. At the turn of the twentieth century Tesla (whose name synchronistically contains the T-L-A significators of Tula) proposed the creation of a global power system in which people everywhere simply stuck a rod in the earth and tapped free energy.

In Jesus' time stones were used to 'acupuncture' or direct the healing energies emanating from the cosmos. Careful attention was paid to solstices, equinoxes and other powerful celestial events. At these times of year, the earth's lines are thought to become revitalized by the energies flowing through them. These healing energies were called 'dragon energies'.

It may be that these dragon energies are central to the new heaven and earth. John, in the Book of Revelation (20:1-2) (the synchronicity of the year 2012 is interesting), tells us: "And I saw an angel come down from heaven, having the *key* [out of] of the bottomless pit [the Labyrinth] and a great chain in his hand. And he laid hold on the dragon, that old serpent, which is the Devil, and Satan, and bound him a thousand years."

It's shocking that when one applies a narrow-minded interpretation, the Millennium seems to represent a time when we destroy our connection to the new heaven and earth.

As we have explained, however, nothing is quite right about the prevailing interpretation of the serpent image in the Bible. In many cultures (such as China, Greece and India), the symbolism of snakes, serpents and dragons form images of life in balance with itself and transcendence. The dragon, a serpent with wings, suggests a marriage of earth and heaven. In the Tao, the dragon symbolizes the harmony of yin and yang, male and female, light and dark. The Hindu serpent symbolizes kundalini or life energy.

Somehow Christian civilization has demonized life itself. Antipathy toward life has thus pervaded Western culture. We have subdued and even raped nature, or as Francis Bacon once said, we have put her to the rack. Mother Earth has become little more than our factory. As individuals, we have repressed, alienated, and imprisoned our sexual feelings: symbols of the dragon.

Here again, the ancient symbolism of the Peacemaker confirms that we are on the right track. According to Malcolm Godwin (*Angels, An Endangered Species*), Thoth ascended to the angelic level of Seraph, becoming one of the Seraphim. Seraphim are closely identified with serpents and dragons. They are popularly known as the 'fiery flying serpents of lightning' who 'roar like lions' when provoked. The Hebrew name 'Seraphim' actually is a blend of *rapha* , meaning 'healer', and *ser*, meaning 'higher being'. The *ser*pent symbol of this order of angels, which I call the Peacemakers, represents their ability to rejuvenate by the shedding their 'skin'.

It is time to reclaim our balance by unleashing the transcendent, rejuvenative dragon-power within ourselves and nature and let loose the regenerative powers of love. *This* is the Key of Life. This is also the secret of the ages which began with Jesus who said: "Be ye wise as serpents and peaceful as doves." This is the means by which we can heal ourselves and the earth in preparation for Salvation.

In the days to come, connection to the natural forces of the world will be as vital to survival as air itself. Each of us will need a tool that crosses political and religious boundaries. John makes it clear that it is not only Christian children who will be admitted to Christ's Holy City, Tula. Before the throne of God, he sees those who have "come out of the great tribulation" (Rev. 7:14) and they are "a great multitude which no man could number, from every nation, from all tribes and peoples and tongues..." (Rev. 7:9).

The Peacemaker's wand, the "blameless tool of peace," the Key of Life, is the tool we need. This technology is capable of delivering highly charged thought forms into the world for the healing of ourselves and the earth.

There was a time when we placed toy guns in the hands of our male children. When we take them away, they fashion guns out of any available medium: bread, cucumbers, wood. They do this, I believe, because they want to express the power of the warrior within them. A gun is an extension of the hand. It is a fist magnified thousands of times. Toy store chains across America have taken the immense step of removing toy guns from their shelves. Why don't we replace them with something more constructive like magic wands and help children release the Peacemaker within? Why don't we turn them from warriors into sacred warriors?

The suppressing of the drive to demonstrate our power is counterproductive. We must channel it. Massively switch it on to the positive. Ancient legends explain that the most significant purpose of the ley line system was for the increase of soil fertility and plant growth. Imagine, millions of children all over the planet with healing rods accelerating the healing of the planet! This same type of healing affects plants and animals. Water can even be made purer with the power of the imagination in conjunction with the Key of Life.

90. The Celtic Right Hand of God.

The wand is the tool of the Peacemaker. It is a tool of spiritual transformation. With an understanding of the power of the Key of Life, the individual child will be empowered to create positive changes on the earth. In so doing, they will redefine what it means to be considered a powerful person. Power by today's standards will seem childish as compared to the *true power* we all have when our minds are channeled into healing and peacemaking.

CHAPTER TWENTY-SEVEN

BUILDING TULA
BEHOLD A WHITE HORSE

The Great Tribulation is immediately followed by the return of Christ, the Earth Teacher. In anticipation of this event, every world religion looks for the appearance of His Prophet. The Hindus, the Zoroastrians, the Moslems and the Buddhists all await a messiah figure who will appear on a white horse. "And I saw heaven open, and behold a white horse: and he that sat upon him was called Faithful and True" (Revelation 19:11). The white horse, as has already been established, is a symbol of the Peacemakers, originating with its founder Enki/Saturn. The horse is frequently associated with the Tree of Life, the connecting link between Heaven and Earth. According to the Kaballah, the role of the Messiah or Christ is to unite the Tree of Life with the Tree of Good and Evil. This is but secret code for reuniting the souls of earth with Tula.

According to the prophecies of Nostradamus and those of the Iroquois Indians, the white horse, the Peacemaker, is on earth today. He is here to lay the cornerstone of Zion/Tula in preparation for the arrival of the Earth Teacher.

The symbol of the white horse closes the loop on a definite symmetry in the synchronicities involving the Peacemaker. 'Chiron', the Wounded Healer, is symbolized by the centaur, a creature that is part man, part horse. Chiron is very similar to "Chyren," the anagram Nostradamus used in his prediction of "the King of Terror," the prophet of Christ, by which he meant a person with the last name of 'Heinrich' or 'Henry'. Mythologically, Chiron is the son of Saturn (Chronos) who was symbolized by a white horse. The Peacemakers were founded by Saturn. By definition a synchronicity involves time: *syn* meaning together and *chrono*, time.

Chiron, like Ezekiel, Enoch, Moses, John and Jesus, is a shaman. The shaman acts as healer, visionary, intermediary and as a source of replenishment of the spiritual life of all. Above all, he is the keeper of a heritage of direct access to sacred realms, inaccessible to most people, and he is the guardian of the soul-history of a people. Chiron acts as a stimulator of initiation who leads those seeking knowledge of resurrection and ascension toward a new beginning. In the Book of Revelation this new beginning is represented by the construction of the New Jerusalem, the new Tula.

It is clear: now is the time for our civilization to begin building Tula.

There are many questions surrounding the building of Tula. According to the Book of Ezekiel, Tula is so large it will not fit on the existing Temple Mount in Jerusalem or even in Old Jerusalem itself. This presents a problem. Does this mean the New Jerusalem will not be built in this part of the world and that the nation of Israel will not be responsible for building Tula?

If not Israel, then who will build the house of the Messiah? For thousands of years Rabbis have held the answer to these questions. Clearly Israel must build the Temple. Exodus 25:8 states: "Let them build me a sanctuary; that I may dwell among them."

Others believe the Messiah will build the Temple himself as was the message of the prophet Zecharia (6:12): "Behold the man whose name is the **Branch**; and he shall grow up out of his place, and he shall build the temple of the Lord."

Bran, in the Arthurian legend, sleeps like King Arthur awaiting the appointed hour of his awakening. Bran is the Celtic Chronos or Father of the Peacemaker. He is linked in Celtic mythology with the time when the earth shifts on her axis and realigns with Ursa Major, the Great Bear.

This argument is taken one step deeper when we recall the Peacemaker laid the cornerstone of the Great Pyramid. The Pyramid prophecy states the Peacemaker will reincarnate to replace the missing capstone (Christ) on the Great Pyramid (Zion/Tula). Zecharia states: "Zerubbabel with his own hands laid the foundations of this house and with his own hands he shall finish it."

If the Great Pyramid is Tula, the reader may be wondering, why do we even need to build a new Tula? Why not simply replace the limestone casing stones and restore the Pyramid to its deserved grandeur?

The reason, Revelation 21:9 clearly states, is the New Jerusalem, the new Tula, is to be "the bride, the Lamb's wife." This statement distinguishes this New Jerusalem from the ancient Israel, the "wife" of Jehovah which, according to Isaiah 54:1-10 and Hosehiah 2:1-17 is yet to be restored.

Peter Lemesurier (*Great Pyramid Decoded*) presents startling linguistic evidence linking the defaced Great Pyramid with Jehovah, making it the "wife" of Jehovah. The name 'Jehovah' is derived from the letters YHWH.

The true vowels of the name are unknown. The same situation applies to Khufu, the supposed builder of the Great Pyramid. When we remove the hypothesized vowels, transliteration of the name yields HWFW.

91. Yahweh, 'God' of the Bible, with serpent legs from an inscription on Jewish amulets of Hellenistic and Roman periods, second-first century B.C. The depiction of Yahweh with serpent legs is baffling given that there was a Hebrew law against graven images and that the serpent was the first to receive Yahweh's curse.

The Hebrews explicitly tell us the name YHWH comes from the Hebrew verb *hava(h)* (I am). As Lemesurier points out, it is an extremely short step linguistically from HWFW (or Khufu) to *hava(h)*. From this he concludes:

> *it is entirely possible linguistically that the name of the Divine 'I am' could have arisen in the first instance on the basis of the Egyptian name HWFW, which is historically the older name of the two. In YHWH, in short, we may actually have a Hebrew version of the Egyptian name HWFW.*

Interestingly, Yahweh/Jehovah equates with Saturn and Enki, the extraterrestrial bio-engineer and founder of the Peacemakers, who was symbolized by the entwined serpents as a reference to our DNA. This explains why Yahweh was depicted with serpent legs and why the entwined serpents signify the builder of the Pyramids.

Lemesurier's findings substantiate my theory that the Great Pyramid was built as the house of the Messiah, that is, as a Tula. When Christ returns it will necessitate building a new house of life, a virgin bride, a new Tula. What does Christ's bride look like?

THE CUBE

The main feature of the New Jerusalem is that she is enclosed in a square: "And the city lieth foursquare" (Revelation 21:16). Whenever the ancient Israelites set up camp during their forty years of wandering in the desert, they always formed a square, with the Ark of the Covenant in the center. According to the wisdom tradition, this pattern was based on the zodiac which we know is a wheel. Presumably, the tribes formed a square around them, but sat in a circle.

92. The New Jerusalem in the form of a cube. The names of the twelve tribes of Israel are written on the lines of the cube. In the center is the Eye of God.

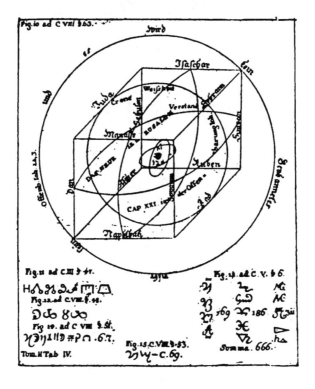

The Wheel of Time signifies man's returning again and again to the earth plane, the Labyrinth, in order to balance his karma. Leonardo da Vinci masterfully expressed this balancing of the cube with the sphere, the physical with the spiritual, the earth with heaven. Leonardo may have been inspired by the same muse as the Siberian shaman who drew the identical lesson in the shape of an egg on a cave wall before the last Ice Age.

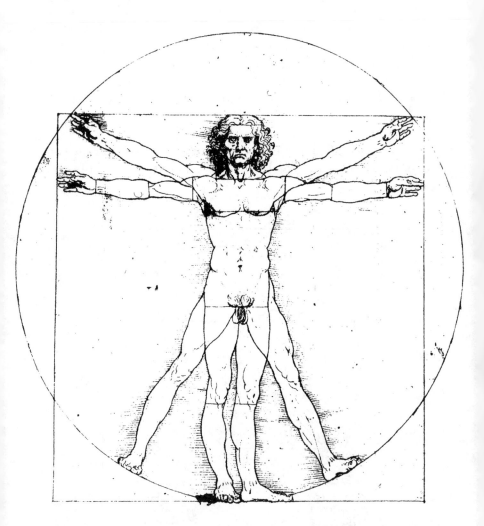

93. Proportions of the human figure by Leonardo da Vinci (1452-1519). The circumference of the circle is the same as the perimeter of the square, thereby 'squaring the circle'. The human body is the place where the synthesis of Earth (square) and Heaven (circle) occurs.

94. Portrait of a shaman holding his drum. The axis of the world on this drum is represented by the vertical line. The crossing horizontal line separates the celestial and the earthly. This drawing bears a striking resemblance to da Vinci's human proportions.

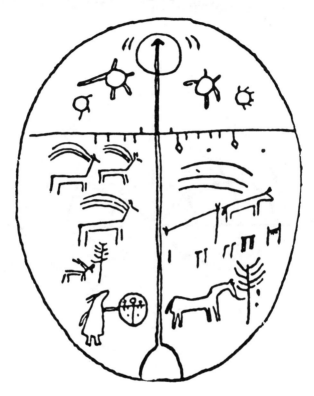

From this we can deduce Revelation is telling us that while the wall surrounding the New Jerusalem is square-shaped, it may enclose an entirely different shape. (What this shape may be will be revealed momentarily.)

This deduction helps us realize that the reference to the square elegantly hides a more significant meaning. In ancient times temples were built based on the Magic or Planetary Squares. These 'living' Squares offer the identical sum when any line of numbers is added horizontally, vertically or diagonally, from corner to corner. Each square is associated with a particular planetary entity.

In the ancient Christian mystical science called Gematria (where letters in names are given numerical values and the sum of the name is the power number for that individual) the number 8 has great significance. Enoch/Thoth, the builder of the Pyramid, equaled the power of 8. His Greek name, Hermes, also adds to 8, as does the Roman God of Revelation, Mercury. In Greek IEOSUS or Jesus has the value of the mystical 8. Many will notice 8 is the symbol of infinity turned north and south. If we turn this 8 sideways it is the lemniscate, an aerial view of the entwined serpents of the staff of miracles and also of the entwined strands of our DNA.

95. The lemniscate.

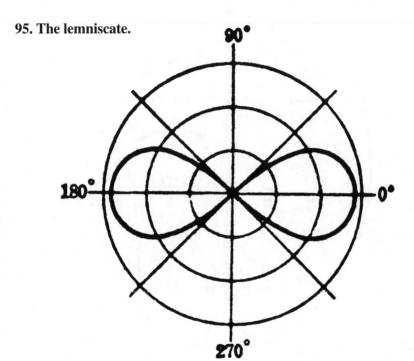

According to the mathematicians of antiquity, the Magic Square of Mercury governed the construction of the Great Pyramid. The Magic Square of Mercury is the square of 8 or 64. 8 is the number of Jesus. The sum of the numbers from 1-64 is 2080. It so happens 2080 is also the number of the first-born, an epithet of Jesus (Revelation 1:5). The number 2080 is therefore associated with Jesus, the Pyramid and the person who laid its cornerstone, Thoth. It is interesting to learn 2080 has the same significance as the number 1080, which is associated with the words *light* and *fire* and the Greek word for Holy Spirit.

When the Book of Revelation tells us the New Jerusalem is laid out as a square, we can only conclude it is referring to the Magic Square of Hermes and Jesus.

The Peacemaker

THE SYMBOLS OF TULA

The Book of Revelation describes the New Jerusalem/Tula in material terms, having dimensions, gates, streets and citizens. In particular, she glows with a precious jasper stone. "Having the glory of God: and her light was like unto a stone most precious, even like a jasper stone, clear as crystal" (Revelation 21:9-11).

Jasper is the stone of fertility and birth and speaks of the feminine nature of Tula. The feminine presence is probably the most powerful significator of Jesus' influence. This presence is the harbinger of the return to righteousness desired by Jesus. Male energy has driven the human race to the brink of extinction. Female energy, according to Jesus, will return us to God. That is, true spirituality. True spirituality means imagination, love, inspiration, divinity.

The city's high walls and twelve gates symbolize the twelve signs of the zodiac and twelve months of the year. The twelve angels, one at each gate, symbolize the power of the spirit world to help humanity through its mystic rebirth. The Female energy is founded upon these twelve apostles. Each one is assigned a precious or semi-precious stone which symbolize the teachings of Tula.

And the building of the wall of it was of jasper; and the city was pure gold, like unto clear glass.

And the foundations of the wall of the city were garnished with all manner of precious stones. The first foundation was jasper; the second, sapphire; the third, a chalcedony; the fourth, an emerald; the fifth, sardonyx; the sixth, sardius; the seventh, chrysolite; the eighth, beryl; the ninth, a topaz; the tenth; a chrysoprasus; the eleventh, a jacinth; the twelfth, and amethyst.

And the twelve gates were twelve pearls; every single gate was of one pearl: and the street of the city was pure gold, as it were transparent glass.

– Revelation 21:18-21

Each stone brings its own corresponding healing energy or vibration to Tula:

Jasper brings clarity and mystic rebirth.

Sapphire is called the Holy Stone and is thought to stimulate the third eye and to induce love. When worn, it promotes peace. A related power is the stone's legendary ability to protect its owner from captivity.

Chalcedony represents beauty, strength and healing.

Emerald is said to grant all knowledge of past, present and future.

Sardonyx promotes the ending of strife and opens communication.

Sardius promotes trouble-free childbirth.

Chrysolite teaches humility.

Beryl prevents deliberate psychic manipulation by evangelists, salespersons and politicians.

Topaz was once worn to help a person become invisible.

Chrysoprasus was used to insure success in new undertakings.

Jacinth brings love.

Amethyst raises hopes and lends courage.

Pearl symbolizes the center of creation.

After this description of the foundations of Tula we learn there are no churches in Christ's holy city: "And I saw no temple therein; for the Lord God Almighty and the Lamb are the temple of it" (Revelation 21:22).

THE SHAPE OF TULA

The glyph I propose to represent Tula is an egg with wings and a heart-shaped head. I believe this pattern represents the new Tula and the machine of the Mandaeans all in one. The egg with wings (the chrysalis, ruled by the heart) is evocative of the process of resurrection and ascension. This shape therefore is the phoenix egg, a massive cocoon for the human race, a womb-egg-heart machine where the Earth Teacher will come to teach the missing keys of ascension and resurrection needed for our journey Home.

There are many teachings enfolded within the egg with wings and a heart-shaped head. The egg or omphalos, e.g. the Omphalos of Delphi, is the symbol for the center. From the center the universe manifests itself in all directions simultaneously. This is a fitting image for humanity's present stage of evolution.

The egg has been an object of faith in every corner of the world since time began, symbolizing new life. Before man created the concept of division (separating and enslaving people by color, nationality, religion, and ideology), every culture, every man, woman and child on the planet shared one common object of faith: the egg. Why? To all peoples the humble egg represented new life. While mankind may have gazed at the sun and stars with awe, it was to the egg that we once turned to express our admiration for life – admiration often expressed by decorating eggs.

In China, Egypt, India, Europe, Greece, Peru, Finland, and North America, people shared a belief that the earth was hatched from a world-egg. Some even call the world itself an egg. All of these cultures ascribe supernatural power to the egg.

In some cultures, such as Egypt, the egg symbolized water (symbolic of transforming the spirit and searching for the god within) and the sun. This tradition continued with the introduction of Christianity, which holds Christ as the light of the world. With the Christian celebration of Easter the egg began to take on new meaning. The term Easter, in fact, means 'dawn', or the 'season of the rising sun'. St. Augustine compared the egg to the hope of eternal life. Both represent potential.

As Christianity spread, so too did the practice of coloring eggs on Easter Day as a symbol of the resurrection of Jesus. By the twelfth century, eggs were officially entered into church creed for use during Easter. Christian chapels were enclosed as Easter eggs, incubating men in preparation for hatching into the next world.

Since early times the oval image of the egg has been produced in virtually every medium known to man. It has been carved from wood, stone and bone, and crafted in porcelain, enamel, glass, metal and wax. Perhaps now we will build a Tula in the shape of an egg.

In 1972, Hopi leader Dan Katchongva (*From the Beginning of Life to the Day of Purification*) described man's Great Purification, the Hopi term for resurrection, as a "mystery egg" that would hatch something mysterious in global consciousness after the arrival of the Blue Star, a distant subgalaxy of our Milky Way which first appeared in 1987.

Richard Leviton writes in *The Emerald Modem* of the prophesied spirits of light released from the buried heart of Quetzalcoatl, the Mayan Peacemaker. "A cordon of angels make an enveloping fence of light around the huge tree (el Tule) which seems to sit like a mother bird on a precious egg of light. Inside the egg are a million crystalline facets . . . I realize this radiant crystalline egg is the heart of Quetzalcoatl, poised for a glorious hatching."

The Egyptians inscribed the rare glyph of *Niw-t Nwtr*, the 'City of God', the Stable Center of the Universe on the first pyramids. Another name for Niw-t Nwtr was the Eternal City and the City of the Divine Transformation. Its glyph was depicted from ground level. It appears as an egg with wings and a radiant head.

THE BUTTERFLY

The butterfly symbol of resurrection is found in Mexico, at Tula, and elsewhere. The stylized butterfly was the original symbol for Jerusalem. This symbol later morphed into the now familiar Star of David or hexagram. This symbol takes the butterfly into the realm of sacred geometry.

If there is one creature on this planet that strikes the vibrant chord of magic within us all, it must be the butterfly. Its ethereal nature and deceptively frivolous behavior triggers our sense of wonder and speaks to our gentler selves. Butterflies are the apotheosis of change.

In ancient Greece, the word for soul was *psyche*, and was often imaged as a butterfly. The emergence of the butterfly from the chrysalis was analogous to the birth of the soul from matter – a birth commonly identified with resurrection and therefore immortality. The winged butterfly with an egg is a natural image for the Age of Aquarius, the age of resurrection, and the Shift of the Ages, particularly if shown on the hand of the Christ child.

96 & 97. Goddess with butterfly wings; seal impression, c. 1700 B.C.E. In Minoan art the double axe symbolized the entwined serpents. The double-axe is exceptionally ancient, being found in Paleolithic caves and in Neolithic depictions. The axe is a symbol of the power of light, originating presumably from the fact that primitive men saw nature altered by the power of lightning. In Crete the double-headed axes stood on shafts 6 1/2 feet high on either side of the altars of the goddess and were held by priestesses much in the manner of the winged lions of the Seal of Ningishzidda. The double-axe, like the entwined serpents, symbolized dominion over life and death, time and space. It predated the metal axe by thousands of years and had nothing to do with chopping wood. In Crete the axe was never shown in the hands of man leading some scholars (Gimbutas) to conclude that the double-axe evolved from the double wings of the Neolithic butterfly, the symbol of the soul. Like the shaft of the caduceus, the shaft of the double-axe both separates and unites.

By metamorphosing (through stages of dissolution) from the mundane caterpillar into a remarkably elegant, almost celestial winged creature, the butterfly symbolizes rebirth, resurrection and the powers of regeneration. The astonishing sequence of events that leads from a minute egg to a winged adult begins with the rays of the Sun – rays from the Sun in our solar system but also, correspondingly, from the Central Spiritual Sun, Tula.

In many legends, butterflies are seen as a metaphor for the soul. The Nagas of Assam, India, believe that spirits of the dead undergo a series of changes in the Underworld, eventually returning to our world as butterflies. In Burma, the word for soul is the same as that for butterfly.

Eight thousand years ago the butterfly conveyed the same meaning it does today: there are two aspects to a single life form. The image of the butterfly is a constant motif in the art of antiquity. Whether in Egypt, China, Japan, or Greece, one finds frescoes or objects adorned with butterflies. Early Greeks employed butterfly imagery to represent the human soul and often ornamented their pottery and other ceramics with winged creatures that were half-human, half-butterfly. It was an easy thing for the first Christians, many of whom were Greeks and part of Paul's personal flock, to lend their symbolism to the Resurrection. Not surprisingly, during the years of Roman persecution, the butterfly, along with the fish, became a visual 'password' among the secret faithful.

THE HEART

The symbolism of the heart is self-explanatory. My only comment in this regard is to direct the reader to Psalm 101. As we have noted, many believe the Psalms contain coded prophecies. Reading Psalms 100 and 101 (which in this theory correspond to the years 2000 and 2001), we find remarkable reference to entering the gates of Tula and life and Tula itself:

"Enter into his gates with thanksgiving and into his courts with praise," says Psalm 100. Next, Psalm 101 states: "I will walk within my house with a perfect heart. I will set no wicked thing before mine eyes... A froward heart shall depart from me: I will not know a wicked person."

The heart, the Book of Psalms is telling us, will rule at Tula.

THE TREE OF PEACE

Finally, in the last chapter of Revelation, we discover the Tree of Peace at Tula:

In the midst of the street of it, and on either side of the river, was there the tree of life, which bare twelve manner of fruits, and yielded her fruit every month: and the leaves of the tree were for the healing of the nations.

– Revelation 22:2

The Tree of Life is one and the same as the Tree of Peace (Atlantis) in Genesis. In Tula, we have the new Atlantis, the new City of God, the symbol of mankind's enlightened steps into the Kingdom of God. Jesus' parable of the Kingdom of God speaks directly of Tula and its prophesied role in mankind's colonization of space and the construction of Tulas on other worlds:

> *It is like a grain of a mustard seed, which, when it is sown in the earth, is less than all the seeds that be in the earth; But when it is sown, it groweth up, and become greater than all herbs, and shooteth out great branches; so that the fowls of the air may lodge under the shadow of it.*

> — Mark 4: 31-31

This corresponds with the verse of the Sanskrit poet Kalidas which was believed to have been inspired by the myth of Atlantis:

> *We planted a noble tree in the forest, it grew*
> *and grew, bearing exquisite flowers and*
> *fruit, and it spread its seed round about,*
> *and other trees pierced the soil.*

The intent of Tula as a staging area, or interdimensional star station, to be used for mass colonization of (or interaction with) other worlds is clear when comparing Revelation with *The Apocalypse of Paul* and the *Book of Enoch*. As Paul looks up into the heavens, he sees the angels "with faces shining like the sun; their loins were girt with golden girdles and they had palms (the symbol of the phoenix) in their hands . . . and they were clothed in raiment on which was written the name of the Son of God." Paul then asks the guiding angel who these extraordinary beings are. The angel replies: "These are the angels of righteousness; they are sent to lead in the hour of their need the souls of the righteous who believed God was their helper."

St. Ephraem the Syrian would have understood, in a spiritual sense, the merging of two or more worlds in the garden of Tula. In his *Hymns of Paradise* he helps to spread the myth of the New Jerusalem where the trees display "limitless fertility," and

> *when two neighboring flowers,*
> *each with its own color*
> *combine together*
> *and become a single flower*
> *they bring a new color into the world,*
> *and when fruits combine,*
> *they yield a new beauty*
> *and their leaves take on a new appearance,*

Within the garden of Tula, which St. Ephraem describes as a "granary of perfumes," "lambs feed, free of fear."

The prophecies and traditions of the ancients agree. Perhaps now we will build Tula and branch into the universe!

I close this book with an invitation written by the ancient Anasazi who inhabited the Mesa Verde, the Emerald Table, the sacred land of the Hopi in Arizona:

> *Come to the City of the Future. Tula shines in all her glory. Here are the buildings unlike those we build, yet they have a breathless beauty. Here people dress in materials we know not, travel in manners beyond our knowledge, but more important than all this difference are the faces of the people. Gone is the shadow of fear and suffering, for man no longer sacrifices, and he has outgrown the wars of his childhood. Now he walks in full stature toward his destiny - into the golden age of learning.*

BIBLIOGRAPHY

I am indebted to the original scholarship of the authors whose works are cited below. Much of the material included in this book found its source and inspiration within the pages of these books.

Alfred, Cyril. *The Egyptians.* New York: Thames & Hudson, 1961.

Anderson, William. *The Green Man: The Archetype of our Oneness with the Earth.* London: HarperCollins, 1990.

Argüelles, Jose. *The Mayan Factor: The Path Beyond Technology.* Santa Fe: Bear & Co., 1987.

Baigent, Michael, Richard Leigh, and Henry Lincoln. *Holy Blood, Holy Grail..* New York: Henry Holt, 1986.

Baigent, Michael, Richard Leigh, and Henry Lincoln. *The Messianic Legacy.* New York: Dell, 1983.

Bailey, Jim. *Sailing To Paradise, The Discovery of the Americas by 7000 B.C.* New York: Simon & Schuster, 1994.

Bauval, Robert and Adrian Gilbert. *The Orion Mystery.* London: William Heinemann Ltd., 1994.

Bayley, Harold. *The Lost Language of Symbolism.* Carol Publishing Group, 1989.

Begich, Nicholas J. and Manning, Jean. *Angels Don't Play This HAARP.* Anchorage: Earth Pulse Press, 1995.

Blumrich, Josef F. *Spaceships of Ezekiel.* New York: Bantam, 1974.

Boissiere, Robert. *The Return of Pahana.* Santa Fe: Bear & Co., 1990.

Carey, Ken. *Return of the Bird Tribes.* San Francisco: Harper San Francisco, 1982.

Cheetham, Erika. *The Final Prophecies of Nostradamus.* New York: Perigee, 1989.

Childress, David Hatcher. *Lost Cities of North and Central America.* Stelle, IL: Adventures Unlimited Press, 1992.

Dannelley, Richard. *Sedona: Beyond the Vortex .* Sedona: The Vortex Society, 1995.

Davies, Stevan, *Jesus: The Healer .* New York: Continuum, 1994.

Devereux, Paul. *Earth Memory Sacred Sites - Doorways into Earth's Mysteries .* St. Paul, MN: Llewellyn, 1992.

Donnelly, Ignatius. *Atlantis - The Antediluvian World*. London: Sampson, Low, Marston & Co.Ltd., 1882.

Fanthorpe, Lionel and Patricia. *The Secrets of Rennes-le-Chateau*. York Beach, ME: Samuel Weiser, Inc., 1992.

Feurerstein, Georg. *Spirituality by the Numbers*. New York: G.P. Putnam and Sons, 1994.

Fideler, David. *Jesus Christ Sun of God*.Wheaton, IL: Quest Books, 1993.

Frisell, Bob. *Nothing In This Book Is True, But It's Exactly The Way Things Are*. Berkeley: Frog, Ltd., 1995.

Gardner, Laurence. *The Bloodline of the Holy Grail*. Boston: Element, 1996.

Godwin, Malcolm. *Angels An Endangered Species*. New York: Simon & Schuster, 1990.

Gruber, Elmer & Holger Kersten. *The Original Jesus*. Rockport, MA: Element, 1995.

Guenon, Rene. *Fundamental Symbols*: *The Universal Language of Sacred Science*. Cambridge, UK: Quinta Essentia, 1995.

Hancock, Graham. *The Sign and the Seal*. New York: Simon and Schuster, 1992.

Hancock, Graham. *Fingerprints of the Gods*. New York: Crown Publishers, Inc., 1995.

Hansen, L. Taylor Hansen. *He Walked the Americas*. Amherst, WI: Amherst Press, 1963.

Hargreaves, Joyce. *Hargreaves New Illustrated Bestiary*. Great Britain: Gothic Image Publications, 1990.

Heinberg, Richard. *Memories and Visions of Paradise*. Los Angeles: Jeremy P. Tarcher, 1989.

Hoagland, Richard. *The Monuments on Mars*. North Atlantic Books, 1987.

Hope, Murry. *Atlantis - Myth or Reality*. New York: Penguin, 1991.

Houston, Jean and Margaret Rubin. *Manual for the Peacemaker*. Chicago: Quest Books, 1995.

Howard, Michael. *The Occult Conspiracy*. Rochester, VT: Destiny Books, 1989.

Lemesurier, Peter. *The Great Pyramid Decoded*. Great Britain: Element, 1977.

Leonard, Cedric. *The Quest For Atlantis*. New York: Manor Books, 1979.

Lorie, Peter. *Revelation* . New York: Simon &Schuster, 1994.

Lorie, Peter. *Nostradamus: The Millennium and Beyond*. New York: Simon & Schuster, 1993.

Lundquist, John M. *The Temple*. London: Thames and Hudson, Ltd., 1993.

Mardyks, Raymond. *Sedona Starseed: A Galactic Initiation*. Sedona: Starheart Publications, 1994.

Mathews, Thomas F. *The Clash of Gods*. Princeton, NJ: Princeton University Press, 1993.

McFadden, Steve. *Ancient Voices, Current Affairs*. Santa Fe: Bear & Co., 1992.

Men, Hunbatz. *The Secrets of Mayan Science/Religion*. Santa Fe: Bear & Co., 1990.

Mooney, Richard E. *Colony Earth* . New York: Stein and Day, 1974.

Norvill, Roy. *Hermes Unveiled*. Bath, England: Ashgrove, 1986.

Osman, Ahmed. *Moses: Pharaoh of Egypt*. England: Paladin, 1990.

Osman, Ahmed. *The House of the Messiah*. England: Paladin, 1992.

Ponce, Charles. *Kabbalah*. Wheaton, IL: Theosophical Publishing House, 1973.

Ravenscroft, Trevor. *The Spear of Destiny*. Newport, ME: Weiser, 1987.

Reinhart, Melanie. *Chiron and the Healing Journey*. New York: Arkana, 1989.

Schaaf, Gregory. *Wampum Belts and Peace Trees: George Morgan, Native American and Revolutionary Diplomacy*. Golden, CO: Fulcrum Publishing, 1990.

Schellhorn, G. Cope. *Extraterrestrials in Biblical Prophecy*. Madison, WI: Horus House Press, 1990.

Schonfeld, Hugh. *The Passover Plot* . Great Britain: Element, 1965.

Sitchin, Zecharia. *The Stairway To Heaven*. New York: Avon Books, 1980.

Sitchin, Zecharia. *The 12th Planet* . New York: Avon Books, 1976.

Sitchin, Zecharia. *The Wars of Gods and Men*. New York: Avon Books, 1985.

Sitchin, Zecharia. *Divine Encounters*. New York: Avon Books, 1996.

Soderber, Sten. *Hammarskjold*. New York: Viking Press, 1962.

Starbird, Margaret. *The Woman With the Alabaster Jar*. Santa Fe: Bear and Company, 1993.

Temple, Robert K.G. *The Sirius Mystery*. Rochester, VT: Destiny Books, 1976.

Timms, Moira. *Beyond Prophecies and Predictions*. New York: Ballantine Books, 1980.

Toth, Max. Pyramid Prophecies.

United States Capitol Historical Society. *We the People, The Story of the United States Capitol Its Past and Promise*. Washington DC: National Geographic Society, 1981.

Van Buren, Elizabeth. *Refuge of the Apocalypse*. Great Britain: C.W. Daniel Company, 1986.

Walker, Barbara. *Woman's Encyclopedia of Myths and Secrets*. New York: HarperCollins, 1983.

Waserman, James. *Art and Symbols of the Occult*. New York: Destiny, 1989.

Waters, Frank. *Book of the Hopi* . New York: Penguin Books, 1963.

West, John Anthony. *The Serpent in the Sky: The High Wisdom of Ancient Egypt*. Wheaton, IL: Quest Books, 1993.

Williamson, George Hunt. *Road In The Sky*. London: Neville Spearman, 1959.

Wilson, Robert Anton. *Coincidance*. Santa Monica: New Falcon Publications, 1988.

Wolf, Fred Alan. *Taking the Quantum Leap*. New York: Harper & Row, 1989.

Wood, David. *Genisis*. England: Baton Press, 1985.

LIST OF MASTER ILLUSTRATIONS

COVER: Seal of the Peacemaker . (from: Harold Bayley, *Lost Language of Symbolism*, Citadel Press)

TITLE PAGE: Heron atop pyramid. (from: Joyce Hargreaves, *Hargreaves New Illustrated Bestiary*, Gothic Image Publications)

INTRODUCTION – APPOINTMENT WITH DESTINY
No illustrations

CHAPTER 1 – THOTH/ENOCH: PROPHET AND PEACEMAKER

1. Hermes/Thoth releasing souls from the underworld. (from: David Fideler, *Jesus Christ: Sun of God*, Quest Books)

2. Thoth with a notebook computer? (from: Manly P. Hall, Th*e Secret Teachings of All the Ages*, p. xxxviii, The Philosophical Research Society, Los Angeles, CA)

3. Wall sculpture of Inanna. (from: Z. Sitchin,*The Twelfth Planet*, copyright Z. Sitchin)

4. Seshet (from: Z. Sitchin,*When Time Began,* copyright Z. Sitchin)

5. Heron atop the pyramid. (from: Joyce Hargreaves, *Hargreaves New Illustrated Bestiary*, Gothic Image Publications)

6. Dog-headed Thoth holding the Key of Life. (from: Manly P.Hall,*The Secret Teachings of All the Ages,* The Philosophical Research Society, Los Angeles, Ca.)

CHAPTER 2 – TULA: THE SPIRITUAL SUN

7. Enclosed sun crosses. The primordial symbol for Tula.

8. Four Flowers of Life form an enclosed sun cross, the symbol for Tula.

9. Pillar-like stream ascending into the heavens. (from: E.A. Wallis Budge,*The Gods of the Egyptians*, Dover)

10. Chinese yin and yang symbol, the Mayan Hunab Ku and a Navajo symbol. (from: Michael S. Schneider, *A Beginner's Guide to Constructing the Universe*, HarperCollins)

11. "Seven stars" of the constellation of the Pleaides. (from: David Fideler, *Jesus Christ: Sun of God*, Quest Books)

12. Overlap the two cosmic fish, often shown as triangles, and you have the Star of David. The Star of David, in turn, "morphs" into a butterfly and back into a Flower of Life.

CHAPTER 3 – THE KEY OF LIFE

13. Tula, the twin peaks, sits atop the Key of Life.

14. Caduceus (from: Anne Baring & Jules Cashford,*Myth of the Goddess*, Arkana Books)

15. Seven human chakras. (from: Michael S. Schneider, *A Beginner's Guide to Constructing the Universe*, HarperCollins)

16. The Key of Life is called in the Orphic hymns "the blameless tool of peace." (from: David Fideler, *Jesus Christ: Sun of God,* Quest Books)

17. Isis, Horus, Thoth and Ra using the Key.. (from: E.A. Wallis Budge, *Egyptian Religion*, Citadel Books)

18. Ptah, "The Developer." (The Museo di Antichita, Turin)

19. The serpent symbol of Enki. (from: Z. Sitchin,*Genesis Revisited*, copyright Z. Sitchin)

20. Enki and Ninharsag with the Key of Life.(from: Z. Sitchin,*Genesis Revisited,* copyright Z. Sitchin)

*21. The Annunciation (from: Rheinisches Landesmuseum, Bonn, Germany)

CHAPTER 4– THE LABYRINTH

22. Hopi drawing of Mother Earth (from: Michael S. Schneider, *A Beginner's Guide To Constructing the Universe*, HarperCollins)

23. Mazes. (from: Michael S. Schneider, *A Beginner's Guide To Constructing the Universe*, HarperCollins)

24. "Impossible" objects. (from: Guy S. Murchie,*The Seven Mysteries of Life*, Houghton-Mifflin)

25. Goddess with the double axe. (from: Anne Baring & Jules Cashford, *Myth of the Goddess*, Arkana Books)

CHAPTER 5 – THE GARDENER: KING OF TULA

26. The Egyptian hieroglyph for "essence of being." (from: Musaios,*The Lion Path: You Can Take it With You*, House of Horus)

CHAPTER 6 – THE EMERALD TABLETS

27. Tesseract or "hypercube." (from: Rudy Rucker,*The Fourth Dimension,* Houghton-Mifflin)

28. The Magic Cube. (from: Michael S. Schneider, *A Beginner's Guide To Constructing the Universe*, HarperCollins)

29. The Holographic Cube.

30. Malachim (from: Z. Sitchin*The Twelfth Planet*, copyright Z. Sitchin)

31. Teraphim (from: Z. Sitchin*The Twelfth Planet*, copyright Z. Sitchin)

32. 'Ptah/Enki, the Creator, wise and kind'. (from: Michael Hesseman,*The Cosmic Connection*, Gateway Books)

CHAPTER 7 – TULA: HEARTBEAT OF THE HUMAN SOUL

33. Great Pyramid: constructed as the "heart" of the earth? (from: E. Raymond Capt,*The Great Pyramid Decoded*, Artisan Sales)

34. Dragon energies atop the Pyramid (from: Z.Sitchin,*The Wars of Gods and Men*, copyright Z. Sitchin)

35. The heron.

CHAPTER 8 – THE SHAPE OF THE HEART

36. Tetrahedral forms. (from: Michael S. Schneider, *A Beginner's Guide To Constructing the Universe*, HarperCollins)

37. The 'Solomonic Pentacle'. (from: Beth Davis,*Ciphers in the Crops*, Gateway Books)

38. The Triune Godhead or Trinity. (from: Beth Davis,*Ciphers in the Crops*, Gateway Books)

39. Three-dimensional tetrahedron crop circle. (from: Beth Davis,*Ciphers in the Crops*, Gateway Books)

40. Five platonic volumes. (from: Michael S. Schneider, *A Beginner's Guide To Constructing the Universe*, HarperCollins)

41. Star of David or Seal of Solomon. (from: Z. Sitchin,*The Wars of Gods and Men*, copyright Z. Sitchin)

42. 'Atlantean' Statue from Tula, Mexico with the butterfly emblem emblazoned on his chest. (from: Charles Berlitz, *Atlantis: The Eighth Continent*, G.P. Putnam)

CHAPTER 14 – AKHENATEN, NEFERTITI AND TULA

CHAPTER 15 – THE HOPI INDIANS, THE PEACEMAKER AND THE CREATION OF WORLD PEACE

CHAPTER 24 – THREAD OF ARIADNE

83. The Arch-Druid In His Ceremonial Robes. (from: Manly P. Hall,*The Secret Teachings of All the Ages*, The Philosophical Research Society, Los Angeles, CA)

84. Djed Pillar. (from: Z. Sitchin, The Stairway to Heaven, copyright Z. Sitchin)

85. Egyptian djed pillar from Abydos.(from: Richard H. Wilkinson,*Reading Egyptian Art,* copyright 1992, Thames & Hudson, Ltd, London. Reprinted with permission of the publisher.)

86. Sri Yantra diagram, 'one arch upon the other' (from: Richard Dannelley,*Sedona: Beyond the Vortex,* from an original drawing by Patrick Flanagan, The Vortex Society)

CHAPTER 25 –THE KING OF ANGOLMOIS

87. Mongolian prayer flag. (from: Henning Haslund,*Men and Gods in Mongolia*, Adventures Unlimited Press)

CHAPTER 26 – TULA: TODAY

88. Prophecy Rock. (from: Moira Timms, *Beyond Prophecies and Predictions*, Ballantin Books)

89. Tesseract. (from: Rudy Rucker,*The Fourth Dimension*, Houghton-Mifflin)

90. The Celtic Right Hand of God. (from: Michael S. Schneider, A Beginner's *Guide to Constructing the Universe*, HarperCollins)

CHAPTER 27 – BUILDING TULA: BEHOLD A WHITE HORSE

91. Yahweh, 'God' of the Bible, with serpent legs. (from: Anne Baring and Jules Cashford,*The Myth of the Goddess*, Arkana Books)

92. The New Jerusalem in the form of a cube. (from: Manly P. Hall,*The Secret Teachings of all the Ages*, The Philosophical Research Society, Los Angeles, CA)

93. Proportions of the human figure by Leonardo da Vinci

94. Portrait of a shaman holding his drum. (from: Roger Cook, The Tree of Life, Thames & Hudson)

95. The lemniscate. (from: David Wood,*Genisis*, Bellevue Books)

96 & 97. Goddess with butterfly wings; seal impression (from: Anne Baring and Jules Cashford,*The Myth of the Goddess*, Arkana Books)

Resource Guide

Earthpulse Press
P. O. Box 201393
Anchorage, Alaska 99520 USA

24 Hours a Day
VISA or Master Card Accepted
Voice Mail Ordering: (907) 249-9900
http://www.earthpulse.com

1. The Peacemaker and the Key of Life, by William Henry is a controversial book which explores and challenges the ideas surrounding the end of the present age. Through careful research, and a new perspective, the author describes the religion, philosophy and archeology of the end times. The book is $22.95 shipped airmail in the U.S. or $27.95 internationally.

2. Pyramid Power, The Millennium Science is the first paperback edition of this title which sold over a million and a half copies in hardcover in the early 1970's. This book ahead of its time remains a classic. The book is $17.95 Air Mail in the U.S. or $19.95 Air Mail internationally.

3. Earthpulse Flashpoints is a Microbook series edited by Dr. Nick Begich. Microbooks cover four major areas: government, frontier health sciences, earth science, and new technologies. The goal of the publication is to get hard-to-find information into the hands of individuals on their road to self empowerment and self discovery. For six issues send $19.95 in the U.S. and $26.95 internationally.

4. <u>Towards a New Alchemy: The Millennium Science</u> is book about the Neurophone™ and other inventions of Dr. Patrick and Dr. Gael Crystal Flanagan. This book will awaken readers to areas of new science which will change the way we live. The book is $17.95 Air Mail in the U.S. or $19.95 internationally.

5. <u>Angels Don't Play this HAARP: Advances in Tesla Technology</u> is a book about non-lethal weapons, mind control, weather warfare and the government's plan to control the environment or maybe even destroy it in the name of national defense. The book is $17.95 Air Mail in the U.S. or $19.95 internationally.

6. <u>The Coming Energy Revolution</u> was written by Angels Don't Play this HAARP: Advances in Tesla Technology co-author Jeane Manning. The book is about some of the more interesting new energy systems just on the horizon which could revolutionize the production and uses of energy. The book is $15.95 Air Mail in the U.S. or $17.95 internationally.

7. <u>The Secret Lives of Plants</u>, by Peter Tompkins and Christopher Bird is a classic on plants and early work in sound stimulation of plant growth. This product is shipped air mail in the U.S. at $19.00 or internationally for $24.00.

8. <u>Living Energies</u>, by Callum Coats. This inspiring book could help unravel Nature's mysteries, rewrite science textbooks, revolutionize politics – and safeguard Earth's future. This book is 320 pgs., has 72 photographs, 36 charts and tables and 321 line illustrations. Available shipped in the U.S. at $22.95 or internationally for $27.95.

THE KEEPERS OF HEAVEN'S GATE: THE MILLENNIAL MADNESS
THE RELIGION BEHIND THE RANCHO SANTA FE SUICIDES

©1997 William Henry

THE KEEPERS OF HEAVEN'S GATE: THE MILLENNIAL MADNESS THE RELIGION BEHIND THE RANCHO SANTA FE SUICIDES is an attempt to elucidate the mystical and prophetic happenings which are fueling the furor of new millennial cultists. The end of the last millennium brought suicides and a rash of prophetic ideas surrounding "the end of the world." Today history is again repeating this pattern. Is this the "age of the end" as some are suggesting, or the beginning of a "new heaven and a new earth" as others believe? Only history will reveal the actuality of future events as yet unwritten.

This book presents the time line of escalating events that led to the suicides in Rancho Santa Fe, California. The time line begins in November, 1996, with the first radio talk show and news reports about a space ship hiding behind the comet Hale-Bopp. The author presents the facts behind this new millennial "end of the world" thinking. Through painstaking research conducted throughout the 1990's, the author presents a thorough understanding of the belief structures of these new millennial groups.

This book includes:

• The complete Hale-Bopp story.

• The core beliefs behind the root idea of ancient astronauts inhabiting a space ship trailing the comet Hale-Bopp.

• The ancient basis for the mystical teachings of the Heaven's Gate cult.

This book brings to light the truth behind the religion which led to the Santa Fe suicides.

AUTHOR'S NOTE

Readers may find parts of this book difficult to believe. This is, however, the true story of the religious beliefs of an extraordinary group of people. The 'illuminations' drawn from their beliefs have been selected from the statements, documents and interviews by cult members. Since the beginning of time, people have sought to answer the questions raised in this book. It is dedicated to all who have ever asked these questions, and written in hopes that all who pursue the answers, in the future, will do so with the healthy understanding that perhaps we are not meant to answer all of life's questions. The key of life may be to simply enjoy it to its fullest while we are here.

ISBN 1-890693-00-6
Available shipped airmail in the U.S. at
$15.95 or internationally for $17.95.
Voice Mail Ordering: (907) 249-9900
http://www.earthpulse.com